❧ MOUNTAIN PASSAGES

An Appalachia Anthology

MOUNTAIN PASSAGES

An Appalachia Anthology

Edited by Robert E. Manning

Appalachian Mountain Club
Boston, Massachusetts

Great things are done when men and mountains meet. ❧

William Blake

To my late father who opened my eyes to the out-of-doors.

TABLE OF CONTENTS

✳ 3

MOUNTAIN LIFE:

THE NATURE OF APPALACHIA   59

�kh'ld 6

❧ *Preface*

THE APPALACHIAN MOUNTAIN CLUB was organized in January of 1876 for the advancement of the interests of those who visit the mountains of New England and adjacent regions. Charter membership numbered only thirty-nine, and total receipts to the Club the first year were just $295. Yet in June of that year the Club published a sixty-two page journal entitled *Appalachia*, Volume 1, Number 1. Five hundred copies were printed, requiring expenditure of half the year's receipts.

That first issue stated in its introduction that "The publications of the Club, of which the present number is the first, will include reports of its meetings, description of trips among the mountains, papers upon the physics, geography, and natural history of these regions, and specific directions for investigations in the field. The results of each year's work will also be given in full."

The first article in *Appalachia* described a system of mountain nomenclature developed by a committee of Club members. At that time many major mountains of New England were unnamed and there was confusion over many others — some had been give several names, while the same name had been applied to many peaks. Such confusion troubled the scientist-members of the Club, many of whom were academics from Harvard, Massachusetts Institute of Technology, and Tufts. They proposed their own system of nomenclature that divided each mountain district into a grid of lettered blocks. Each major peak in a block had a number, and subordinate peaks on radiating ridges had subnumbers. Under this sytem every summit was designated a unique symbol — Mount Adams, for example, became F.3.1.a and Mount John Quincy Adams was F.3.3.a. While the system was used for a number of years in topographic work, it failed to gain general acceptance, being described by a popular monthly of the day, as "dry and unaesthetic to the last degree."

Other articles included a geology of "The Atlantic System of Mountains," a report on "Two New Forms of Mountain

Barometer," a description of a homemade plane table for topographic work used to construct a "New Map of the White
Mountains," a description of the "East Branch of the Pemigewasset" and a geological expedition there in 1871, and an account of
the adventures of "A Day on Tripyramid." All articles were
written by Club members and had been read by them at previous
Club meetings. The last half of the journal contained reports by
the councillors of the Club's various departments and records of
Club meetings.

Today's *Appalachia*, while graced with glorious photographs and other features, is strikingly similar to that first
number. It is the same familiar octavo, each issue containing a
series of major articles — still most often prepared by Club
members — on climbing, natural history, conservation, and
related subjects. The back matter is a less formal account of Club
affairs and notes of interest.

Thus, *Appalachia* is quite literally a journal, a day-to-day
account of the Club and its activities. Charles E. Fay, editor of the
journal for forty years, wrote that "The history of *Appalachia* is
the history of the Club. What the Club has accomplished, apart
from the enrichment of the lives of its members, has formed a
complete expression upon its pages." It is also a remarkably rich
source of history about the mountains of New England and
beyond. This is especially so in regard to matters of conservation
and outdoor recreation, for the Appalachian Mountain Club is
the oldest organization of this type in the nation. *Appalachia* has
been published continuously since 1876, at first once a year, then
twice in June and December.

Turning the pages of *Appalachia* one learns much about the
Club and the mountains it is named for: the evolution of the Club
from its fledgling beginnings to its current membership of over
twenty-five thousand; the exploration and opening of the White
Mountain "wilderness"; development of an intricate network of
mountain trails, huts, shelters, and camps; early and continuing
concern over conservation of natural and scenic areas; and, development of outdoor recreation from simple mountain tramping
to technical rock climbing, snowshoeing, nordic and alpine
skiing, white-water canoeing, and contemporary backpacking.
Woven through these stories are informed descriptions of the
natural history of the mountains and sensitive feelings for the role
these mountains and their environments play in modern society.

But this history is best told by those who made it; and this is the purpose of *Mountain Passages*. An anthology of *Appalachia*, it is necessarily an eclectic collection of writings ranging from harrowing tales of early first ascents to thoughtfully reasoned pleas for conservation, and from philosophical musings about the meaning of mountains to rather technical descriptions of natural history. The writers are as diverse as the articles. Some are Club luminaries, little is known of others beyond their names.

The most difficult part of assembling the anthology was selecting articles to be included, or more precisely, setting aside those that could not be included if this book were to be of reasonable length. Each selection represents one aspect of Club interest and activity. Yet for nearly every subject, place, and time, other articles might just as rationally have been chosen. The articles included are only a few dozen chosen from over a thousand. Those not included have contributed substantially to the series of introductions and editorial comments prepared to integrate the anthology. Taken together, the book highlights the history of the mountains of New England and of the Club devoted to their well-being.

For accuracy, it should be noted that all of the articles appearing in the anthology have been condensed and edited, in some cases quite heavily. In additon, I have relied on many sources, too numerous to mention, in developing my editorial remarks. Of special importance, however, were Rod Nash's *Wilderness and the American Mind, The AMC White Mountain Guide,* and, as noted earlier, the many worthy articles published in *Appalachia* that do not appear in the anthology.

Appreciation is expressed to several people who assisted in preparation of this book. C. Francis Belcher generously shared his encyclopedic knowledge of Club history to ensure factual accuracy of the book, and Phil Levin enthusiastically offered selections to be included in the poetry section. Finally, heartfelt appreciation is expressed to my wife, Martha, who offered sensitive and sensible reviews of the manuscript at critical stages.

Robert E. Manning
April, 1982
Burlington, Vermont

On Millbrook Mountain, AMC Catskills Trip 1905

✳ 1

THE FIRST HUNDRED YEARS

Annals of the AMC

IN THE LATE 1800s there were many New England peaks that had never felt a mountaineer's boot. Indeed, much of the White Mountain region was unexplored, unmapped, and unknown, except to a few lumbermen, fishermen, and hunters. To most New Englanders the mountains were an untamed wilderness that only disrupted transportation and slowed economic progress. But, at the same time, Americans were beginning to be shaken into a consciousness of nature. The powerful writings of Emerson and Thoreau that suggested a philosophy of religious naturalism were capturing the attention of eastern intellectuals. Romanticism was flourishing in the arts. And a popular nostalgia for the suddenly vanishing western frontier was beginning to take hold.

Against this backdrop a few dozen men interested in mountain exploration were invited to meet in Boston on January 8, 1876. The purpose of the meeting was to consider the advisability of forming a society or club devoted to mountain exploration and kindred subjects. Three preliminary meetings were held that month to build the foundation of the Club.

Professor E. C. Pickering, in the first paper in this chapter, describes the early debate over the Club's name and its purpose. It is not known who first suggested the name Appalachian Mountian Club. It is recorded only that the first comment from the floor was "How do you spell it, two p's or one?" Nevertheless, it was favored by the group, principally because it provided a wide geographic scope to the Club's activities. The purpose of the Club was agreed to be "for the advancement of those who visit the mountains of New England and adjacent regions, whether for the purpose of scientific research or summer recreation." This was a deliberate compromise between those who wished for a scientific or geographical society and those who favored emphasizing exploration and simple mountain "tramping." It has proved a happy marriage: each interest has benefited from advances of the other. The term "adjacent regions" was added to placate those who wished to widen further the scope of Club activities, though Pickering wryly observes that this may be interpreted as including the Himalayas and even the lunar mountains. He has, of course, been proven only half correct.

Time has shown the name and purpose of the Club to have been thoughtfully chosen, and the same is true for its organization. While boasting the usual complement of general Club officers, the day-to-day work of the Club was divided into five departments — Natural History, Exploration, Improvements, Art, and Topography — each headed by a councillor. While the outward structure of the Club has evolved with growing size and complexity, these five basic interests remain at the heart of Club functions. Each has claimed its share of pages in *Appalachia.*

Over a hundred years of mountain exploration and conservation is an impressive record. A skeptic, of course, would point out that a hundred years is but a moment in the history of mountains. Yet these have been especially important years during which American attitudes toward wild mountains have evolved from fear and exploitation to appreciation and preservation. The first two papers in this chapter briefly outline the ways in which the Club and its activities have contributed to bringing people and nature into harmony. The final paper addresses two of the more important aspects of Club organization.

THE ANNUAL ADDRESS OF THE PRESIDENT

E. C. PICKERING

1877

"*THE ANNUAL ADDRESS of the President.*" *The very title suggests a quiet sense of history, an understated assuredness about the role to be played by the Club in mountain exploration and conservation. This review of the founding of the Club and its first year's accomplishments concludes with the optimistic observations: "Of the future of the Club I should speak with hesitation, had not our greatest expectations at the outset been more than realized. . . . From a small beginning we steadily advanced until we have now an active, well established Club, supplying a clearly marked want of the community, and therefore almost certain of success."*

Indeed, this paper proved to be the first of many opportunities for the Club periodically to review its progress and plan its future. As a formal feature of Appalachia, *however, the Annual Addresses appear regularly only through 1881 when, through a change of the Club's bylaws, they were no longer required. This change may have been due in part to the evolution of these papers into lengthy discourses, laboriously prepared, on special scientific or aesthetic subjects. The address of 1881, for instance, was a thirty-nine-page essay on barometric measurement of heights. Incumbent presidents considered preparation of these papers to be the least enjoyable perquisite of their office.*

Professor Edward Charles Pickering is justly regarded as the founder of the Appalachian Mountain Club. He issued the simple cards of invitation on the first of January 1876:

Dear Sir: You are hereby invited with your friends to attend a meeting of those interested in mountain exploration, to be held at the Institute of Technology on Saturday, January 8th, at 3 P.M.

Yours truly,

E. C. Pickering

Pickering was elected the Club's first president at its first regular meeting in February 1876. He was later to serve the Club again as president, Councillor of Topography, and as a member of the Publishing Committee and the Standing Committee on Honorary and Corresponding Membership. His contributions to the early topographical work of the Club are particularly noteworthy. The efficiency of the topographical instruments he invented is proved in his 1886 Appalachia *paper, "Heights of the White Mountains," in which accurate altitudes for one hundred seventy-five principal peaks and their subordinate summits were tabulated. This work developed directly from his profession of physics and from his distinguished career as director of the Harvard College Observatory.*

IN RETIRING FROM THE POSITION of President of this Club it becomes my duty, at the same time that it is a pleasure, to make a farewell address. As the first to whom this privilege has fallen, it seems advisable that I should give you a brief history of the origin of the Club, what it has accomplished, and suggestions of work yet to be done; or its past, its present, and its future. The first suggestion of our Club must date back many years. Almost any person exploring the mountains with a definite end in view must have wished for some means of bringing his results to the notice of those most interested. On first suggesting our Club to our present Councillor of Exploration, I found that he had had in mind such an organization for many years. Our Councillor of Improvements also, having made my acquaintance by seeing my name on the Mount Adams register, was on the point of writing to me to suggest our Club, when he heard that it was in process of formation. In 1873, when passing my first summer among the mountains, I often discussed the advantages of a Mountain Club. I remember in particular the ascent of one of those many summits said to be unascended and inaccessible, which we have all gone up, only to find them frequently visited and presenting no difficulty. Discussing with my companion the advantages of such an organization, we said we would make a path up this very mountain were there a Club who would appreciate it and find it of permanent value. Passing the summer of 1875 in the same house with our indefatigable

Secretary, we brought the plans of a Club into a more definite shape. On the 1st of January, 1876, we issued twenty or thirty invitations to those interested in *Mountain Exploration* to meet at the Institute of Technology. In organizing, we met with our first difficulty, the rock on which we came near splitting. The question was on our name, and the kindred but more vital problem of our objects. Some wished to form a Geographical Society, and that our work should be mainly scientific, with the walks and explorations as a secondary feature. Others wished for a White Mountain Club, or a Mountain Exploration Society, with mountain walking and excursions as a prominent feature. The Alpine Club also had its advocates, while at one meeting the New England Mountain Club was unanimously recommended in an informal vote, no one else being bold enough, on so important a question, to venture even informally to express what he thought! The adoption of the name Appalachian Mountain Club, with the objects given in our Constitution, seems to have been a wise step. It gives us, and was intended to give us, a very wide scope. By Appalachian, whatever the geologists may say, we should include everything east of the Mississippi, while by adjacent regions some insist that the Himalayas and even the lunar mountains should be included. If our own members had such difficulty in determining our objects, it is no wonder that the public misjudged them. One gentleman told me that he would like to join our Club were he not already connected with so many *gymnastic* societies! Many others would have joined us, but they feared that they had not the requisite scientific knowledge! In reality all interested in mountain work are welcome to our ranks, from the man of science to the simple pedestrian and explorer.

Of the ten meetings we have so far held, we have every reason to be proud. The large attendance and the interest shown prove that I have not over-estimated the value of the papers presented. The large number of persons who have taken part in the discussion is another evidence of their general interest.

The work of the Club that will most interest the public has been in the Department of Improvements. The unwearied efforts of the Councillor of this Department could scarcely fail to bring forth good results. That we should have succeeded in rendering Mount Adams, previously a difficult and rarely visited peak, now easily accessible to any good pedestrian, is certainly a triumph for the work of one year. I need only call your attention to the fact that probably more persons visited this summit last summer than in all previous years, and that the almost unequalled prospect was also enjoyed by several ladies. The substantial character of the path will form a good precedent for our future work, and the excellent plan of marking at short intervals the distances and elevations is to be recommended. The work on Carter Dome also promises valuable results with a comparatively unknown and unvisited, but almost equally interesting mountain. The excellent camp on Mount Adams will doubtless soon be followed by others, which will add greatly to the comfort and convenience of those visiting the more remote regions. Several explorations have been carried out successfully, and the interest in this portion of our work seems to be widespread.

Of the future of the Club I should speak with hesitation, had not our greatest expectations at the outset been more than realized. Our year's record has been one of continued progress. From a small beginning we steadily advanced until we have now an active, well established Club, supplying a clearly marked want of the community, and therefore almost certain of success.

A CENTURY OF THE APPALACHIAN MOUNTAIN CLUB
C. FRANCIS BELCHER
1976

ON JANUARY 17, 1976 the Club held its hundredth annual meeting. Those attending were treated to a warmly personal history of the Club by C. Francis Belcher. The paper presented here has been transcribed from his spoken words and retains much of the flavor of that special evening.

Belcher's feelings for the AMC are reflected clearly in his description of the Club as " . . . a working family . . . a friendly working family." Such feelings are mutual, for he won the respect, esteem, and even affection of those with whom he worked. In addition to his numerous official capacities with the Club, he is generally acknowledged as the

Club's "unofficial" historian, possessing a legendary knowledge and interest in White Mountain history. His seven-part series on the logging railroads of the White Mountains, appearing periodically in Appalachia, *has recently been published by the Club in book format.*

Belcher began his official duties with the Club early in life, working three summers in his Dartmouth College days for Joe Dodge in the hut system. In 1948 he was appointed to the Hut Committee, thus beginning thirty-two years of uninterrupted service to the Club. Later he was elected Councillor of Huts, chairman of the Hut Committee, and Club treasurer. In 1956 he accepted his most important position with the Club as its first executive director. This position was particularly challenging, and sometimes controversial. How would the first salaried professional executive director control the direction of the Club and yet remain sensitive to the thoughts and initiatives of volunteer members? Fortunately, Belcher remained firm in his conviction that the Club derives its strength from the membership. His nineteen-year tenure as executive director is testimony to the grace with which he balanced the powers within the Club.

Belcher begins and ends his paper with fond reminiscences of John Ritchie, whom he credits in part for his introduction to the outdoors. On its fiftieth anniversary in 1926, Ritchie, who had been an active member for forty-five of those fifty years, was, like Belcher, called upon to prepare a history of the Club. To many, he is most closely associated with the Club's outings and excursions. Not a passive lover of outdoor life, he thought it only natural that when so many people interested in the outdoors became acquainted, outings into the country would result. These trips, often led by Ritchie himself, became one of the Club's more popular visible activities. As Councillor of Art, Ritchie presided over the Club's renowned photograph collection — mountain scenery, acquired from Italian photographer and alpinist Vittorio Sella — and began a collection of local mountain photogaphs, stimulating amateur photographers in the Club to become interested in nature photography. As corresponding secretary and librarian, Ritchie supervised expansion of the Club's library in 1896 to the new quarters in the Tremont Building. He also served as president of the Club in 1904.

Indicative of the Club's spirit and of his own personal outlook, Belcher ends his history with an optimistic look to the future. He notes the recent expansion of Club headquarters from 5 Joy Street to adjoining 3 and 4 Joy Street, a project he personally supervised as the Club's director of special affairs. This merely confirms that "We are planning for the future . . . we are busy. We're planning for growth, we're planning for a more active organization."

Photographs for this selection appear on pages 1-5 of the center insert

W ELL, I'VE WONDERED since I've known of this talk, "Why am I doing it?" I've done some reflecting. I'd like to share it with you. First of all, I had a family that loved the mountains. I am the third generation of Belchers that has climbed our mountains. I now have two more generations following me. My father loved the mountains. My mother tried once but she was a valley hound. That didn't stop Dad. We climbed many places.

I had a paper route in the late twenties on both sides of the railroad tracks in Malden. On that route was one John Ritchie, a distinguished gentleman with a smile and a white beard at that time. John Ritchie somehow kindled my interest in the out-of-doors. Through the help of him and others I went to Phillips Andover Academy, and it was there that I first saw *Appalachia*. It opened horizons for me. Joe Dodge came down while I was president of the outing club, with all his color in his most colorful days, and spoke to us. Joe ultimately hired me, and I worked three years in the hut system. Later on I became a member of the Hut Committee. Ultimately I was chosen by the Council for the job of running the Club office. I have a lot of people to thank for the opportunity of being here with you. It's a great organization. It's a working family — then, now, and in the future.

Well, let's go to the mountains. In 1875–76 the Maine Central Railroad finally cracked through Crawford Notch, but before that you had to take the train to Dover and Alton Bay, transfer to a steamer to Center Harbor, put up in the Center House overnight, and then take the coach north into the hills. It must have been quite a ride. Thank goodness for the "Puffin' Devil." When the "Puffin' Devil" showed up, people went to the mountains by train directly out of Boston, either through Woodsville or up through North Conway, originally with the wood-burners, and later on coal. Then engines got more sophisticated. Before and during the second World War we had the

Mountaineer running up there into the mountains, and this was a very popular way to get there. I have been at Fabyan's where these trains turned around and have seen, in 1946 and 1947, four or five seventeen-car Pullman trains on the siding bringing people from the New York-Philadelphia area to the White Mountains.

People got to the mountains, but the trails had to be found. You had to create them — there weren't any, or very few. Volunteers created fine trails. The Valley Way up to Madison was beautifully waterbarred. It was one of J. Rayner Edmands' great paths to the hills. There is a plaque put up by the Club to honor Edmands in the col between Jefferson and Adams. If you go there, go over and read the plaque and take your hat off and thank J. Rayner for what he has done for all of us who came in later years.

The shelters went through a system of growth. We've gone from bark shelters to the horizontal peel logs. In between we built shelters with the bark still on them at the Liberty Springs. And then we built cairns. The whole Presidential Range was cairned by the 1930s.

I'd like to switch over to other facilities in the mountains. AMC members who'd been to Europe had already become acquainted with the system of alpine huts. Harvey Shepard, who was with the Trustees of Real Estate for many years, went over there on a number of occasions to see how they built their huts and how they operated them, and there was a good deal of contact between some of the alpine clubs there and AMC people in the period around 1900. I'm only going to take one hut, Madison, because it does show you how several of the major huts evolved. Madison Number One was built in 1888; here it is with an AMC group outside of it in 1892. In 1906 an addition was put on. In 1911 we put up another building, which we knew as Number Two: in recent years it was used for storage until the roof caved in. In 1929 the kitchen/dining room was added to the 1922 unit. In 1929 the old Number One building, the 1888 and 1907 units, were torn down. We had a disastrous fire up there in which everything but the masonry burned in 1940. This represents essentially what is there today. There was quite an evolution here to create a mountain hut. Carter Notch had the same evolution; Pinkham, of course, has had it; Lakes of the Clouds has had additions; the western huts and Mizpah are the only ones that were built by themselves and have not changed in size.

How do we get equipment and food up into the mountains and to the huts? In the early days they used as much of the native rock as possible, of course, to avoid the carrying of timber and other building supplies. In the back of Boothman's barn in the 1920s we had big horses that would take material up through some logging roads that the Brown Company had long since given up from their cuttings in 1908. In 1929–30, with a lot of construction facing us, Joe Dodge sent some boys off down into the southwest, and they ultimately found this string of jackasses, and brought them back. They had to go up into Maine to find a guy who could teach us how to use them. Joe always claimed this was one of the wholly owned subsidiaries of the Appalachian Mountain Club — the "White Mountain Jackass Corporation."

Well, the back was also a way of getting stuff up and down. Then we went to the helicopters and we've been helicoptering ever since. But we will still forever backpack.

The camps. August camp, first of the Club camps, is a nomad. It knows no home; it owns only tents. It has moved and roamed around the world. Here we are at Byron Notch in Maine some years ago, when it was a lot more difficult to get there than it is today. Notice the wood fire, the tent — that kept the people fed after their long walks. We purchased Three-Mile Island in 1900, our first permanent Club camp, and we've been there ever since. Only the common buildings were permanent structures in those days, and everybody slept around the perimeter of the island in tents. Today there are smaller cabins around the island. We didn't have any electricity on the island until about 1952.

The Club owned reservations scattered in three New England states. By gift, we acquired a number of properties. At one time we owned summits of quite a few mountains. These properties were eventually turned over to the state, federal, or local communities.

Well, let's take a look and see what people did in the old days. I'd like to show you a few people in their clothing. Walking in these long skirts was no easy job. In fact, it discouraged my mother, I think, among others. Then we have the "high brass" on the porch of the Franconia Profile House for afternoon tea — they really dressed it up then; going on a canoe trip to the Allagash in 1900; sportswear modeled in the Canadian Rockies in the 1920s; skiing garb in the early 1920s — no poles, hands.

The Club in the teens, the twenties, right down to World War II, was a great promoter of fine equipment. We actually sold equipment. You could not get outdoor equipment then that you can today; World War II did a tremendous amount to make advancement in equipment, and after World War II we stopped making it. It's only been a very few years ago that somebody called up wanting to know if we were still making sleeping bags. They'd purchased one in the thirties and it had finally worn out.

Well, let's take a few winter excursions. Here we are at a three-legged snowshoe race. You'll notice the snowshoes are all different, which makes it even more interesting. We didn't have down equipment then — it was good old wool and layers of it. Our hardy forebears really did well, and they climbed many mountains. They used to climb without rope early on — long ice axes and no rope. Then the times changed and they tied every-body on the rope. They did make the summit in droves in our winter trips.

After World War I the AMC was really a pioneer in several forms of outdoor pleasure. The AMC was terribly active, first in cross-country skiing and then in downhill skiing in the twenties and thirties. Prior to World War II the Club sponsored and conducted major Eastern races on the Wildcat Trail.

Canoeing was another sport which took off in this period. The Club was really the prime organizer in the beginning of white-water downriver canoeing.

Then we come to rock climbing, which again as a technical sport bloomed in the twenties. These slides are taken from a teaching collection: "Too close to the rock" and "just about right."

The Club has had a lot to do with natural history. Many of the names of peaks, of flowers, and so on, bear the names of AMC people who identified them or did some research in our moun-tains. The Club has also been directly allied to the Mount Washington Observatory.

And as we close, here's 3, 4, and 5 Joy Street. We now own the buildings — the three of them. We are planning for the future. I wanted to show this because we are busy. We're plan-ning for growth, we're planning for a more active organization.

Someone in the 1901 issue of *Appalachia*, the twenty-fifth, called the AMC a "Working Society." Somehow I feel that we are more than just a working society. We are a friendly working family which cares for the outdoor world, and that is a challenge for us in the future. John Ritchie's paperboy of the late 1920s has been honored to stand in his place fifty years later.

OUR GOVERNING BODY, THE COUNCIL/THE GROUPS OUTSIDE THE HUB

CHARLES W. BLOOD/DEAN PEABODY, JR.

1953/1951

THE STRUCTURE OF AN ORGANIZATION as complex and diverse as the AMC often determines how smoothly it will function. The degree to which an organization should be centralized or decentralized is an inherent problem. Within the AMC, the Council represents centralization, and the chapters represent decentralization. The original constitution of the Club established the Council, consisting of Club officers and the councillor for each department, as the Club's governing body. It was directed to control all expenditures, to make rules for the use of Club property, and generally to act in the interest of the Club at large. The Council remained the managing board and has evolved to meet increasing complexity. The actions of the Council, which operates out of the Club headquarters in Boston, sometimes appear mysterious to the outlying membership. Charles W. Blood, in the first part of this article, brings his nearly forty years of service on the Council to unravel some of these mysteries. He first served as Councillor of Trails, and in this role we learn more about him in the following chapter.

The second part of the article discusses the Club's chapters. Prior to the formation of chapters, members residing some distance from Boston could participate in Club outings and excursions only infrequently, their visits to Club headquarters in Boston were even rarer, and communication in general was restricted to the official level. In answer to these difficulties came the idea of local chapters, and the New York Chapter was formed in 1912. New York proved to be a successful model, and the number of chapters expanded. An article on the history of the Club's chapters in the 1926 fiftieth anniversary issue of Appalachia — *there were then five chapters — suggests that those "whose misfortune it is to live so far from the Hub of the Universe" owe a great deal to the concept of local chapters.*

Chapters have continued to grow and prosper: there are eleven that range from eastern Pennsylvania to the Canadian border. They have their own meetings and programs, sponsor extensive schedules of outings and excursions, and often own and operate their own camps and reservations. They complement and further the overall interest of the Club, and their members are its very roots.

It is especially appropriate that this history of the Club's chapters was written by Dean Peabody, Jr. During his three terms as president of the Club, he devoted much effort to promoting closer ties between the chapters and the Club. He was a frequent and favorite guest at annual chapter meetings.

TO MOST MEMBERS of the Club the Council is a mystery. They read the reports of the Council meetings as published in the monthly bulletins and wonder how the Council could possibly have spent an hour or more coming to the reported decisions. Of course, the fact is that it didn't, for the reports cover only a small part of the deliberations of the Council. One of the most important functions of the Council is to prevent things from happening. When you are trying to prevent things from happening, you don't advertise the fact.

Councils differ as much as people. Some have transacted their business with a minimum of discussion. Others have been loquacious and have spent hours of time thrashing out problems without accomplishing much. You will remember that *Hamlet* is nearly twice as long as any other play of Shakespeare's and, in spite of all the talk, almost nothing happens till the last act! However, regardless of the route followed, Councils have almost always acted with substantial unanimity in the end. I cannot recall half a dozen instances where any matter has been decided by a close vote.

Sometimes, though rarely, the Council has not agreed with the Membership Committee and, in its policy-making role, has elected to membership someone who failed to receive the endorsement of the committee. Once the only objection seemed to be that the applicant was "a nut." The members of the Council looked at one another and almost simultaneously blurted out, "Aren't we all?"

The Club has been fortunate in its ability to draft younger people for membership on the Council. Many organizations tend to become static and unprogressive because their officers and executive group are recruited largely from the older members of the organization. This has never been true of our Club. The Club was formed by a group of young men and the younger groups have always been in control. As a result, the Council has been able to meet every opportunity for service with an open mind. It has encouraged rock climbing and white-water canoeing. It has provided for skiers. On the other hand, after due consideration, it has never hesitated to abandon once-popular activities that have become outmoded.

However, in spite of all the changes that have taken place in the world and in the activities which the Club has from time to time sponsored, the Council has kept in view the primary purposes which inspired the founders of the Club. In making out its annual budget, it has always provided funds for publishing our *Appalachia* magazine; it has always provided funds for trail maintenance; it has always been liberal in its appropriations for hut construction; it has always found money to finance our *White Mountain Guide* with its valuable maps.

Although the Council contains representatives of its leading activities, who can thus speak for these activities, its obligation is and has always been to the Club as a whole and to the public, for it must never be forgotten that the Appalachian Mountain Club is a public charitable corporation. If the Council continues to act in the future as it has in the past, the Club will be in safe hands.

T|HE POLITICAL HISTORY of the Appalachian Mountain Club resembles in many ways that of the United States. Both started as a compact group of members, or citizens, and subsequently expanded until their geographical extent was so greatly increased that a consequent difficulty fulfilling the objectives of the organization resulted. The AMC member living at a distance from Boston rightly felt that he enjoyed fewer privileges as a member than those nearer the center. It was inevitable then that at other centers of membership local groups would come together.

The result has been that we have a chapter (state) organization for local affairs and, superposed upon that, a federal government handling the commonwealth of the AMC: the trails, huts, camps, and excursions. The AMC has had, as yet, no destructive Civil War, so the States-Rights party is in full control of each chapter. So much so, that it is the favorite witticism to introduce a freshman president on his first visit to the annual meeting of a chapter as "the Chairman of the Boston Chapter."

New York was the natural focus for the appearance of the first chapter, for a large group of active AMC mountaineers lived there. After some preliminary rumbles the chapter was organized in 1912. Frank S. Mason, as president and later as chairman of the AMC Committee on Regional Chapters, was the leading figure in the formation of the next four.

From what was formerly considered an underprivileged status, the chapter member is now in a most-favored situation. He is one of a group small enough so that he may know all his associates. There are local excursions and meetings, as well as all the general Club activities available for his choice. Practically all of the chapters possess, or have owned previously, local "huts" or camps. Such places as Berkshire's "Noble View," Worcester's "Chapter Lodge," the "Bantam Lake Camp" of Connecticut, and "Fire Island Shelter" for New York have been centers of social life and the terminal objective of walks. Many of the chapters have developed trails in their areas; the most notable being the Manning Trail on Mount Cardigan laid out by the Merrimack Chapter, just before the advent of the skiers, and the various sections of the Appalachian Trail cared for by the three western chapters.

The chapter members have increasingly participated in attendance and in committee membership on our general excursions, at the camps, and on our special activities, such as rock climbing, white-water canoeing, and skiing. I clearly recall from my rock-climbing days the pleasure of my first attempt of the prize routes of the Connecticut and New York rock-climbers, and the good fellowship enjoyed with these newfound friends.

Blest be the tie that binds, and blest be the good sense and tact that have minimized possible friction between chapter and Council, so that all members may wander throughout the realms of the AMC unarmed and fancyfree, fully participating in the various activities and sharing in the comradeship which our Club has to offer.

On top of Mount Liberty, 1907

✻ 2

BLAZING
THE TRAIL

AMC Manages the Mountains

Trails

THE BUILDING OF "PATHS," as they were orig-
inally called, was one of the first priorities of the Club. C. Francis
Belcher, in the previous chapter, has already alluded to the
generally pathless condition of the White Mountain area in the
late 1880s. To be sure, there was the Carriage Road on Mount
Washington, completed in 1861, and the Mount Washington
Railroad, first used in 1869. Beyond these, however, there was
little except a few ancient bridle paths and several short foot-
paths, maintained by hotels, which led to a nearby waterfall or
other attraction.

In the spring of 1876 William G. Nowell, AMC's first
Councillor of Improvements, suggested that twenty paths be
made, seven of them "speedily." Among this latter group was a
route up the main northern ridge of Mount Adams. With well-
known local guide Charles E. Lowe, Nowell began cutting the
path that autumn, and the project was completed the following
summer. In August of 1976 a ceremony at the foot of Lowe's Path
commemorated one hundred years of public use and continuous
maintenance of this, the first, AMC trail.

Emphasis on trail building, almost frantic at times, continued for several decades and opened the White Mountains for the first time to the public at large. Howard Goff, in "The Pace of the Grub-Hoe," written for *Appalachia* in 1951, calculates that in the AMC's first seventy-five years, an average of 23.5 miles of trail per year were developed in the White Mountains, much of it by the AMC. However, maintaining these trails proved to be an increasing problem for the Club, in part because they were so widespread. Each Councillor of Improvements, it seemed, tended to focus his efforts on new areas that were personal favorites. An observer in the early 1900s noted that if there were an original plan for the trails, it had vanished into "innocuous desuetude," and the trails, like Topsy, "just growed."

As the sheer volume of trail work demanded of AMC volunteers became too burdensome, the Club experimentally hired a local woodsman for trail clearing in 1917, only to encounter numerous problems. In 1919 there was a new experiment. Paul Jenks, Councillor of Trails, hired several of his high-school pupils, along with a student from Dartmouth College — Sherman Adams, later governor of New Hampshire — to spend the summer working on trails under his supervision. Pay was a dollar a day plus expenses. This arrangement was most satisfactory, and the trail crew became an AMC institution. Today the trail crew has grown to twenty or more, mostly "college huskies" — not all of whom, notes an early report, are "of the axe-wielding sex." Crew members spend the workweek living in the field, clearing blowdowns, cleaning waterbars, arranging 175-pound rocks into stepping stones, and other difficult and occasionally dangerous tasks. All this for a modest $45 to $78 per week, plus room and board. Nearly all return for at least a second year.

As with all Club activities, there are a handful of individuals over the years who contribute far beyond the call of duty. With trails it is the "Old Masters," two of whom wrote the papers included in this section. Nathaniel Goodrich writes of the attractions and rewards of trail making, perhaps partly explaining why so many trails were opened in the early years of the Club. His rationale seems just as valid, if not more so, today. Dean of the Old Masters, Charles W. Blood, writes some of his personal reflections on his nearly seventy years of association with the trails of the White Mountains.

Today the Club maintains several hundred miles of trails in the mountains of New Hampshire and Maine. Certainly the most widely known portion is the segment of the Appalachian Trail that traverses the backbone of the White Mountains. The Club contributed substantially to the early progress of the trail as noted by its "father," Benton MacKaye, in a 1922 article in *Appalachia*. MacKaye was closely associated with the Club, volunteering his time in the summers of 1907 and 1908 to assist the AMC in managing its recently acquired Rhododendron Reservation. He personally led parties of workers in clearing slash left by previous logging from the site to reduce the risk of fires. He later prepared the first comprehensive forest management plan for the same site. In 1975, the year of his death, he was voted honorary membership in the Club.

THE ATTRACTIONS AND REWARDS OF TRAIL MAKING
NATHANIEL L. GOODRICH
1918

NATHANIEL GOODRICH WAS A CHARTER member of the "Old Masters," a group of ex-Councillors of Trails so christened by the AMC trail crowd for their experience and expertise. He was a contemporary of Charles Blood and Paul Jenks, whom we meet in the final paper of this section. Together they spent more than twenty summers in the White Mountains dreaming, prospecting, and making the AMC trail system.

This paper was read by Goodrich at the annual meeting of the New England Trail Council in 1917. The council had been formed the previous year to coordinate regional efforts in trail development and maintenance. The AMC was, and still is, a principal participant. Goodrich engagingly describes some of the more romantic aspects of trail work — its concreteness as opposed to the abstraction of the everyday world, its enduring quality, and the delight and enthusiasm of tramping "one's own trail." One must wonder if his objective in preparing this paper was simply to enlighten the uninitiated with these personal observations or rather to entice more volunteer workers into the woods. In either case he seems to have succeeded.

OF TRAIL MAKING there are three stages. There is dreaming the trail, there is prospecting the trail, there is making the trail. Of the first one can say nothing — dreams are fragile, intangible. Prospecting the trail — there lies perhaps the greatest of the joys of trail work. It has a suggestion of the thrill of exploration. No one of us but loves still to play explorer. And here there is just a bit of the real thing to keep the play going. Picking the trail route over forested ridges calls for every bit of the skill gained in our years of tramping. There is never time to go it slow, to explore every possibility. Usually there is one hasty day to lay out the line for a week's work. For a basis there is the look of the region, from some distant point, from a summit climbed last year, perhaps. For a help, there is the compass, but in our hill country we use it little. Partly we go by imperfect glimpses from trees climbed, from blow-down edges, from small cliffs — but chiefly we feel the run of the land, its lift and slope and direction. The string from the grocer's cone unwinds behind — an easy way of marking and readily obliterated when we go wrong. We pay little heed to small difficulties, those are for the trail markers to solve. Only a wide blow-down, a bad ledge, a mistake in general direction, cause us to double back a bit and start afresh.

There is an edge, a tenseness, about this work. The day is a long strain of keen concentration, of quick decisions, of driving through scrub and blow-downs. The unexpected may appear at any minute — an outlook, a spring, a trail. It gets done at length, and so back to camp.

Making trail is the more plodding work; yet it has reliefs and pleasures of its own. Each day, as the gang works along the string line, problems of detail arise. Ours is no gang of uninterested hirelings. If the line makes a suspicious bend, the prospectors have to explain or correct. If it plunges through a blow-down, their intelligence and motives receive pungent criticism, and someone is likely to take a vacation for explorations of his own.

So there is scouting ahead and shouting back, running of trail lines in doubtful places, argument, decision. If we go through the blow-down, we lose much of the limited time in slow cutting; if around, we lengthen the trail. If we go over a hump in the ridge instead of slabbing around, we keep a straighter line, but cause posterity to climb up and then climb down again. And all is complicated by the requirement that the footing shall not be too rough for men under heavy packs.

Decision made, the gang scatters along the line, each to a rod or two, for we find working together is not efficient. Each then finds that he has in little the problems of the general line. He casts ahead over his section, picks his line over a bit of ledge, decides whether to loop around a small snarl of down timber or drive through, aware that few will ever know the difference whatever he decides, but thinking always of the future trail crank who might inspect his work with critical eye. In thick growth where it is impossible to see ahead it is sometimes necessary to break, head down, through a rod or two of country four or five times before the line is right. Then he settles to the job, and the odor of fresh-cut fir arises. He works in a remote little world of his own, a way through lengthening behind him, happy, intent, and oblivious, until quite suddenly he finds a fresh-cut way ahead — and that stint is done. He looks back and sees that it is good, looks forward up the next man's job and sees that it is very bad, shoulders tools and disappears up the line to start another section.

One dismal noon of wind and intermittent rain found us cutting high on the shoulder of Lafayette, in the scrub belt below timber line. The trees were little more than head high and drenching wet. The cold gusts swept through, but little broken by the low growth. The most strenuous exertions hardly kept us warm. Each as he finished his section turned to the next man's, until all were together on the final stretch. The last tree fell, the last branch was tossed aside. "All done above?" said one. "All done, she's through to timber line."

The next day dawned brilliant and still, a mountain day, a day of days for the last of our work, cairning the line up the ledges beyond timber line. High on the shoulder of the world, our gaze sweeping a crystal horizon, revelling in the incommunicable joy of the great sunlit hills, the hours passed unnoticed. We picked our line up ledges and around low cliffs, carried rocks and built our cairns. The old tall cairn at the summit drew near. "One more will do it," we said. Then we dug from the pack the sign, long since painted for this very spot, and wedged it into the summit cairn. We gathered there — "Garfield Ridge Trail" it read, "To Garfield and S. Twin." Our work was done. We were all professional men, dealers with books and papers, with the abstract and the intangible. Here, at least, was one concrete thing done, a visible result of labor, not unlikely to endure. So we sat in the sunlight of Lafayette, and were happy.

Other trails, other scenes. What will recall to each of you his best days on the trail? Camps by the pulsing, insistent rushing of a brook; nights in the open, with moonlight in the firs; drumming rain on the tent; noon halts by a spring; monotonous hours of blazing, chopping, sawing; the smells that work so strongly in our memories — wood smoke, balsam, fly-dope, wet clothes drying. Each to his own woods. If mine are the low firs of the high levels, yours may be the great hardwoods, the old growth spruce, the second growth country of old logging roads, the oak scrub of the Massachusetts hills, with rustling leaves under foot and a riot of autumn color.

And what of the trail itself, of the pleasure of tramping it? Any trail is a delight, sometimes; one's own trail is an enthusiasm.

THE EVOLUTION OF A TRAILMAN
CHARLES W. BLOOD
1965

IN THIS ARTICLE, *written the year before he died, Charles Blood describes his personal evolution as a trailman. His remembrances span nearly seventy years of experience with White Mountain trails, from early trial-and-error approaches to latter-day bridge-building. He notes the Club's important reassessment of trail policy in the early 1920s. Until that time trail mileage had been added to the system quickly and sometimes indiscriminately, which compounded the problem of trail maintenance. The expanding hut and shelter systems also meant more trail use and more maintenance. A special Club committee was formed — a process Blood took under personal control — that recommended that the AMC concentrate its efforts on major trunkline and connecting trails and turn trails predominantly of local interest over to local hiking organizations and appropriate public agencies. In this way the Club consolidated its efforts where they were most needed and it has retained this policy to the present day.*

Blood's story is liberally punctuated with references to Paul Jenks, his congenial trail companion of thirty-five years. Jenks was known as AMC's "Sign Man," because he assumed responsibility for the Club's five thousand trail signs. With help from his high-school pupils, he experimented with different types of signboards and paints and eventually developed today's system of trail signs. He summered in the White Mountains every year, placing new signs prepared the previous winter and collecting old signs worth saving for repair. Writing of his experiences in Appalachia *in 1945, he remembers one incident in particular. Two guests of the Mount Washington Summit House spotted Jenks returning one evening from the trail with an armload of signs and inquired about him at the desk. Leaving for another day on the trail with an armload of new signs, he encountered the same guests at six-thirty the next morning. This time they questioned him directly: "We saw you come in yesterday afternoon with a load of signs and go out with some this*

*morning. Now, do you do that regularly, bring in the signs at night and
put them out again the next morning?"*

*Blood, or "CWB" as he was popularly known, served the Club in
many capacities. He was president, vice-president, Councillor of Improvements, Councillor of Topography, Trustee of Special Funds, and
treasurer for twenty-two years. By his own admission, though, Blood
was above all else a trailman.*

M Y FIRST GLIMPSE of the White Mountains was
from the Maine coast when I was a small boy. I was told
that the dim blue outline I saw was Mount Washington.

My first visit to the mountains came when I was ten. With
my father and mother I spent two weeks at Littleton. I remember
the impression I got as we came up through Crawford Notch on
the observation car. The ride through the Notch on the train was
much more spectacular than the view one gets today from the
highway. I had prepared for the trip by bringing a small stone
from home to drop from the Frankenstein Trestle.

Like all small boys I was eager to climb Mount Washington, but my father — wisely, I now realize — refused to take me.
The east side was too far away for a day's trip from Littleton and,
although my father had walked up the Carriage Road a few years
before when vacationing at Gorham, he knew nothing about the
west side of the mountain, where the Crawford Path was the only
footpath.

For several years following this we spent our summer
vacations at the seashore and I did not return to the mountains
until I was halfway through college, when I spent a July at
Waterville. We liked the place so well that I returned to it every
summer for the next twenty years.

On fine days we usually climbed one of the neighboring
mountains. Waterville was then, as it is now, one of the best
tramping locations in the mountains. The hotel was and is one of
the few where you can step from the piazza into the forest. Before
the days of automobiles and blacktop highways, tramping was
largely local and Waterville boasted four fine 4,000-foot peaks. (I

include Sandwich Mountain, although without the summit cairn I believe it is only 3,933 feet high.)

For the first few years I did not attempt to leave the regular, well-kept trails. As a matter of fact I had a peculiar dread of being alone in the forest. It was purely psychological; there was nothing of which I was afraid. While I have seen innumerable deer and porcupines, a few rabbits, an occasional beaver and one or two foxes, in the sixty-seven years I have roamed the White Mountains only once have I seen a bear and on that occasion the bear and I went in opposite directions. The most startling thing one encounters in the White Mountain forests is the sudden shirr of a partridge or the chatter of a squirrel.

In the early days I had only a vague sense of topography. I was not interested in the location of the trails. To me they were merely routes by which to reach attractive peaks and waterfalls. I used trails that had been made by others. The idea of locating and opening a new trail never occurred to me.

The first new trail out of the Valley in my time was one opened in 1901 leading from Cascade Brook to Whiteface. I formed an unfavorable opinion of this trail the first time that I used it. For the first time I was carrying a pack with blankets and provisions for an overnight stay. Up to that time when I went off for a day's trip I carried my lunch rolled up in a sweater tied around my waist. This trip was also my first experience spending the night on fir boughs in a log shelter. I had heard that such a bunk was very comfortable. I did not find it so, for during the night I kept digging out pieces of wood under me. In the morning I discovered that I had been sleeping on a pile of kindling wood.

A few years later Paul Jenks took me out in front of the hotel one morning and pointed to a slight sag in the ridge to the east and suggested that a trail from the Valley through that gap would shorten the Woodbury Trail and avoid the loss of elevation on the old route by way of the Cascades. This was an interesting idea, and we prospected the new route. We had never heard of "stringing" a trail and we marked our proposed location by small blazes. Cutting the trail proved quite a task. I had never swung an ax and my only tool was a small Boy Scout hatchet. Up the hillside from the Valley our trail was serpentine for, although the young hardwood growth was quite thick, we did not attempt to cut any trees more than an inch or two in diameter. Above that point the woods were fairly open but infested with hobblebush. If a person has ever attempted to cut hobblebush with a hatchet or ax he knows what a task we had. We had no better luck with a bush scythe, and it was not until years later that we realized how simple a task it is to cut hobblebush with long-handled pruning shears.

About this time we began a series of tramping trips outside the Waterville Valley, including tramping trips to Franconia, Carter, and Mount Washington ranges and camping trips to Carrigain, the Twin Range, and the Lowell, Anderson, Nancy, and Bemis group. In all these trips we were becoming oriented throughout the mountains. We learned not to be dependent upon familiar trails but to tramp cross-country by sun and by compass, and camp where we found water.

After three years of local tramps about Waterville and a camping trip in Huntington Ravine, my real trail work began in 1913. Paul Jenks suggested that we camp at a little spring below the cone of Mount Jackson and cut a trail from Jackson to Clinton. The previous year he had cut a rough trail between the summits of Webster and Jackson. By this time I had graduated from hatchet to ax and Paul had acquired a pair of long-handled pruning shears. However, we were still very much amateurs. That night Harry Tyler, who was then Councillor of Improvements of the AMC, joined us. He had brought a small ball of string and initiated us in the idea of stringing a trail.

The opinion that Harry Tyler formed of me, due I believe more to my cooking than to skill in trail work, caused him to recommend me as his successor as Councillor of Improvements the next year. I had joined in 1912 because I was using the Club's trails and thought I ought to "pay my taxes." I had not intended or expected to take any part in the work of the Club.

In order to become thoroughly familiar with all the AMC trails, I made it a point during my term as councillor to visit the trails that I had not previously tramped. In 1914, Paul and I camped at the old shelter in Carter Notch. The trip over the Carter Range the next day was a hectic experience. The range trail up Moriah was well marked through a burn-over on the south side of the mountain, but we completely lost the trail through the burn-over on the Gorham side, and we finally came down without trail to the logging roads in the Moriah Brook Valley and landed completely exhausted after eight o'clock in the evening.

In 1918 it was suggested that there should be a trail from Wildcat over the ridge running west to Pinkham Notch. Dr. Larrabee reported that the view from the lawn (now known as Larrabee Lawn) across the Mount Washington ravines was in itself worth a trail. As a result Paul and I spent a day stringing a route from Glen Ellis Falls up through the ledges, and a second day stringing from Wildcat west over the "Kittens" to the end of our first day's line. Considering its length, the route is much harder than would be expected, as I found out later when going over the trail after it had been cut out.

Later in the same week, while spending two days at Lakes-of-the-Clouds Hut, I located and cairned the Camel Trail. Stringing was not necessary; it was merely a case of aiming the cairns toward the Camel.

In 1922 we moved to Zealand Notch in order to make a connection from the Twin Range to the east. The ledges on the west side of the notch presented some interesting problems in trail location. Gary Harris had run a string line up the face of the cliffs, but this seemed to us an impossible route for what would presumably be a through tramping trail. After a good deal of study, I discovered a little shelf which afforded a satisfactory route, and we led the trail up that way. The forest from the top of the ledges to Zeacliff Pond had been burned over in the big forest fire many years before while the trees were still standing. Although these fire-killed trees had fallen they were still sound, easy to cut with a saw but difficult to cut with an ax.

In 1923, we came back to the Mahoosuc country, and Paul and I ran a string line from Gentian Pond across to Dream Lake. I have always regarded this as one of the best bits of stringing I have ever done. The distance was about two miles; the country was rather flat and irregular with no well-defined ridges. We knew only approximately where Dream Lake was located but we were able to strike the inlet brook within one hundred yards of the lake. This section was later cut out by the Trail Crew.

Up to this time there was nobody to consider the relationship of the Club's trails, shelters, and huts. The Councillor of Improvements opened trails and built shelters wherever he wanted to and for which he had sufficient appropriations, and the Trustees of Real Estate were building huts with their own financing and without even notifying the Council of their plans. It was felt that this situation should not continue but that there should be some committee to which all plans for new trail, shelter, or hut work should be submitted in order that there should be coherent development of our system. After a preliminary study by an *ad hoc* group it was agreed that the Club should have a regular standing committee for this purpose. As I was president of the Club at this time and wanted to make sure that this committee got off to a good start and would not be sidetracked or ignored, I appointed myself chairman of the committee and for thirty years I suppose I dominated the Trail, Hut, and Camp Extension Committees.

By 1930 the management of the AMC trails had passed from the Old Masters to the Young Masters, the trail system was pretty well established, and no new trails of major importance appeared in sight. The problems had become more those of improving existing trails.

In 1937, a party of us camped at Eliza Brook Shelter on the Kinsman Ridge Trail. This trail, as originally constructed, had not gone over Wolf Mountain, but had followed some Forest Service trails to the east of it. For a number of reasons it seemed wise to carry this section over the mountain. The last morning we were there, instead of going up on the trail for more cutting, I spent about an hour at the junction. The new trail did not leave the Forest Service trail exactly opposite the point the old trail from the north came down. After a good deal of study and some cutting, I made a clean crossing. When Fred Fish came back he looked at it and said, "I see the Old Master Mind is still at work."

By the late forties I found it took longer for me to get into real tramping condition than formerly and I did not want to have a strenuous climb more than once or twice a week. On the other hand, I was just as eager as ever to get into the forest and work on the trails. By that time Schmeck (Dr. Schmeckabier) had quit climbing entirely but was also anxious to work in the forest and we formed a sort of partnership which lasted until his death. We had worked together on trail clearing in Randolph and about 1947 we began to build bridges on the Moosebank and other trails near the Ravine House. Like most of my early trail work, the development of our bridges was a matter of "trial and error."

As I look back over my nearly seventy years of experience with the White Mountain trails, several things stand out. Except for tramping, which I often have done alone, though I prefer to have a congenial companion, the trail work has depended largely upon the cooperation of other kindred spirits. Without such assistance I am afraid I should have accomplished very little. For thirty-five years Paul and I worked together as a harmonious team — each having perfect confidence in the other. When, after a trip over the Baldface range putting up signs one April, we landed on Eagle Crag at sunset with several feet of snow on the ground and all blazes covered, we were not in the least concerned, although neither of us had ever been on that trail before. We merely put on our snowshoes, came down where we thought the trail ought to be and when we got to the bottom found we were on the trail.

As each opportunity came along, I was physically able to take advantage of it, and my previous experience had given me a reasonable foundation for the work. For thirty years I never had to consider whether a trip or expedition would be too much for me. On a one-day trip Paul and I took in 1905 from Waterville to Whiteface and Passaconaway, I learned to take a pace that I could hold without frequent stops to rest — "the pace that kills" the distance, not the man. I still take that pace, although it is half as fast as it was fifty years ago.

I have never made any records for speed or tried to make any. Probably I could not have even if I had tried. I have never tried to "collect" all the 4,000-footers, although at one time or another I have been on all but three of these mountains and have been on about seventy-five peaks in the White Mountain country from Kearsarge and Cardigan on the south to Magalloway, Aziscoos, and Baldpate on the north. Gathering *records* has never interested me particularly. Some peaks and some trails are worth repeated visits. In recent years, when I realized that the time would soon come when most climbs would be beyond my capacity, I chose each year some mountain or trail that I would particularly like to climb again. I am glad I did.

I am happy, however, just to go into the forest and put a new handrail on a bridge or putter over a few rods of trail, for, above everything, I am a trailman.

Huts and Shelters

THE EXTENSIVE HUT and shelter system of the AMC had its beginnings in a concept considerably different from its popular image now. The original structures were built for safety rather than recreation and convenience. The first hut constructed at Madison Spring in 1888 was erected simply as a refuge for persons caught on the mountain by night or by a sudden storm. The refuge along the exposed ridge of the Crawford Path between Mount Clinton and the summit of Mount Washington was constructed in 1901 as a direct result of two tragic deaths in that area the previous year. The structure was, in fact, posted "Not for pleasure camping."

But with AMC trails attracting more trampers to the mountains, the huts evolved into popular camping destinations. As early as 1895 the Councillor of Improvements reported that "The (Madison Spring) Hut has been more used this season than ever before, at one time, at least, sheltering more than twice its complement." To control the use and sometime abuse of the hut, the Club stationed a keeper there in 1906 and asked compensation for using the hut; $231.60 was collected that year from 469 campers. That first hutmaster, on his own initiative, occasionally prepared meals for guests, which became so popular that it soon became a regular feature of hut life. The continuing popular use of the Madison Spring Hut led the Club's Trustees of Real Estate to suggest in 1908 that it might "be of great advantage to the community if a few additional huts shall be constructed, with good paths thereto, so that an interesting walk of from three to seven days may be made without the incumberance of the carrying of blankets or provisions." And so the concept of the modern hut system crystallized. The huts' expansion era lasted from 1914 to the early 1930s, personally supervised first by Milton E. MacGregor and later by Joe Dodge, who describes some of his experiences in the first paper of this section.

There are now nine AMC huts in an area stretching more than fifty miles across the White Mountains. All are open to the public; each offers bunks, blankets, and hearty meals. There are also twenty AMC shelters.

If hut life is a pleasure to the average camper, it is something much more intense to the hut crews. Mostly college students, these hardy individuals spend their summers at the huts, where they do maintenance and provide basic services for visitors. They are a close-knit group, bound by a common love of the mountains and also by a common need to tolerate the exploits of the ubiquitous "goofer" with good humor. To be called a goofer is not an insult: the term is descriptive, not pejorative; it refers to the characteristic behavior of a mountain novice, and so, we are all goofers at some time.

AN OLD HUTMAN REMINISCES
JOSEPH B. DODGE
1963

IF IT IS POSSIBLE for one man to be the quintessence of an organization, then for the Appalachian Mountain Club that man is Joe Dodge. Mayor of Porky Gulch, First Citizen of the North Country, twentieth-century pioneer, co-founder of the Mount Washington Observatory, honorary Master of Arts from Dartmouth — these are a few of the ways that Dodge is remembered. To thousands of White Mountain trampers, he was the AMC. Dodge was often described as a rough man, like the mountain country he loved. But when he died in 1973, he left "nearly as many friends as trees in New Hampshire." His reputed roughness stemmed from Dodge's directness and his fluent and creative use of colorful language. According to his friend Bill Whitney, "There was no doubt Joe was a churchman. He referred to the Lord in nearly every sentence and in a greater variety of ways than I ever thought to."

The Old Hutman's reminiscences begin in 1922, when he accepted his first position with the Club as hutmaster at Pinkham Notch. In those early days he was the protege of Milton E. "Red Mac" MacGregor, whom he succeeded as huts manager in 1928. Dodge briefly describes the expansion of the hut system — opening Pinkham Notch on a year-round basis for the first time, developing and constructing four new huts, and rebuilding, adding to, and improving the four existing huts. But that is only part of Dodge's story. Not included is the fact that he co-founded the Mount Washington Observatory in 1932 and served as its managing director and treasurer until his death. Neither space nor Dodge's modesty would permit a record of his mountain search and rescue activities or his evangelistic work for skiing and other winter sports. In recognition of these and other accomplishments, Dartmouth College honored Dodge along with the poet Robert Frost at its 1955 commencement. Prior to awarding Dodge an honorary degree, President John S. Dickey of Dartmouth said,

Long-time mountaineer, student of Mount Washington's ways and weather, you have been more than a match for storms, slides, fools, skiers, and porcupines. You have rescued so many of us from both the harshness of the mountain and the soft ways leading down to boredom that you, yourself, are now beyond rescue as a legend of all that is unafraid, friendly, rigorously good, and ruggedly expressed in the out-of-doors. And with it all you gave this college a great skiing son. As one New Hampshire institution to another, Dartmouth delights to acknowledge you as Master of Arts.

I
T WAS ON JUNE 9TH, 1922, that I bid adieu to my folks in Manchester-by-the-Sea and climbed in the only piece of rolling stock the Club owned at the time, a model T Ford truck, with Red Mac, Johnnie White, and Ed Nelson. It was a real expedition to reach the White Hills in those days as there was no paved highway north of Rochester and we had the usual tire trouble that hot June day. We finally arrived late, just ahead of a thundershower, at Pinkham Notch Camp, where I was to be the hutmaster that summer.

The two log buildings were built at Pinkham Notch during the summer of 1920; Bill Loker was the first hutmaster and I was the second. When I looked over the interior that June day, it looked pretty bare, so I immediately started building various pieces of equipment, shelves, benches, and so on. Many small changes were made between daily cookery and the duty of killing the excessive numbers of porcupines that bothered us. Mac and I built new facilities for the men and women out in the woods and a much appreciated wooden canopy over the guests' washstand. Such jobs were sandwiched in between the preparation of meals for the registered and the unannounced guests. It always gave me a thrill to see how far I could stretch the soup and open a few more cans of this or that to expand a meal prepared for a dozen to serve sometimes three times that number. In those days we cooked entirely with wood at Pinkham, and it was another chore to work up wood ahead to be sure of good dry hardwood for the hot fires we needed. At Pinkham we got on nicely with the hardwoods, mainly beech, killed by the porcupines that girdled these trees three or four feet from the ground, working on winter snows.

The great numbers of porcupines caused Ed Nelson, the truck driver that summer, to call the place Porky Gulch, a name that has stuck through the years, replacing Pinkham Notch, even on incoming correspondence. Many a night we killed a dozen porkies. We clipped the noses for the 25¢ bounty, which was put in our meager kitty of those days. In the spring, we would collect the bounty from the town clerk in Gorham, buy strawberries and cream, then go home and make what we called a porcupine shortcake. Several years later, when I had been given ether for a leg injury, I was told that coming out of the effects I raved about porcupine shortcake and I had to make a complete explanation of what a porcupine shortcake was.

The next spring marked my arrival in the hills for good, as on May 7, 1926, I opened Pinkham Notch Camp, after bucking the snowbanks halfway up old Spruce Hill, where Tom Baker and I abandoned "Asma," my mountain-going Ford, and hiked into camp slumping deep in the thawing snows. We threw the key away that day, and Pinkham Notch Camp has been a year-round part of the Club activities in the White Hills ever since.

In October the Hut Committee called me to Boston. We had a very pleasant luncheon at the City Club, with light conversation, and I was awfully uneasy as I had misgivings that I was being hauled up on the carpet for something I had done that summer. Conversation ran on until George Rust asked me if I would be interested in keeping Pinkham Notch Camp open for the winter and make periodic trips to the other huts, Lakes-of-the-Clouds, Madison, and Carter Notch, to try to prevent the vandalism that had been rampant for several years when the huts were unmanned. I told the Committee that I would love the chance to keep Pinkham open for the winter. I could visualize the necessary work to make the camp livable for the winter and I determined that I would equip myself with some radio gear for communication.

Before Christmas we were snowed-up until the next May for wheel travel in any direction, and this gave a real feeling of isolation. But we made frequent trips to the Glen House for fresh milk and once every two weeks we skied into Gorham. Because of the fact that we could not anticipate our volume of business we had to backpack many heavy loads all the way from Gorham to camp, and eleven miles of uphill on skis is quite a chore with 100 pounds on your back. Owing largely to a very nice story in the old *Transcript* concerning the pioneering of the Club in Pinkham Notch, we had enough guests so that the camp lost only $119 that first winter of 1926-27.

The spring of '29 was all activity. The Committee had commissioned me to take over the log buildings at Lonesome Lake for a hut, build a hut of a new type of construction at Eagle Lake on Mount Lafayette, and add a kitchen, dining room, and hutmen's quarters at Madison. This indeed, in addition to the regular huts operations, was a large order for a young feller, but I was eager and willing and wanted to make good so that I took everything in stride.

The summer was certainly a very busy one, and many a night I lay in my bunk planning the morrow, but we completed, as far as possible, the scheduled jobs and closed in Greenleaf Hut on Mount Lafayette by October 12, just ahead of an early fall snowstorm. The next spring we completed this job, moved over to Carter Notch, and added a kitchen and hutmen's quarters to the stone hut.

Now we had a discontinuous hut chain, the four original huts in the Carter and Presidential range and Greenleaf and Lonesome Lake huts far to the west, with a gap of thirty-odd miles separating the Lakes-of-the-Clouds Hut from Greenleaf Hut on Mount Lafayette. What to do about it? The fall of 1930 was spent cruising much of the territory along the Twinway and Garfield Ridge trails, and two locations were chosen by the Committee, one at the head of Gale River and the second on the side of Whitewall Brook in Zealand Notch. To complete these two jobs in one year was a pretty big order, but we carried on. These were true pioneering jobs, back a long way from the usual forms of transportation and offering a real challenge.

Construction was quiet for the next few years until we launched into the big changes at Pinkham when we built the new Lodge in 1934 and in 1935 moved the log lodge and attached it to the former cookhouse making the Trading Post. These were home jobs and offered no great problems, but all the time we were increasing our demand for electrical power and after inventorying the Cutler River for over a year, we made an application to the Federal Power Commission for a permit to build a miniature Hoover Dam. Because we were on Federal land, the document issued the Club for a 15 HP plant on the Cutler River was the same as issued for the gigantic dam in Nevada. Isn't that something? This was a very interesting project and with additions and improvements served the Club nobly from 1939 to 1960, saving, over the years, many thousands of dollars. It wasn't the best regulated power but with reasonable care and attention served its purpose very well. This little plant was one of my crowning achievements and I was very fond and proud of its performance.

A major change was made and many conveniences were added to the kitchen at Pinkham in 1940. This was the year we took some of the drudgery from the hut boys and girls by installing a second-hand dishwasher and made the cooks happy with an upright baker and new cooking ranges. This year also marked the first catastrophe to the huts, the burning of Madison Hut on October 7. I was really sunk when I was called on the telephone and told of this fire. Fortunately for us no water was available to put on the fire, and consequently the masonry was not split but came through in good shape. We had old #2 hut to house a construction crew the next spring and we were able to get the hut functioning again that next summer.

The next major construction came in 1947, when we added a wing of two bunkrooms and additional toilet facilities to the Pinkham Lodge and practically made a complete face-lifting of the Lakes-of-the-Clouds Hut. The Pinkham job started early in May but was interrupted in early July to take advantage of the good summer weather to do a real big job at the exposed site of the Lakes hut. After a hectic summer but a fruitful one, we returned to complete the job left at Pinkham and connected up a new heating system to the rooms.

May of 1950, we had another unfortunate fire when Tuckerman Ravine Shelter, which we took over from the U.S. Forest Service in 1945 to run, burned completely. The skiers had to do without shelter the next winter, but, as the Forest Service had demolished a large building at their Bartlett depot, the usable materials were made available and in the winter of 1951–52, we toted most of the necessary lumber and other durable items over the snow on the Tuckerman Trail and during the summer the present structure was built.

This was the last big construction job I did for the Club, but over the years I often wonder how were we able to do so much with so little. But the spirit was there and until I was required to slow down in the late fifties I was always in with the gang pitching, swearing, but making the jobs percolate. I am very proud to have been a part of the work of developing a chain of huts in the White Mountains that the Club can feel is making it possible for thousands of persons to have a healthful and inexpensive vacation on the ridges of New England.

PACKS AND PACKBOARDS:
A HUTMAN'S REMINISCENCES
JOHN C. WHITE
1939

OF JOHN WHITE'S REMINISCENCES of hut life, "packing" is the most vivid. Somehow those tons of supplies — fresh laundry, fifty-five-pound cases of soup, even the stove to cook it on — must be moved from the valleys to the cols and ridges where the huts are located. The traditional conveyance is the backs of the hut crews. John White explains why packing is an important ingredient in the glue that binds the hut crews together.

Over the years, packing has provided many excuses and opportunities for mountain heroics, especially during periods of hut construction, when tons of additional materials must be hauled. The single-day record must be held by the anonymous packer who, in ten round trips, packed 1,000 pounds of cement in to Lakes-of-the-Clouds in 1927, traveling a combined total of thirty miles, while climbing and descending 13,000 feet. No wonder that in 1938 a number of Club members expressed their concern over adverse effects of packing in a petition to the Club president. The Hut Committee's subsequent investigation concluded that there was no inherent medical danger. Indeed, most former hutmen surveyed reported that the rugged physical condition they acquired during their years of packing was a valuable asset in later life.

White worked in the hut system from 1921 to 1924 and has returned to the White Mountains nearly every year since.

THE STOREHOUSE FOR THE SUPPLIES for the Madison Spring Huts was in the Ravine House barn. You went in the side door on the lower level, through the stable room where the two big work horses were stalled, climbed up on a barrel to get the key and then unlocked the storeroom door. Here everything for the huts was piled up in a heap. Blankets back from the laundry were piled up on the shelf, clean and dry and good-smelling. A stack of new post cards, some shoe nails, a shiny new swill-pail, and several boxes of chocolate bars were lying about. But most everything else, the big bulk of the supplies, was in unbroken cartons. Soup and more soup. Klim and cocoa and canned fruits and all the vegetables, carton piled on carton, and more boxes of soup. One big box held a miscellaneous assortment of foodstuffs, salt and pepper and catsup and dates and breakfast foods and rice and macaroni and more such. Roughly there might be a ton of food and other articles locked up here in the Ravine House barn. Through the back window of this little storage closet you could look out over the lush meadows to the single-line train tracks and the wooded hillsides of Adams and see the valley of the Snyder Brook winding upward to the shoulder of Madison. Up to the top of that valley this stuff had to go, up to where the shoulder of Madison broke the skyline, and then a few hundred feet more into the hollow of Madison Spring.

A case of soup weighed about fifty-five pounds. With a little urging it would go whole and unopened into the packsack. If you put it in first it would tend to be bottom heavy in the pack and bump you in the small of the back. Better to put in a blanket for softness and two big cans of Klim at the bottom, then the soup, and at the top something not too big or heavy, something perhaps that should not be crushed. Then if you stuffed in the woolly shirt that you needed for the down trip and tied up the throat strings you were all set and ready to go. You knew what it ought to weigh but you took a test heave to sample it: you set it on the barrel and got into the straps. You were off.

All this ton of supplies and plenty more had to go up to the huts year after year. Most all of it has gone up on the backs of hutmen. There have been times, although not many, when the packers could hardly keep up with the demand at the huts. The shelves at Madison grew pretty bare toward the end of July in 1923. I had been at the Carter Hut that summer. Milton Mac-Gregor, Joe Dodge's predecessor as Hut Supervisor, sent someone in to take my place at Carter for a few days while I went to Madison along with four or five others to help with the packing. The August rush required a good stock.

Construction of the additions to the huts created a special problem. At those times the amount of material that had to be transported, naturally, was greatly increased. Part of the new building at Madison was started in 1922. The building crew finished up the cellar hole for the new hut about the end of June and began to call for a steady flow of sand, cement, and lumber of all sizes from the pine flooring and the shingles to the big two-by-six planks for the supports. Nails and tools and window glass had to go up the trail and, worst of all from the packers' point of view, the great steel window frames. A pair of stout horses dragged most of this up from Randolph through a rough roadway to a point on the Valley Way about half the distance from the bottom to the huts. Here it was dumped and covered from the rain with tarpaulins. From that point it was packed on man-back up the last mile-and-three-quarters to the Madison Spring. Up and down this stretch of the Valley Way there passed daily a gang of fifteen or twenty French-Canadians from Berlin and vicinity, loaded down with bags of sand, more bags of cement, and now and then boards and hardware and tools. What harm the packing may have done to the men we shall never know but I recall that they regularly brought in loads weighing up to 150 or even 175 pounds.

The hutmen usually carry their loads either with a rucksack or a packframe. The sack is convenient. Whatever you put into it stays secure and is protected from rain. Such a pack will hold enough, more than enough if it is stuffed with canned goods. It makes a world of difference how it is loaded, for if it is too heavy at the bottom it will tend to drag you over backwards, and if it is loosely stuffed it will sway and flop about. A good pack must lie snug at the back, well above the hips. Such a pack will stick to you and soak the sweat from your skin. A little of the walnut-colored dye from the pack cloth melts into your clothing and becomes a fixed and enduring part of it. In turn the pack itself becomes bleached and aromatic.

The pack-frame is nothing but a wooden corset for the back, all set about with hooks. It accommodates itself nicely to the carrying of boxes, stoves, kerosene tins, and wheelbarrows. To fit a load onto it you heap the boxes or what you will on its back and lash them securely with a rope to the many hooks. Many a mean and awkward load has been hauled up the trails by means of the packboard.

The pack up the Valley Way to the Madison Spring Huts has always been considered the hardest pack in the mountains. From the place where it leaves the highway and crosses the rich, wet meadows of the Randolph valley until it reaches the bleak grassy col of Madison Spring it is three-and-one-half miles. The Valley Way is not a favorite with the tramper; as a rule he finds it too monotonous for his liking for it has too few vistas, little novelty, and nothing like precipitous inclines. But after the one hundredth trip, more or less, it begins to be appreciated like an old friend. No doubt every familiar trail comes in time to be treasured for its associations. For a mile or more the Valley Way passes through deep forests of evergreens and hardwoods, sometimes hot and often buggy; but there is the agreeable sound of Snyder Brook always at hand, and frequent crossings where you may stop and get a drink. Next you cross the burnt patch and start the dreary climb up the hillside by the graded path, turning first to the left and then to the right, back and forth countless times. But here is where you may find the Canadian warblers and the black-throated blues. On this pitch is where Lew Hall, bitterly harassed by a bad pack load, tore away the legs of his long green breeches and tied them in a tree, where they hung in the breeze as a milepost to greet the sweaty packer for years to come. At the top of this pitch I once saw a bear cub scamper into the deep woods and here I always expect to see another.

The grade becomes more moderate now, but it is this middle section that seems endless and more discouraging. The brook has dropped away to your left and is heard as a muffled distant roaring. You look across the ravine to the rocky shoulder of Madison, steep and remote, rising higher with each stride you take, and yet you know you must meet that ridge at the top. Even so you finally reach the spruce woods and the place where the juncos had a nest and where the dancing song of the winter wren drifts through the trees like mist. Here is the clear flowing spring just a thousand feet from the huts. The trail above this spring is rougher and steep, the hardest work of all, but the down-flowing mountain air currents chill you and keep you going. The little twisted spruces shrink on each side and with every step the horizon opens up to the north so that when you stop and turn you see that your hard-earned trail has dropped away behind you and you look down into the misty valley.

Presently you are at the hut. You roll your pack off onto

the doorstep and you stand up. There are some visitors at the hut but what of it. You earned this moment and it is precious to you. You see the sun hazy and low in the west and the glint of Cherry Mountain Pond. The Bicknell thrushes are whistling somewhere in the scrub on Adams. For a few moments you soak it all up; then you know you are a little cold and will be stiff, and that you need a rubdown and a cup of tea. Gradually you descend, little by little, to the prosaic duties of the hut, yet not quite losing that inward sense of satisfaction with your job, a tough job done.

Packing is, withal, a good job. Most of the men have liked it and would not care to give it up. The only real trouble with it is that the packs get too heavy at times. They get too heavy before the hutmen get the loads firmly lashed to the board or in the pack, and they stay too heavy over every inch of the trail. Of course, you may say there is no need of this loading so many pounds. The seasoned packer, however, will hardly make up a light load if there is plenty at hand to pack. Here at the base of supplies he regards a light pack as hardly worthy of his efforts, though he may fret under his burden on the pitches. And you may say that if the load is too heavy it should be possible to lighten it en route, to remove some imperishable part of the burden and stow it conveniently behind a boulder. On occasions, I have seen some two-by-six planks left alongside the Valley Way during the period of construction. Now a two-by-six plank, eight or ten feet in length, is a mean load. It rides badly, however you adjust it, and it bumps and catches in trees. I have the utmost compassion for the packers, whoever they were, who foundered and cast their burdens by the side of the trail. But, for all that we admit a man may lighten his pack, it remains that it is very seldom done.

In the mind of the packers, if I may speak for them out of my own experience, there lies a sullen defiance of the pack, a single and unquestioned idea that the load, once securely bound and got up onto the back, somehow will go. I think those who worry about the carrying of big loads must look into the mind of the packer. Doubtless they have done so, and with little reassurance. The packer has a measure of sense at times, but it is a queer sense. It has little to do with necessity; it disregards convenience. It is not wholly without regard for effect, a kind of strutting, if you please, although for the most part it is done without comment or observation from anyone but the packer himself. If, on the other hand, he is plodding along doggedly under a good load and he overtakes a party on the trail and is given the right of way, what a lift he gets. The stretch of the path goes with renewed speed and power, although a pounding heart presently reminds him that it was not done without costs. Mostly the packer lives in a solitary world of this own thoughts. His mind perceives things dully and without keenness — the drip of sweat from the tip of the nose, the fatness of the veins of his hands. Ideas flit in and out, and phrases are annoyingly repetitious. Hunger and fatigue grow slowly and do not greatly disturb the languid mind. Sharp chill does hurt and awakens him to the reality of the annoyances. But hunger and chill and fatigue come toward the end and give keenness to the great pleasure of finishing the job.

Camps and Reservations

THE LATE 1800s are generally recognized as the period when America's great conservation movement began. Easterners could witness first hand the devastation that resulted from wasteful and exploitive lumbering practices; land, water, and wildlife resources of the country's great western public-domain lands were being exploited on an even grander scale. Natural resources — the nation's economic foundation and part of its cultural heritage — could no longer be considered super-abundant or unlimited: action needed to be taken to conserve them.

At this period in history, virtually no organizations existed to work toward conservation. There was no National Park Service, no U.S. Forest Service, no state forest or park agencies. The AMC played a pioneering role in conservation and preservation of New England lands — directly by acquiring and preserving significant properties and indirectly by supporting the creation of public agencies to carry out this work.

The earliest indication of the Club's interest in land conservation is in an 1886 recording secretary's report. The report, by Rosewell B. Lawrence, author of the first paper in this section, suggests that ". . . it is not unreasonable to expect that our Club will someday own mountains for the purpose of protecting Nature and enabling man to enjoy her beauties and grandeur." Shortly thereafter, in 1888, the Club acquired its first property, an acre of land located between Mount Adams and Mount Madison, the site for Madison Spring Hut. The property was donated by the Brown Lumber Company of Whitefield, New Hampshire.

Concern about land and resource conservation continued to grow, and in 1893 the Club held a series of discussions on forestry and other conservation issues. It was also resolved that year that "The Appalachian Mountain Club proposes not only to discuss but to act, and it is accordingly preparing to take the most important step since its organization in 1876 — to qualify itself to receive, hold, and administer real estate." The Club appealed to the Massachusetts legislature for permission to hold land in the public interest under tax-free status. Permission was granted immediately, and in 1894 the Club established its Trustees of Real Estate to oversee property. The new trustees had to act quickly when the Club learned of plans to log a tract of virgin timber along Snyder Brook in Randolph, New Hampshire, that included part of the path to Madison Spring Hut. Individual contributions from Club members funded purchase of a thirty-six-acre tract surrounding the path. Over the years the Club acquired many properties in New Hampshire, Massachusetts, and Maine through purchase or donation.

While the Club was acquiring lands of historical and environmental significance for preservation, it also led efforts to create public agencies dedicated to conservation. In 1890 the Club appointed a special committee to study the problems of preserving scenery and historical sites in Massachusetts. The Committee produced a short report with a long title — "An Outline of a Scheme For Facilitating the Preservation and Dedication to Public Enjoyment of Such Scenes and Sites in Massachusetts as Possess Either Uncommon Beauty or Historical Interest." The report proposed that a Massachusetts Board of Trustees be created to acquire land in the public interest, which the legislature voted into law in 1891. The Metropolitan Park Commission, a similar agency that focused exclusively on the

Boston metropolitan region, was created shortly thereafter. These were the first of many regional and national conservation agencies which the AMC has supported.

By 1933 managing the lands it held had become an overwhelming financial burden for the Club. By that time, however, there were numerous public agencies that held land in the public interest, and in 1933 the Club passed a resolution to donate its holdings to appropriate agencies. Today, nearly all of the Club's lands have passed into agency keeping, with the provision that they revert to the Club if their purpose of conservation is violated.

The AMC lands are classified as reservations or as camps. Reservations are lands held for preservation; of the many the Club once owned, all but two have been donated to public agencies — Madison Spring, the original Club property, and the thousand-acre Cardigan Reservation in Alexandria, New Hampshire. Camps are also manged for preservation, but the land is available to AMC members and guests for camping.

In 1900 the Club established its first camp at Three Mile Island in Lake Winnepesaukee. The camp's principal benefactor, Rosewell B. Lawrence, describes Three Mile Island in the first paper in this section. At present the Club owns five permanent camps. In addition, there is August Camp, a transient camp with a long tradition. It is described in the second paper of this section.

THE CLUB AT
LAKE WINNEPESAUKEE
ROSEWELL B. LAWRENCE
1901

O*VER THE FIREPLACE* in the *living room of Three Mile Island Camp hangs a tablet inscribed "Rosewell Bigelow Law- rence, Organizer and Constant Benefactor of Three Mile Island Camp."* *A photograph of Lawrence hangs over the door. Lawrence spurred the Club to establish a permanent camp on land it had acquired in 1899 and 1900 and personally contributed ten of the island's approximately forty acres. At his suggestion, August Camp of 1900 was held on Three Mile Island, and its success convinced the Club to raise funds to purchase the balance of the island and to erect a permanent building there — all in time for the 1901 summer season. Lawrence's interest in Three Mile Island never flagged during the many years that he was active in the Club, and he left a substantial bequest for a Three Mile Island Fund when he died in 1921.*

Three Mile Island, a heavily wooded ledge at the northern end of the "Upper Broad" of Lake Winnepesaukee, has attracted enthusiastic campers throughout the years, and its success led the Club to develop additional permanent camps — Cold River Camp in North Chatham, New Hampshire, in 1919, Ponkapoag in the Blue Hills of Massachusetts in 1921, and Echo Lake on Mount Desert Island, Maine, in 1923.

D|EVELOPMENT OF CAMP LIFE is a natural out-growth of the Club's activity, and an important part of its missionary work in the community. In 1885 the need of a Club-room in town for business and social purposes was felt; in 1888 the Madison Spring Hut was erected as a mountain refuge;

so now the growth of the camping spirit has come to demand a permanent home for outdoor life. Camping parties will still be organized to reach otherwise inaccessible peaks, and tents will occasionally be pitched by other waters, but Three Mile Island, situated in New England's most beautiful lake, and watched over by Ossipee and Belknap, Passaconaway and Chocorua, will be the Club's camping home.

In 1899 Mr. and Mrs. Edson C. Eastman, of Concord, N.H., offered the Club a lot of land on this island. The Trustees of Real Estate selected the southwest corner. Early in the past summer the southeast corner was added to the gift. Moreover, a member, the writer of this article, has purchased and conveyed to the society an additional area of ten acres. The island comprises about forty acres, and the remainder, consisting of about twenty-five acres, has just been purchased for eight hundred and fifty dollars, so that its entire surface, together with the islet called Rock Island, is now the property of the Club.

In August of 1900 the island was the scene of the summer camping party. Under the direction of the Committee, J. Ritchie, Jr., and R. B. Lawrence, a cook-house was erected, and twenty-four tents, including a large dining-tent, were pitched. A week or two was spent in camp by thirty persons, while those visiting for a shorter time brought the total to forty. The camp was a decided success, and all the participants were enthusiastically in favor of establishing here a summer home.

In the early autumn an appeal was issued, by authority of the Council and Trustees of Real Estate, to raise $2150, wherewith to purchase the remainder of the island and build a permanent camp. The subscription was successful and the camp has been erected.

It has been decided by the Trustees of Real Estate that the island, together with the camp, shall be under the charge of a committee. It is not intended that the project, either in its inception or its continuance, shall be an expense to the treasury. The original outlay having been raised by subscription, the property is to be so managed that it will pay running expenses.

The Committee has not yet formulated any definite plans for the use of the camp and island. Experience must determine the needs of the Club. It is very probable, however, that during the first season the camp will be kept open by the Committee for six or eight weeks, and that members of the Club to the limit of accommodations will be received, a certain rate being charged per day.

We have called this our Club's "camping home." The word "home" signified permanence, and therefore many improvements of a sort not in harmony with camping ideals. The serious question therefore comes, How far from nature shall we allow civilization to allure us? Most important of all, the forest must be preserved, only such cutting being allowed as will give a better growth to the more valuable trees and open to the campers finer views of the beautiful scenery. Nature intelligently assisted will produce the desired results. No exotic should be planted, no orchid plucked up by the roots, and, without the careful consideration of those in charge, no tree should be cut or bush destroyed.

Moreover, all buildings should harmonize so far as possible with the surroundings, and nothing should be obtrusive to the sight or inappropriate to its intended uses. Already we are fortunate in the architecture of the camp, for the building looks as if it belonged where it has been erected. So far as it is possible for a framed structure, it harmonizes with its environment. Sites for tents must be selected among the trees and back from the water's edge, and the alder and witch-hazel must be allowed to fringe the shore. If small camps are ever erected, they too must be lost in foliage to the passerby in boats. Moreover, that choicest spot, Chocorua Point, should not be desecrated by tent or camp, but remain as nature made it with the beautiful view it commands.

But not only should the natural beauties of the island be protected and no work of man allowed to mar; the campers also should live as close to nature as the rules of hygiene and a reasonable regard for comfort will allow. Golf and fine clothes should be tabooed; early hours, camp costumes, and simple fare should be the rules. Canoeing and swimming, fishing and sailing, tramping and climbing, resting and communing with nature should be in order every day. Briefly, the Island Camp should never become a hotel, but remain a camp, pure and simple, where Club members may find rest and live as close to nature as possible.

Much might be written concerning the attractions of Three Mile Island and the region of Lake Winnepesaukee. The beautiful views, from various points, of Belknap, Copple Crown,

Ossipee, and Chocorua, must be seen in order to be appreciated. Many are the delightful excursions upon the lake. Undoubtedly there are attractions enough to last for many years, while the island itself will fascinate all who love nature and enjoy life in the open air.

AUGUST CAMP IN THE MOUNTAINS
MARY B. SAWERS
1958

AUGUST CAMP, A COLLECTION of white canvas tents, cots, buckets, and basins, is pitched each August at a new location throughout the mountains of New England, in the Adirondacks, or occasionally as far west as the Rockies. One of the oldest and sturdiest Club institutions, August Camp was first held at Katahdin Lake in 1887. Nineteen Club members attended, "ten of them ladies." All ascended the mountain. The ten ladies must have had a difficult climb wearing long tweed skirts, even if they did roll up to the knee and pin them with blanket pins as the Club Equipment Committee advised. An August Camp has been held nearly every year since.

What is August Camp life like? M. Gertrude Gould, in a 1936 Appalachia *essay, "What August Camp Has Done for Me," describes the daily regime — an early morning plunge into a cold mountain stream, punctual attendance at breakfast, pleasant agonizing over the several daily outings, "culinary triumphs" of camp dinners, and impromptu entertainment and companionship around the evening campfire. Perhaps it is not so strange that the chores and occasional hardships of camp life are quickly forgotten when compared to these "moments of ecstacy."*

The transient August Camp has been directly responsible for several of the Club's permanent camps. In the previous paper Rosewell B. Lawrence noted that the 1900 August Camp on Three Mile Island generated enthusiasm for that as the site of the Club's first permanent camp. Similarly, the 1913 August Camp at Cold River, New Hamp-

shire, and the 1922 August Camp at Echo Lake, Maine, led to permanent camps on these sites.

In this paper, Mary Sawers surveys seventy years of August Camps. She was a frequent August Camper and a member of the Club's August Camp Committee for four years.

WHETHER THE LOCALE be Riley Lunn's pasture and the Percy Peaks in New Hampshire or an aspen clearing in the shadow of the Maroon Bells in Colorado, August Camp is a way of life. The seasoned August Camper may find the familiar arrangements of tents nestled amid unfamiliar peaks, their wild and tempting outline promising new delights. He knows well that he will find such comforts as camp life affords, experienced leaders to show the way and, above all, companions whose feeling for the high country matches his own.

August Camp is not limited to a few hardy seasoned campers. Anyone who is active and likes to share camp life will find himself at home. To the first-timer, August Camp offers high adventure. It provides a chance for those who might otherwise never become acquainted with the high country to live in the mountains for a time at small expense. Each year newcomers find themselves caught up in a swiftly moving drama from their first day on the heights to the final one with its farewells to friends proven by every test which life in the open offers.

Cooperative endeavor is the theme, as in all AMC activities. The camp manager and crew are full-time paid employees but the leaders are Club members, or occasionally guests, who receive no pay beyond their expenses and are just as much on vacation as are the campers. Their skill, care and contagious enthusiasm have gained untold new friends for the wilderness. Trips of varying degrees of length and difficulty are offered, three or more each day, so that each camper may find his own level of strength and skill. Under this system, the victim of "August Camp fever," who wants to go everywhere and do everything, is faced with making a daily decision on which trips to forego.

A nomad camp without a home, August Camp is stripped to the essentials to such a degree that the Club's permanent camps seem luxurious by comparison. "Simple but adequate" furnishings in each tent consist of a cot, a water-bucket and a basin. This Spartan setting presents no hardship to the August Camper. His primary concern is a full day on the mountains in company with like-minded friends. In his scale of values, climbing companions and nearness to the peaks at low cost outweigh such amenities as hot baths and electric lights. He appreciates, too, an early start in the morning, with breakfast under his belt, lunch in his pack, and the knowledge that dinner will be forthcoming on his return with no effort on his part.

Evening dress at August Camp is likely to be long johns, ski pants and a wool shirt; the pervading odor a blend of "bug juice" and wood smoke; the view a dark mountain profile against a starry sky.

The sounds which emanate on a summer's night from the group gathered under the shelter tent at the campfire cover a wide range. A voice relates the day's adventures or tells of trips to come; the strains of a favorite song pour forth in mighty melody; or a single sweet voice sings a haunting lay. The sounds are frequently joyous, for camaraderie and friendliness, traditional at August Camp and a natural result of the sharing of adventure, are strengthened by the spirit of unity common to all August Campers — committee, campers, and crew alike.

August Camp's table has long been noted for its high quality and generous supply, appropriate to the appetites it must satisfy. For the past several years campsites accessible by road have been chosen in order to meet problems of equipment and supplies, and the commissary is replenished daily. The quantity has always been generous, but up until the late 1930's lumber-camp food was the rule. In recent years, under the capable management of Lee and Emma Jameson, the fare has reached new heights.

Whenever campers of pre-1954 vintage talk about August Camp the names of George, Charles, and Phil invariably come up. The three Learneds of Andover, Maine, were an August Camp institution for a span of thirty years. They were so much a part of it that their departure marked the end of an era.

During these years the three Learneds made up the entire paid staff of August Camp. They were up at daylight getting the fires ready, having their own breakfast, making hot bread or muffins, preparing for the hungry horde. By rising time for the customers, 6:30, they had done a day's work. "Sleeping their lives away!" George would mutter as he circled camp blowing the rising whistle, always careful to avert his eyes as he passed the women's tents. The whistle disappeared long ago, and in recent years camp has been wakened by a moose horn. Blown enthusiastically by a member of the crew, this has the virtue of getting through to the deepest sleeper within a distance of a mile or so. The boys always go all-out on this chore, possibly prompted by the same thought which George had.

George and Phil retired at the end of the war and the following summer (1946) at Katahdin, on a site near the confluence of Abol Stream and the West Branch of the Penobscot where the bridge now stands, the first crew of boys was brought in. By the end of that season it had become apparent that operating August Camp had reached such proportions that a full-time paid camp manager was necessary.

That same year saw the end of the picturesque open cook-fire which under Charles' skillful hand has produced so many delectable dishes — meats, hot breads, pies. The fireplace was made with a backwall of fieldstone to take four-foot cordwood, and the fire burned twenty-four hours a day. During rain a large tarpaulin would be rigged high overhead. The cookfire was a rallying point for campers, who enjoyed watching Charles, wearing heavy asbestos gloves, tend his big kettles and manipulate his Baker ovens with a long-handled shovel. But as camp increased in size this method became impractical and the committee reluctantly shifted to two Maine camp wood-stoves.

Charles continued to cook for August Camp through 1954. On the occasion of his 25th anniversary in 1952 at Abol Pond, some of the members of the first section presented him with a wool shirt one night at campfire, with an appropriate speech. Charles was pleased and thanked them warmly, then remarked, with Yankee humor, that perhaps the second section would provide a pair of pants.

August Camp has covered the White Mountains in thirty-three visits, from Waterville Valley on the south to Dixville Notch on the north, from Kinsman Notch to the Wild River. The attractions of the Katahdin region are evident in the regularity with which the Camp returns to that area. The Adirondacks proved popular in 1940, in a break with New England, and have been visited repeatedly. Nineteen-fifty-six saw a more ambitious venture, with August Camp based on the shore of Maroon Lake near Aspen, Colorado, amid the 14,000-foot peaks of the Elk Range of the Rockies. This proved to be the largest and one of the most popular August Camps ever held.

The August Camper, leader or follower, is rich in memories. He has roused at first light to the song of the hermit thrush. He has known the quiet of deep woods, the smell of sun on pine, the joy of a windswept ridge. He has watched sunrise drench mountain tops with liquid gold and lake reflect the rose and saffron of alpine glow. He has stood, breathless, on top of the world, looking out over a sea of tumbled rock, past the unblinking eye of a tarn, to distant green valleys. He has knelt beside a pool lying amid fern and moss; legend says he who drinks its waters is ever after bound to the hills. He has trod the trails countless miles in sun and rain with friends who, when they meet again, be it next year or ten years hence, will find their friendship unchanged.

August Camp has seen many changes in its day but the purpose for which it was founded remains unaltered: to enable more than the hardy few to experience, each year, mountain days and nights; to visit forest and meadow and stream; to stand on a peak and feel that exhilaration mingled with humility which is the mountains' spell.

PUBLIC RESERVATIONS
OF NEW ENGLAND/
THE CLUB'S RESERVATIONS
ALLEN CHAMBERLAIN
1914/1904

ALLEN CHAMBERLAIN'S TWO ARTICLES,
written ten years apart, outline the AMC's role in preserving significant
lands in New England. The pioneering nature of this work is evident in
that it preceded the formation of England's prestigious National Trust for
Historic Preservation by several years.

The Club's work in this area was led by Charles Eliot, Council-
lor of Topography in the early 1890s. He and noted landscape architect
Frederick Law Olmstead led the movement to develop public parks in the
United States. Olmstead's design for Central Park in the mid-1800s
brought the concept of large landscape parks with a strongly rural flavor
into prominence. In the late 1800s Eliot expanded this idea to a regional
park system and brought it to fruition through his successful advocacy for
the Metropolitan Park commission in Massachusetts, which he later
served as secretary.

Chamberlain, the author of these articles, was himself a notable
conservationist. He spent ten years working to have Congress pass the
Weeks Act, which established the White Mountain National Forest and
other national forests in the eastern United States. He was also a strong
supporter of creating a national park system.

IF PROOF IS WANTED to confirm the recent statement of Lord Bryce that "the love of nature is increasing
among us," it is only needful to witness the achievements in
systematic scenery-saving in the public interest, made in this

country, and in England, during the past twenty to twenty-five years. Coupled with this love of nature has come also a renewed veneration for landmarks in human history, picturesque relics of earlier days that should prove inspiring to present and to future generations.

To New Englanders it may well be a cause for proper pride that the thought which led to the creation of these reservations of "beautiful and historic sites" originated and was developed here, only to inspire others, even across the seas, with a zeal to undertake this work, the need for which was already manifest to many minds. A few reservations had previously been made, notably in New Hampshire, in Connecticut, and in Rhode Island, but to Charles Eliot of Boston belongs the credit for the inspiring thought, and for the diligent and intelligent effort as well, upon which the really systematic work was founded. By reflected glory, at least, our Club may shine in the annals of this enterprise, since Eliot was then our Councillor of Topography, and chose the Club as his medium for arousing the public to timely action.

IT WAS IN MARCH 1890 that Charles Eliot, then a member of the Council of the Appalachian Mountain Club, began, through the instrumentality of that office, to enlist public interest in a plan to preserve beautiful and historic sites in Massachusetts. That effort, to which the Club lent its full strength, resulted first in the organization of the Trustees of Public Reservations through a special act of the Legislature. It also contributed to the creation of a similar body in England. By this act a corporate body was established "for the purpose of acquiring, holding, arranging, maintaining, and opening to the public, under suitable regulations, beautiful and historic places and tracts of land within this Commonwealth." Such property was limited by statute to a value of one million dollars, and the Trustees were further empowered to acquire personal property to a like amount, the income from which was to be devoted to the maintenance of the real estate, all this property to be exempt from taxation so long as it is open to the free use of the public, subject only to suitable regulations prescribed by the Trustees.

The second result of the above-cited effort was the organization of the Metropolitan Park Commission. This was accomplished directly through the agency of the newly organized Trustees of Public Reservations. To this last, and most important movement, the Appalachian Mountain Club also gave its support. Through the Park Commission the cities and towns of the so-called Metropolitan District were provided with ample powers and funds for the acquiring and developing of reservations of wild lands. Still the usefulness of the Trustees of Public Reservations was not in any way diminished by the establishment of the Park Commission. The latter stands for a specific local purpose. The Trustees remain to care for such other lands, within or without the Metropolitan Park District, as private or public interests may bring to it and dedicate to public use. The board of Metropolitan Park Commissioners is a creative organization subject to legislative direction. The Trustees of Public Reservations is a guardian body purely.

With Massachusetts so well provided for, the Appalachian Mountain Club wished, for most natural reasons, to see a similar work begun in the State of New Hampshire. Although a Massachusetts corporation, one of the chief fields of the Club's activities had always been the mountain districts of the Granite State. Why should not the Club undertake the work directly? This question was presented to its Council in 1893. The answer was a petition to the Massachusetts Legislature that its charter rights might be extended to enable the corporation to hold real estate. This was at once granted, the act providing that where such real estate lay within this Commonwealth and was unproductive of revenue to the Club beyond the cost of maintenance, and was kept open to public use, it should be exempt from taxation. In 1903 the New Hampshire Legislature also passed an act exempting from taxation such real property of the Club as lay within that State at that time, provided that it be kept open to public use under suitable regulations.

❧ AMC camp at base of Imp Mountain, 1905 ☙

⚜ 3
MOUNTAIN LIFE

The Nature of Appalachia

FEW CLIMBERS WHO TOIL UP Mount Washington or skiers who race down realize that the ravine which their most popular route traverses honors Professor Edward Tuckerman, an early AMC member. Tuckerman, whose studies of lichens in the ravine gained world recognition, was one of the many technically or scientifically trained people who dominated membership in the Club's formative years. The Club roster contained many faculty members from MIT, Harvard, and Tufts — geologists, botanists, entomologists, engineers, and mathematicians. So, early on, the Club had an interest in the study of natural history, one of the five departments around which Club activities were organized.

Before the automobile, Club members on extended summer holidays were restricted to relatively localized areas, which often led to intensive surveys of the natural history of their immediate surroundings. At Three Mile Island Camp, for example, lists prepared and published by Club members show that 209 species of native plants, 400 species of beetles, and 136 species of spiders were found. These surveys were raw material for many of the Club's natural-history activities, including exhibits, lectures, outings, and papers carefully prepared for publication in *Appalachia*. A selection of those papers appears in this chapter.

Writing thirty years ago, Roy E. Davis seems to capture the Club philosophy toward natural history. "Many prefer to walk merely that they may arrive, but the way thither is also worthy of attention for one may gather inspiration in the fields and woodlands as well as from the mountain top."

LAY OF THE LAND
W. KENT OLSON
1978

*T*HE MAN WHO TRAVELS *the mountains and knows each peak and landmark at a glance is likely to say he knows the mountains. Yet he knows them "only as he knows the face and figure of a stranger who regularly passes his door." To truly know the mountains, one must know their life history.*

The White Mountains proved an especially attractive area to early geologists. Louis Agassiz, founder of the science of glacial geology, roamed the flanks of Mount Washington regularly in the mid-1800s looking for evidence of the great ice sheet. In 1875 Professor Charles H. Hitchcock of Dartmouth College, a charter member of the AMC, discovered foreign boulders and other signs of moving ice upon the very summit of the mountain. His paper in Appalachia *of 1878 demonstrated the complete glaciation of the White Mountains by an ice floe moving southeastward from Canada. Through the years geologists have contributed generously to the pages of* Appalachia.

W. Kent Olson brings this development of the White Mountains to life. He focuses on the glaciers and how they shaped the land — U-shaped valleys and notches, imposing ravines "plucked" from the mountainsides, and gentle symmetry of northern and western slopes contrasted to the suddenness of those to the south and east.

This paper is excerpted from New England's White Mountains: At Home in the Wild, *published in 1979 under joint imprint of the AMC,* Friends of the Earth, *and the New York Graphic Society. Olson was editor of* Appalachia *from 1977 to 1978.*

O VER SIX HUNDRED MILLION YEARS AGO, when North America and Africa were one continent, there was no Atlantic Ocean, nor any mountains on what is now our eastern seaboard. Great oceans surrounded the merged continents which over eons split and drifted apart on the earth's fluid mantle. Into the opening between these plates the ancestral Atlantic flowed, disappearing later as the continents joined again. Their slow forceful collision, with its attendant heat and incalculable pressures, made mountains — the ancient Appalachians. The continents drifted once more and the modern Atlantic flowed in. Over two hundred million years of erosion have worn this old range to its roots.

But even before that wearing process was fully underway, another range had begun to form. The new Appalachians grew of sediments deposited west of the old range by the ancestral Atlantic, and by eonic upwellings of molten rock — magma — which fairly lifted this lesser range into the sky. Under continued pressure, from which nothing was immune, the land went plastic, its liquefaction the result of great geologic hiccups. More magma rose. Streams and the inland sea pared away the land as hot pliant rock continued to rise from eight to nine miles below the earth's surface.

The wearing down exceeded the welling up, but for all that was carted away the bedrock remained, forever rising, shoving the inland waters eastward with every cant. Freshwater runoff from the higher bumps chiseled the land and quickened with each steepening cut. Streams carved Vs in the high rolling surfaces that would become Bigelow Lawn, the Alpine Garden, and the Gulfside Ridge. Something like the present White Mountains of New Hampshire came of this aqueous sculpting.

Nearly two million years ago — a mere instant in geologic time — a process began which gave the White Mountains the character they have today. What had been a warm climate became cooler. The mean annual temperature dropped only a few degrees, but that was enough of a change to begin an ice age. No human eye witnessed what happened to the White Mountains, but we can imagine what man might have seen had he been there . . .

Glaciers are born of the sea. Dry snow robs water from the air, moisture that in a fairer climate would find its way back to the ocean. Snow building on itself compresses the lower tiers into a gelid mass that under continued pressure fails to support the load. And the whole thing moves.

Winds from the west prevail on Mount Washington. They lift snow from the western flank and the narrow gullies of rivers like the Ammonoosuc, and carry it eastward for a second drop on the equally featureless valleys of the Dry, Cutler, Ellis, and Peabody, where the snow, in the lee, is protected from further removal. High in each eastern river course, snow accumulates and begets an alpine glacier, whose weight carries it downward, taking pieces of the mountain with it. Each glacier scrabbles up loose rocks as it moves, grinding them along underneath. Crevasses on the upper surfaces accept melt-water, which percolates downward and freezes in rock joints and foliations, popping apart rocks and ledges. But the big work is the making of vast natural bowls. Inching forward, the dense ice cleaves whole rock faces from the mountainsides. Pluck, Tuckerman, a fine symmetrical ravine. Pluck, Huntington, craggy and good for climbers. Pluck, the Great Gulf, a steep cul-de-sac with a half dozen smaller ravines contributing to the main one.

Temperatures cool enough to excite local glaciers have grander effects in Labrador, where snow and ice are amassing. So large is the growth that the snows assimilate whole glaciers. Several merge to form a single ice sheet that, as it crawls in all directions, enlarges to continental dimensions. Its movement south through Canada is slow, perhaps three or four feet a year, but inexorable. The glacial wall is not uniform but lobed; amoebic, it advances podia. The ever broadening front creeps south to upper New Hampshire. Colloidal snouts follow riverbeds, nose into notches, ride part way up hillsides. They are not yet large enough to surmount peaks, but the sheet builds as it goes, fed by more snow in the Laurentian uplands. It is a river flowing over itself, now nearly as deep as the surrounding peaks are high, and still rising. As the valleys fill, the ice sheet takes for the summits, braiding around the highest peaks, making temporary islands of them. Finally, they disappear altogether.

Mount Washington lies buried under a thousand feet or more of blue and white ice. Gone are the summits, gone even the suggestion of mountains: hardly a bump is left on a snowscape as flat as the Antarctican plateaus.

Though encased in a moving continent of ice, the mountains are quite stable. The southward flow tears at bedrock, having its greatest success in the notches. In Pinkham, Dixville, Carter, Franconia, Crawford, Zealand, and the others, the glacier digs away sidewalls and valley bottoms, rounding each V into a U. High up, the ice work gentles the western and northern slopes of the big mountains, makes the southern and eastern sides more precipitous. It cleaves the eastern edges of Monroe and the southern Presidentials, giving them cornices. The ice cuts passages through which water will fall during the thaw: Crystal Cascades, Glen Ellis Falls, Thoreau Falls, and many others. It digs two hollows at five thousand feet: Lakes of the Clouds. Dirt and vegetation are carried oceanward by subglacial streams.

A slight rise in temperature is enough to stop a glacier; as soon as melt exceeds build-up, the wall retreats. So it is with the ice sheet, which comes and goes four times in two million years. The last flow and ebb, the "Wisconsin Stage," is a cycle of fifty thousand years, more than half spent in recession. At its scalloped southern edge — some two thousand miles from its source — the front deposits most of Long Island, Nantucket, Martha's Vineyard, and, as an afterthought, Cape Cod.

Under uncountable tons of ice, northeastern America sinks a few hundred feet. The Alantic, having given up so much water to the ice sheet, is also low, but it rises more rapidly with glacial melt than does the land. For a time southern New Hampshire's coast lies under water, and much of Maine's. The fattened St. Lawrence is an ocean extension that hooks down into Vermont. The receding glacier leaves sandy outwashes, glacial till, broken rock.

It is a stuttering retreat at best. Capricious temperature changes cause reformation and quick advance, then equally sudden melting. New Hampshire gets all of its lakes, some scoured, others formed by the weight of ice chunks sheared, then abandoned. Rivers flow under the stagnant ice, only to be glutted by shorn rock that forms serpentine ridges — eskers — in the glacial path. New Hampshire's valleys bulge with water at the withering edges of glacial tongues. The lateral runoff cuts terraces in the Zealand Valley, among other places, and pushes sand into the bottom lands — the Saco Intervale. Neighboring Vermont gets — gift of gifts — a whale trapped inland as the land rises. The ice sheet is gone.

From immediate post-glacial times to nearly twenty centuries after the birth of Christ is a flickering of twelve to fifteen thousand years. But it is time enough for many changes. Trees return, mixed hardwood and conifers to the lowlands and diminutive twisted krummholz up high. The climate assumes some consistency, and a timberline settles at forty-five hundred feet. Tiny flora, including some arctic genera, claim eight square miles or so of alpine tundra. Frost fractures the blocks of gneiss, making talus slopes and talus stripes, frost terraces and scree piles. Rivers and pebbles carve potholes and round out the rough work of the ice. Tarns and bogs form, and ecosystems succeed one another, making soil in the process.

There is time enough for Indians to build eastern nations, name mountains, and succumb to white men. Enterprisers strip the land bald, governments buy it back, and enlightened men try to conserve it. Geologists postulate that the most recent ice sheet may not have been the last, and that we may be enjoying an interlude between glaciers in this, the land of microseconds and millennia.

This is but a rough sketch of the geological history whose details still escape even the experts. But ordinary New Hampshire folks have known the outlines of the history for years. Newcomers to the mountains often ask, "How did all these rocks get on Mount Washington?" And it's a pipe-smoking, hardscrabble Yankee who answers, "The glacier brought 'em, of course." The city man thinks on this a moment and says, "And what happened to the glacier?" "Why," says the old man, with a wink, "it's gone back for another load."

Virgin Forests in the White Mountains
FREDERICK L. STEELE
1961

Forests are dynamic systems that change constantly in response to their environment. The forest in its turn often influences the environment, becomes the agent for the very changes to which it must respond. The process describing this interrelationship is called succession.

In the classic case the first species of trees to become established on open ground are called pioneers; they tolerate or even depend on direct sunlight. Once established, however, they shade their own seedbed, which, ironically, precludes further pioneer species perpetuation on that site. Succeeding stages of forest development have more shade-tolerant intermediate or subclimax species — beech, yellow birch, sugar and red maple, ash, and hickory among them. A final stage may occur in appropriate environments, for example, under the harsh conditions at higher elevations or on steep ravines that remain shaded and cool. Climax species are highly shade-tolerant — balsam fir and red and white spruce.

Once a forest has developed to the climax stage that its environment dictates, it becomes relatively stable: each generation of new trees has essentially the same species as the last. Only disturbances that alter the number of trees — fire, wind, disease, or harvesting — can cause the composition of the forest to change. It was indiscriminate harvesting, exacerbated by slash-fed fires, that caused wholesale changes in most of the New England forest in the mid- to late-1800s. While the region has successfully reforested, these forests are still in early stages of succession. It is only because of their remoteness or inaccessibility that a few remnants of the once vast, virgin forests still exist.

Frederick Steele combines his knowledge of forest succession with firsthand study of the few remaining tracts of virgin forest in New Hampshire to describe the kind of forest that originally covered much of the White Mountain area. These were majestic forests, quite unlike the second growth through which today's hiker travels. When he wrote this paper, Steele, an AMC member and passionate amateur botanist, was a science teacher in Littleton, New Hampshire.

AT THE TIME of the arrival of the first settlers, most of the state of New Hampshire was covered with forest. So far as can be determined, only salt marshes, swamps and a few natural openings were unforested. At present nearly all the original forest has disappeared, much of it many years ago. In the central and southeastern parts of the state, where no traces of it are left, plant ecologists cannot even agree on the composition of the original forest. Presumably much of it was dominated by oaks and hickories. In the southwest a small tract belonging to Harvard University contained primeval forest until 1938, when it was all destroyed in the hurricane of that year.

In the mountainous parts of the state, from the Sandwich Range northward, the history of the forest is much better understood. The mountains at elevations above 2,000 feet were covered by woods consisting primarily of red spruce and fir balsam. North of the Presidential Range, white spruce formed a significant part of the plant community, probably, however, occurring only on the lower slopes. It is not easy to determine how common it was. As the logging operations in the mountains have been relatively recent, beginning a little more than 100 years ago, many people still living can recall seeing fine stands of primeval forest. An example is Sandwich Dome, also known as Black Mountain in reference to the dense stands of spruce which formerly covered it.

In the areas where spruce and balsam are the climax trees, a virgin forest can usually be rather easily distinguished from second growth, even though the latter may be quite old. Stumps, which may persist for fifty years or more after a logging operation, are of course the clearest proof of former cutting. Moreover, the second growth will be characterized by trees all of approximately the same age and diameter, although there may be scattered large trees which were not harvested because they were of poor quality. In an early stage in the succession fire cherries and other short-lived trees will be mixed with the evergreens. In the virgin forest there will be many large straight trees with no branches for the first twenty or thirty feet. However, where natural openings have once occurred, there will be trees of all ages and sizes. This is the most characteristic feature of a virgin forest. When a mature tree eventually dies it falls to the ground and remains there for many years, perhaps supporting a growth of young trees from its prostrate trunk.

What is left of the once extensive and beautiful forest which formerly covered the White Mountains? In the first place, on the higher ridges, where trees are ten feet or less in height and not much more than six inches in diameter, cutting was not economically feasible. Thus a number of small patches of diminutive primeval forest remain, as on the Twin Range or on the top of Mount Whiteface. Occasionally a small tract of larger trees would be left, either because it was in some inaccessible location or because the land was too steep to make logging practical. Below the top of Mount Passaconaway there is a small plateau area, at the top of a steep ravine, where some of the spruces are two feet in diameter and may be 150 years old. Elsewhere in the mountains there are a number of ravines with steep slopes rising from the central brook, where patches of trees have been left.

There are at present in New Hampshire two very interesting tracts of virgin forest which contain trees of large size and great beauty. One of these lies in the township of Pittsburg, in the northernmost part of the state. This tract, of about 100 acres, is located just to the northwest of Norton Pool on East Inlet of the Second Connecticut Lake.

The forest is composed of red spruce and fir balsam, with some white spruce on the lower swampy areas and scattered white birches, of a type mostly restricted to higher elevations, known as variety *cordifolia*. Many of the spruces are large, up to two feet in diameter, straight and tall, with no branches for the first twenty or thirty feet. The red and white spruces look somewhat alike, and are most easily distinguished by the cones, which are usually found in abundance under the trees. The white-spruce cones tend to be long and cylindrical, in contrast to the shorter egg-shaped red spruce cones. Interspersed in the forest are openings, presumably left by the fall of large trees. Some of these openings contain only alders and viburnums, with a few young spruces coming up underneath. Other openings have trees of various sizes, some of which are already losing out in the upward race for light. When a single tree falls, a number of years are required for it to decompose into soil. One of the most picturesque features of the forest are the trunks of fallen trees of a decade ago, covered with dense layers of moss out of which grow more than a hundred miniature spruces and balsams. A striking feature of the floor of this forest is the covering of moss. Much of the soil is swampy, and the combination of abundant moisture and heavy shade seems to provide ideal conditions for promoting a moss flora of great variety and beauty. On parts of this covering there are numbers of small trees ready to take immediate advantage of any openings that might occur. Much of the ground, however, is covered only with moss and a few shade-tolerant northern herbs.

The largest stand of primeval forest in the state is an approximately 1,000-acre tract along the upper reaches of Nancy Brook. This is located primarily on the 3,000-foot plateau area above Nancy Cascades, but it extends almost to the top of Duck Pond Mountain and on the steep slopes of this mountain reaches the south side of the brook well below the cascades. Apparently the area was beyond the boundary of the Pemigewasset Valley timber sale, and it was not logged from the Crawford Notch side because of the steepness of the terrain and inaccessibility of much of it. The steep north side of Nancy Brook, which has been logged, is now scarred with a number of landslides. The forest is reached from Notchland by following the AMC Nancy Brook Trail.

Red spruce and fir balsam are the dominant species in this forest. White birches (variety *cordifolia*) are scattered among the evergreens. Shrubs are rather sparse, but include hobblebush, mountain shadbush, and viburnums. As in all virgin forests the trees are of various sizes and probably, on the average, not so large as those of the former primeval forests on lowland sites. The average diameter of the mature spruce is fourteen inches, but some run up to two feet. In contrast to the thick, close-packed, second-growth woods, it is easy to walk through this forest, in which the trees are widely spaced, although in places passage is blocked by trees which have been subject to windfall, struck by lightning, or have died from disease or old age. These woods are markedly different from any others which would be encountered on AMC trails and a trip to the area would be well worth the effort. Here one may view the kind of forest which originally covered much of the White Mountain area.

THE FLORA OF MOUNT MONADNOCK
WILLIAM H. STONE
1885

THE ROCKY EXPOSED SUMMITS of New England's higher mountains have always held a special attraction for climbers: not only is there a grand view upon completing the ascent, there is also a flora strikingly different from that found elsewhere in the region. When the last glaciers retreated to the north, ten to fifteen thousand years ago, small arctic plants invaded the first areas to be uncovered. Most perished as the temperature continued to warm, but those on the highest summits, where the climate has remained roughly equivalent to that of arctic regions, persisted.

These slow-growing, arctic-alpine plants have adapted to exceedingly harsh conditions — extreme cold, occasional pockets of shallow soil, high winds, short growing season, and heavy precipitation — but they cannot protect themselves from the most recent threat to their existence, trampling by thousands of hikers who visit their habitats each year. The AMC and other concerned groups have attempted to educate hikers to walk only on marked trails or on bare rock outcrops.

William Stone describes the arctic-alpine zone on Mount Monadnock. A monadnock is a geologic term for a mass of erosion-resistant rock that rises abruptly above the surrounding land, which has eroded to a nearly flat plain. Mount Monadnock, in southwestern New Hampshire, is a classic example, an isolated mountain 2,000 feet higher than the surrounding country. Mount Monadnock's prominence and proximity to population centers earned it an affectionate nickname, "the poor man's Everest."

ON THE SIDES OF THE MOUNTAIN the dark conical spruces arise among the lighter deciduous trees, or by themselves impart to great patches their sombre hue. As the trees grow higher on the mountain, they decrease in size, until finally the forest disappears, leaving a wilderness of bare or lichen-covered rocks, with only scanty soil in the hollows and fissures. On this barren, wind-swept tract, extending a mile or two along the mountain ridge, and elevated three thousand feet, more or less, above the sea, there is a flora that is at once seen to differ, either in the species which it comprises or in the peculiarities of its plants, from that of the surrounding country.

The extreme summit of the mountain is treeless, and there are no trees of any considerable height above the forest; but scattered over the tract under consideration are clumps of mountain-ash, and some spruces and paper birches. But the last two present a marked contrast to the beautiful trees of the same species in the lower forest. The spruces increase in size and number until they mingle with the forest below. Here they often take very peculiar forms. Instead of having the tapering, symmetrical shape which this species usually assumes, they are dwarfed and often half dead except for a few feet above the base, but close to the rocks throw out a most luxuriant growth horizontally. A tree that grows about a mile from the principal summit, on the long ridge that runs to the northeast, may serve for an illustration. From its position, the upper part of the tree is exposed to the full force of the winds that sweep over the mountain. The height of the tree is only about eighteen feet; but, growing in a depression among the rocks, its lower branches are sheltered from the winds, and have made a very thrifty growth close to the ground, so as to form a dense carpet in the hollow, and measure thirty-six feet from tip to tip. Above these branches the tree has only a moderate diameter, and is partly dead. Another tree is only about three feet in height, but covers a circle nearly eight feet in diameter. The paper birch rises only a few feet, but throws out branches near the base, and forms a dense head. Before the leafing, were it not for the characteristic bark, one would be unlikely to recognize these misshapen and stunted trees as members of the graceful birch family.

Emerson well calls this mountain-peak

That barren cone
above the floral zone,
Where forests starve.

And yet, excepting some spots of reddish gravel apparently washed bare by the rains, such soil as has accumulated in the fissures and depressions among the rocks is densely covered quite to the summit with flowering plants — and with plants, too, some of which bear most beautiful flowers. One climbing the mountain about the first of June might be surprised to find this mountaintop, that from below looks so bare and desolate, bright with such great masses of a beautiful purple flower as would be no discredit to the fairest garden. Very beautiful they are, growing among the wild gray crags. The plant is the rhodora, a low shrub, with rose-purple flowers resembling in form those of the purple azalea so common in swamps in some parts of New England. It is confined to mountains and swamps, and damp cold woods. It here grows only a foot or two in height, and bears its flowers in little tufts, at the ends of the branches, just as the leaves are coming forth, and is afterward covered with purplish pods. It is very abundant, and may be found on the very summit of the mountain. While the rhodora is in blossom on the top of the mountain, the pretty white flowers of the common shake-berry cover large patches in the pastures below the mountain-house; and gradually the bloom climbs the sides of the mountain till it quite reaches the summit. This little shrub, which on top of the mountain seldom attains the height of more than a foot, though growing from two to three feet high at lower elevations, is widely spread over the mountain.

But "Cheshire's haughty hill" seems to reserve some of its gayest bloom for those who climb to its summit on the anniversary of our national independence. *Potentilla tridensida* and *Kalmia angustifolia* are then in flower. The first, the three-toothed cinque-foil, may be recognized by any one by the two very conspicuous notches at the apex of each small and otherwise entire wedge-shaped leaflet. It is a humble little plant, rising here only an inch or two above the soil before flowering. It is to be found on the coast of New England, and on mountain-tops from the Alleghenies northward. Rooting, as it does, in cracks in the rocks into which it would be scarcely possible to thrust a knife-blade, it seems peculiarly fitted for bare mountain-tops and wild crags. One notes the fitness of things when he finds this little plant growing on the edge of that stupendous precipice standing at the head of the White Mountain Notch. Its star-like, snow-white flowers are borne on stems rising six inches or less. Blossoming everywhere on the top of the mountain, its flowers, infinite in number, are very noticeable against the dark rocks. The other plant is a sheep-laurel, so common in pastures and on hillsides. It is to be found from Hudson's Bay to Georgia. On the mountain its rose-red flowers form a striking contrast with the white blossoms of the cinque-foil. In the spring its leaves, which persist through the winter, have a soft brown color; and large masses of this plant are then very noticeable on the upper slopes of the mountain, and quite pleasing in contrast with the dark gray rocks.

Neither the cinque-foil nor the laurel continues long in blossom; and there is no more very conspicuous bloom on the upper parts of the mountain until autumn. Together with some grass, the four species that have been mentioned — rhodora, choke-berry, cinque-foil, and laurel — with dwarf blueberries and the cow-berry, constitute by far the greater part of the vegetation over the "bald" mountain.

Perhaps the most interesting plants on the mountain are the Greenland, or mountain, sandwort (*Arenaria Groenlandica*), and the Labrador tea (*Ledum latifolium*). Both are to be found only sparingly. The first is a little tufted plant, with thread-like stems and leaves and pretty white flowers. It is an arctic plant; Dr. Kane found it growing at Upernavik, five hundred miles beyond the Arctic Circle. It continues to blossom from spring or early summer until autumn. On the top of Mount Washington, where it occurs in comparative abundance, it has been found in bloom on the 11th of March. It is there called by the hotel people the mountain daisy. It grows on the summits of all the higher mountains of New England. The Labrador tea is a strange-looking plant. It is an evergreen shrub, and has the under, concave sides of the thick leaves, and the new shoots, densely covered with rust-colored wool. In the early summer it bears white flowers crowded in terminal clusters. In New England it is to be found only in cold bogs and on mountains, but grows in all the countries north of us. On Monadnock it is quite abundant in a little swamp southeast of the summit, where it rises eight or nine inches from deep beds of moss. In Labrador its leaves serve as a substitute for tea; and Thoreau's Indian guide in the Maine woods told him that the Indians there used it for the same purpose.

In the early autumn it is the berries that will be most remembered. Perhaps the first to catch the eye on emerging from the forest may be the great clusters of berries, white, red, or blue, according to the degree of advancement, borne by the withe-rod (*Viburnum nudum*), a shrub having handsome cymes of white flowers in early summer; or the pretty red berries of *Nemopanthes canadensis*, the "cheerful but modest mountain holly." Even without its berries, this low, much-branched shrub, with clean light-green leaves and ash-gray bark, is not likely to be unnoticed by him who observes the mountain flora. It is frequently to be found, and sometimes forms dense thickets. One will probably not need to look far to find the large glossy-black choke-berries, astringent in taste; and near the summit the fruit of the cowberry, the mountain cranberry, glows red among the shining leaves. But most refreshing to the thirsty climber are the very large blueberries that grow plentifully among the rocks; and the relish with which they may be eaten will not come entirely from the condition of the feaster, for there is a saying that the higher the bushes are the sweeter is the fruit, and Thoreau, I remember, says that the blueberries on Katahdin had the spicier flavor the higher they grew.

Beside the plants that have been mentioned, the red-berried elder and the small bush-honeysuckle — one flowering early in the season, the other throughout the summer — may occasionally be found; and the clintonia, with its two, three, or four oval leaves rising from the base, grows almost to the summit. A few willows may be seen; and, perhaps, rarely the high blackberry. But flowering plants other than those that have been mentioned will seldom be seen much above the forest. The common plantain, so abundant about dwellings, and the yarrow, so often seen in fields, though they are seldom if ever to be found elsewhere on the top of the mountain, grow in somewhat sheltered spots on the very summit.

Monadnock is not of sufficient height to exhibit fully the transition from temperate to arctic regions. Yet, as one ascends

along the path from the mountain-house, through the noble
forest of yellow birches, and sees the trees gradually decrease in
height and at length become dwarfs with spreading bushy heads,
and finds the hardy spruces shrunk to low and stunted trees, and
finally emerges on the bare crown of the mountain with only
mosses and lichens and such vegetation as has been described, he
may realize that one who ascends to one of our higher mountain
summits has much the same opportunity for botanic study as he
would have "if he made a journey to the north, passing first from
the noble forest with which we are familiar, to those of stunted
growth, and finally leaving them behind altogether, at length
arriving at the barren and bleak regions beneath the Arctic
Circle."

FUNGIGENIC MOUNTAINS
MARGARET H. LEWIS
1963

*THE ANCIENT MONOLITHS of the virgin forest and
the exotics of arctic-alpine summits are not the only mountain vegetation
worthy of notice. Margaret Lewis reminds us that even the lowly fungi
provide an opportunity for observation and appreciation as well as a
convenient excuse for the hiker to catch his breath while stopping to take
note of them. Though some mushrooms grow in the "Garden of Eatin',"
Lewis cautions against eating wild fungi until one is an old and
experienced hand at identification.*

*Lewis's interest in mushrooms began when she was introduced to the
mountains by her husband, a former AMC hutman. She later became
president of the Boston Mycological Club. This paper was prepared as she
recuperated from a skiing accident.*

I T'S SO EASY TO SEE SOME MUSHROOMS. Their spectacular colors, strange forms, peculiar locations, and large dimensions never fail to attract attention. Some are detected by their fragrance, which is not the usual fungus one. Have you ever noticed the sweet odor of spice on a trail (and nary a flower in sight) or the scent of garlic as you crunched over dry needles, looked for soap you thought some camper had accidentally dropped, wondered who was carrying so many apricots in a pack, or hurried along because of a pungent smell? These unlikely aromas indicate the presence of mushrooms nearby.

Fungi grow in well-defined communities, as well as in special seasons, traits saving time and footwork for their searchers. We find a limited few in early spring; usually those with thin caps which can't stand summer's rays. Some like the hot months, and these have thicker caps. Many prefer late summer and early autumn when moisture and temperature do not fluctuate too much. One or two come out in winter, with a glutinous covering to insulate them against freezing. Extreme heat destroys them, while extreme cold prohibits growth and holds them in check.

Fungi seen beside the trail one day are apt to be gone the next. They disappear after the reproductive spores fall from the mature plant. Hot sun and drying wind will destroy them. Squirrels, snails, and insects devour many. Heavy rains leave a glutinous mass, as you already know if you've taken an undignified and blasphemous toss on a slippery one. Such is their ephemeral existence, but they leave behind, each of them, millions of spores which are dispersed by the wind, water, mammals, birds, and insects. Ultimately, a very few of these land on a favorable spot and begin a new colony of mushrooms.

Without these denizens of the forests and lowlands you could neither walk nor climb with ease. After a heavy wind or hurricane, fallen timber litters woods and trails. Fungi quickly begin their work of decay in the timber, breaking it down into forest soil within a few years. Since mushrooms possess no chlorophyll for the manufacture of food, they must get their nourishment from other plants. In their search for it they bring not only decay and destruction, but beneficial changes as well. Some fungi live in close partnership with certain trees, exchanging nutriments with them. A good example is the bolete under the pine.

Hardly a climber has refrained from leaving his art work, some time or other, upon the bracket fungus, *Polyporus applanatus*, which grows in semicircular form, attached to a tree or stump. One finds it knocked from trees, beside the trail, bearing a thumbnail sketch on its white, porous underlayer. These usually large, gray-brown, crusty shelves with brown spore powder on top are found throughout the year on oak and poplar, birch and maple. There are huge ones on the Kancamagus Highway side of the Greeley Ponds Trail, smaller ones on the way to Greenleaf Hut. No forest trail is without them. Not all shelf fungi have tiny round pores beneath. Don't be surprised to find some species with gills, angular pores, bristles, or even a thick-walled maze instead. Look for these types on old logs around New Hampshire lakes and ponds. Comments from those who observe your posture while peering at the underpart of fungi will be fully as interesting as your find.

Very quickly the ubiquitous *Laccaria laccata* starts its passage every which way, meeting climbers right through to fall. Its wet, rather thin, reddish-brown cap fades when dried. The pale flesh-red gills, thick and far apart, are powdered white by spores. The stem, colored like the cap, is fibrous and frequently twisted. Occasionally some are a pale lavender.

Lentinus lepideus gives telltale evidence of old railroad beds, for it has destroyed or is still destroying the ties, especially if they are of evergreen wood. This "railroad wrecker" was much in evidence during the early logging days. A good many are still to be seen from May to October on trails which pass through old logging country. The hard and tough white caps crack and form brownish scales growing in concentric rings, the serrate-edged gills run slightly down a white stem of recurved scales. Some of this genus are still found along Franconia Brook and of course by the East Branch in the Pemigewasset Wilderness.

Few can ignore Caesar's Amanita, which stands in exquisite beauty within a loose, eggshaped white sheath. The orange cap is marked with distinct furrows along its margin, gills are bright yellow, and a broad yellow ring hangs from the upper part of the yellow stem. Admiration of this "Roman delicacy" can't possibly turn you into a godlike creature or out of the Garden of Eatin'. Though considered rare elsewhere, they are found in groups and fairy rings in New Hampshire, especially in thin pine and beech woods along brook banks. The Passaconaway region and the Pemigewasset Wilderness put on quite a showy display of them from July through to September.

Many other species of the striking, but poisonous, genus *Amanita* may be observed in New Hampshire forests. From time to time the Sabbaday Falls area features a beautiful white one, *Amanita virosa*, the so-called "Death Angel." All the members of the notorious genus have three things in common: white spores borne on the radiating gills, which are not attached to the stem, a ring or collar near the top of the stem, and a bulbous cup at the base. This is entirely a white-spored genus.

When rock-climbers gather at the foot of Cathedral Ledge, North Conway, in July, they uncoil their ropes a goodly distance from some bright fingers called stinkhorns, which rise from dead leaves near the boulders. These belong to a species aptly called *Mutinus caninus*. This mushroom emerges from an "egg" just below the surface of the soil. The stem is white and pitted, the cap slimy and dark green at first, changing soon to an attractive rosy or orange red.

The rare and deep purple *Cortinarius violaceus* intrigues even the most casual observer. Though startling enough in color to catch the eye, it is difficult to photograph because of its dark habitat in hilly and mountainous districts. There are those who have hung upside down in the dimly lighted recesses of Mahoosuc Notch trying to capture its royal splendor on color film. There are better places to find it on the trails to Zealand Hut or Lonesome Lake. This uncommon fungus wears a cobweb veil over its gills at first. When this cover separates it exposes dark violet gills covered with rusty spores. When the light is just right, you will find it, in July and August, scattered among fallen leaves near the pines.

While amanitas may appear striking, the spongy boletes have their attractions too. How many times has a saucy red squirrel scolded you for interrupting his meal of boletes? He rarely finishes one, but nibbles many, caching a few tidbits between evergreen boughs or in the crotch of a tree. Boletes are easily recognized by their soft, fleshy, rounded caps. Instead of gills they have a spongy underlayer of tube-like pores upon which spores are borne. Their stout stems have beautiful marking. Colorful networks, glandular dots, rough scales, and rosy streaks are some of their distinguishing features. Those which turn blue when cut or bruised are the most spectacular, though not the most frequent. In summer one always finds a bolete in the pine woods.

There's nothing like an old, mossy log to regiment the puffballs. In August and September, they push through the ground or decayed wood in tufts, sometimes scattered or alone, and generally out in the open. The rind of these globular or pearlike forms peels easily. As they age the inner white cream-cheese consistency changes to powdery brown spores which disperse through a single mouth at the apex. It takes little pressure to force the spore dust to fly up in clouds from these "snuff boxes." One walks through fields of puffballs around Cardigan Lodge in autumn.

These descriptions of the more spectacular fungi found in our mountains act only as a guide for observation. Until you are an old and experienced hand at identification, do not eat wild fungi, but notice their frequent appearance and enjoy the form and color of these strange and beautiful plants. This is but one of the many subsidiary aspects of our New England mountain heritage. Individuals who will take the time to develop a seeing eye as they climb will be richly rewarded by the many facets of nature that are available to the seeker.

ANIMAL LIFE IN THE WHITE MOUNTAINS

ALLEN H. BENT

1915

THERE IS AN INTIMATE RELATIONSHIP between wildlife and wild country. The very etymology of the word wilderness contains its connotation of creatures not under the control of man. In the early Teutonic and Norse languages, "will" meant self-willed or uncontrollable. The Old English term "deor" referred to an animal or beast. Thus the word wilderness has evolved to describe literally the place of wild animals.

In spirit too, wildlife is synonymous with wilderness. Wilderness without wildlife is greatly diminished. Louis Crisler in his book Arctic Wild *says, "Wilderness without wildlife is mere scenery." Similarly, Aldo Leopold in his classic* A Sand County Almanac *describes the killing of the last grizzly bear in the high country of Arizona. Of the mountain where the bear had last roamed, Leopold writes "It's only a mountain now."*

Allen H. Bent takes an early survey of the animal life of the wild country of the White Mountains. While it is the large mammals — the deer, bear, wildcat, and moose — that attract most of our romantic attention, it is two of the smallest inhabitants — the black fly and midge — that the average visitor comes to know most intimately. All of the species noted still reside among the White Mountains, though some in fewer numbers.

Bent contributed frequently to Appalachia *in the early 1900s. His special interest was the history of mountaineering on which he was a recognized authority.*

L ONG BEFORE THE RED MEN came to New England and centuries before the white settlers looked upon our northern hills the White Mountains were teeming with life. Upon the subsidence of the ice that covered this region in the glacial epoch the lower forms of life that love the Arctic cold pushed forward and today on Mount Washington there is a colony of butterflies, the *Chinobas semidea*, whose nearest relatives are in the wilds of Labrador. These little brownies were probably the first inhabitants of the White Mountains. The next family to move in has not been ascertained, but it was presumably some of the smaller winged insects, and the families kept coming until, as Mrs. A. T. Slosson, who has made an exhaustive study of the subject, says "there are now nearly three thousand species of insects that inhabit the barren cone of Mount Washington above the tree line." How many individuals of each species there are no census enumerator will ever be able to tell us. Most of the three thousand species are quite unknown to the average traveller, but two of them — the black fly and the midge — have succeeded in forcing themselves upon the attention of everyone who visits the mountains in June or early July. The midge, the only insect that can go through the eye of a needle, carries something related to the gatling gun with him. He loves the beautiful twilight hours and at some places incense is burned after sundown as an offering to him. This incense is called by the unpoetical a "smudge." Fortunately his season is short. As to the black fly opinions differ, some insisting that he appears with the melting snows in spring and that he goes out of the woods on snow-shoes in early winter. Nowadays people who want to discourage the attentions of these insects and are not particular as to their looks use a mixture of sweet oil, pennyroyal and tar to smear on their faces. If this is laid on thick it will keep the beasties away, but this is a modern invention. I have often wondered what the early visitors to the mountains did and I have recently found out. Rev. Jeremy Belknap in his "History of New Hampshire," written nearly a century and a quarter ago, says:

> *Of the immense variety of insects with which both the*
> *land and sea abound, it is impossible to give a particular*
> *description. There is ample range for the curious naturalist,*
> *both on the seashore, in the open land, and in the woods, but*
> *if he engages earnestly in the pursuit it may be advisable to*
> *defend himself after the manner of the Indians, by smearing*
> *the exposed parts of the body with the oyl of the beaver.*

The butterflies of the human race have often been blamed for leading men astray. Winthrop Packard in a delightful volume about his personal experiences on "White Mountain Trails" has told us how fascinating and potent the winged varieties can be, for a beautiful white admiral butterfly politely showed him the wrong road when he was starting for Mount Kearsarge and gave him more of a tramp than he was looking for. In the same book he also tells how a rare woodpecker led him from the primrose path when he was on his way to the Giant's Stairs, with the result that he reached the top by way of the roundabout and uncertain back stairs.

After the insects came the birds. Bradford Torrey and Frank Bolles have told us of the intimate doings of the birds they have seen, and recently Horace W. Wright has published a list of one hundred eighty-six species that he has seen near his summer home in Jefferson. He has even counted as many of eighty species in one day. Of course this large number includes some that are found only around the farms in the valleys and a few others that are spring and fall migrants, but most of them are woodland birds, whose ancestors have been spending their summers in the mountains for centuries. The pine grosbeak, the red poll and the snow bunting, whose summer homes are still farther north, are now winter residents only, while the dear little chickadee is one of the few permanents residents, equally cherry winter and summer. Near the upper limit of the trees live several of the best singers on earth: the hermit thrush, the olive-backed thrush, the Bicknell's thrush, the white-throated sparrow, and the winter wren. All of these, except the Bicknell's thrush, also inhabit the valleys, but, as most of the singing is done in June or early July, comparatively few people have a chance to enjoy their music. Of what are called game birds the Canada ruffed grouse is the most common. Naturally on the mountain tops birds are rather scarce. Mr. Torrey in the course of a week's visit on the summit of Mount Washington saw only six species — the sparrow-hawk, the sharp-shinned hawk, the snow bird, the myrtle warbler, the goldfinch, and the nuthatch. Occasionally a bald eagle is seen soaring far above the mountain tops, and in one of my mountain-top visits I had the rare pleasure of watching a hawk dive from great heights.

In the mountain brooks lives but one kind of fish, but they are beauties: the speckled trout, the theme of many enthusiastic literary fishermen.

So much for the inhabitants of the air above and waters beneath. Of four-footed animals that walk upon the solid earth, the most familiar figure is the squirrel, who chatters and scolds all intruders. Several years ago, walking leisurely down the Mount Washington carriage road with my wife, we stopped about a mile below the Halfway House to eat our lunch. A red squirrel soon came to look the intruders over and, after circling about us several times and making dashes part way toward what to him must have seemed a tremendous food pile, with palpitating heart came within reach. A moment later, coming from a different direction, he was on my wife's knee and off with a part of her sandwich. As we did not move, he made numerous calls, filling his cheeks and carrying off his plunder, and when we left he was deep in the box that had contained our lunch, greedily devouring the sugar that remained.

Above the tree line there are a few, and only a few, small animals. Not many years ago Gerrit S. Miller, Jr., combed the cone of Mount Washington looking for such small game. He found five species of mice, two of shrews, and one mole, besides chipmunks and woodchucks. The only animal that was at all common on the summit was the red-backed mouse. Lower down in the woods there are, or rather have been, many large animals.

Ethan Allen Crawford, who in 1817 took his grandfather Rosebrook's house, near what is now Fabyans, was one of the first guides and trailmakers in the mountains and, like all pioneers in the wilderness, was by necessity a hunter and trapper. In "The History of the White Mountains," written down for him by his wife, he tells of getting rabbits, fishers, wild cats, wolves, deer and bear. One fall he trapped seventy-five sable and in the fall of 1829 he caught ten bears. The same year he saw signs and tracks of moose at Willey Pond. A year or two later two moose crossed the road near his house.

At the Glen House, one of the best climbing centers in the mountains, Henry W. Shaw used to be a prominent and picturesque figure, and a little roadside spring not far away in the Pinkham Notch bears his more familiar pen name. Over this "Josh Billings" spring is, or was, a sign bearing the warning,

> He who steals this little cup
> The bear shall come and eat him up.

Underneath someone scrawled,

> The cup is gone we know not where
> And now Josh Billings bring on your bear.

Bird Lore of Forest and Mountain
WENDELL TABER AND LEON AUGUSTUS HAUSMAN
1941

To WENDELL TABER AND Leon Augustus *Hausman, mountain climbing had less to do with attaining the summit than with enjoying the climb itself. In their writings they urged mountain lovers to think of their objects as masses of insensate rock to be conquered, but to cultivate a regard for the natural mountain phenomena — geology, flora, and fauna. While they recognized that mountains may speak to their lovers in myriad tongues, to Taber and Hausman, "none speak more clearly than through the voices of the birds," and they described the curious characteristics and behavior of the birds of New England in several contributions to* Appalachia.

Toward the end of this article, Taber speaks of the winter wren with its song "which would make even a canary listen in awe." This often-heard but seldom-seen bird especially fascinated Hausman. A shy, diminutive, high-nesting species, the winter wren may be found by persistent birders in the mountains of central New England at elevations of 2,000 to 3,000 feet, and at lower elevations northward. Hausman searched the mountains for thirty years to find a winter wren's nest. He eventually discovered one on Mount Monadnock. The nest, in a pocket of soil held by the roots of an upturned red spruce, was lined with minute spruce twigs, feathers, and bits of moss and lichen. It had been ravaged recently, and only pieces of shattered eggshell remained.

PITCHING CAMP AT SUNSET, high up the mountainside, in the quiet stillness of the golden twilight you hear arising from the ravine below a chorus of olive-backed thrushes, their songs rolling rapidly up the scale as if each bird were vying with its rivals to see which could reach the end first. The tempo slows as one bird after another retires for the night. Now fragments of the pipe-like song of a hermit thrush drift up. Later, when darkness falls and, tired, you crawl into your sleeping bag, the air suddenly rings with a reedy wood-wind song that meanders up, down, and all over the scale. Secretive resident of the higher conifers, frequently heard yet rarely seen, a Bicknell's thrush expresses his satisfaction with the day just ended.

Here morning breaks — that symphony in which each instrument in turn takes up the refrain, warblers, vireos, flycatchers, woodpeckers, against the background of the violin-chickadees and the 'cello-nuthatch. The novice grumbles as he emerges from his tent to view the havoc wrought amidst the food he so carelessly left loose. Harsh cries from the hitherto stealthy robber barons, the moosebirds, greet his appearance. Attracted by the smoke of the breakfast fire, a red, sparrow-like bird appears from nowhere; then another, and yet another. Soon an inquisitive flock of crossbills takes its stand in a circle surrounding the camp. The loud drilling close at hand turns out to be merely a hairy woodpecker, but on rare and lucky occasions a three-toed woodpecker may flit back and forth between its nest and hunting ground beside you, disdainfully ignoring your presence as it silently pokes about, now ten feet up a live spruce, now almost standing upon the ground.

Mountain, forest, stream, or lake, each has its own inhabitants. Canoeing far out in the lake you may amuse yourself and cause much excitement between that pair of loons as you imitate their wild ringing call. Paddle inshore to that treacherous, floating grassy bog from whence came another call, low, mellow and rolling. Close to the bank and swimming low in the water is a tailless freak, a pied-billed grebe. Try to shoot it, though — it's gone with the flash of your gun, and gone once and for all. If you are experienced, you may recognize that floating object some distance off as the bird's bill. The grebe is holding itself stationary, submerged indefinitely and breathing with only bill exposed. At last the object begins to travel; the grebe takes no chances as it swims off for cover. Talk about your submarines!

Left to its own devices meanwhile, your canoe drifts up and swishes against the soggy bank. Your start nearly capsizes you as a harsh and raucous squawk causes you to turn in time to see one of the marsh reeds suddenly get up and fly away. Alarmed by your presence, the bittern (or stake driver as it is called because of the extraordinary resemblance its mating call, made with laughable contortions, bears to the sound made by a man driving piles) points its head straight up in the air and thins out its body. Thus appearing like any other reed in the marsh, it passes unnoticed. Although generally considered as a marsh bird, I have on several occasions flushed one from a small bog in the midst of deep woods or from a flooded grassy area in a small clearing.

The lanky great blue heron has little protective coloration but, armed with a powerful six-inch bill at the end of a long neck, has little to fear. One day, attracted by a sudden noisy splash, I looked around in time to see swirling water behind a low-flying red-shouldered hawk. A few seconds later a black-duck emerged, and a black-duck dives only as a last resort. The hawk, which ordinarily disregards the duck family, continued its way skimming the water and heading directly toward a great blue heron standing knee deep. At the last moment the hawk seemed to realize discretion might be the better part of valor. I don't suppose one can say the heron's ears were back; its neck certainly was.

On a quiet night at the edge of a large pond or other open area, you can, if you know how, imitate the call of the barred owl so successfully that the air will ring with answering hoots and diabolical gabbling. Near at hand may be the whispering undertones of a pair of tiny saw-whet owls and far off the single bass hoot of a great horned. If you think you hear a bob-cat meowing, there is no cause for alarm; it's only a long-eared owl calling. If you are unable to imitate owl calls you can sometimes obtain good results by using a wooden whistle with a pitch near "High C." Don't wear a white hat unless you are willing to be mistaken for a skunk and pay the penalty of a badly scratched head. And don't make the mistake I once did of pitching tent underneath the nest of a saw-whet. Both owl and I spent a sleepless night: the owl was used to it.

We accept the woodpecker family in an offhand way, with never a thought of Nature's masterpiece, a brain located inside a battering-ram and power drill. We've all used our heads occasionally to bang some door, but it doesn't work so well with us. The woodpecker's specialized equipment includes as well a stiff pointed tail to use as a prop, and an extraordinary tongue barbed at the tip and covered behind with a sticky saliva to entangle ants and other insects. This tongue commences at the top of the skull or even over the right eye and passes down the back of the head before reaching into the bill. In use the tongue stretches like an elastic, extending far beyond the end of the bill to forage through the insect channels tapped by the powerful bill. The tongue of the flicker, for example, reaches beyond the tip of the bill for a distance much greater than the length of the bill itself.

Retiring and somewhat rarely seen is the crow-sized log-cock or pileated woodpecker. Yet its handiwork on dead trees, great trenches perhaps three feet or more in length and six inches deep with individual holes another several inches deep inside, is a common sight throughout the forest. With a rolling call much like that of the flicker, it answers readily to imitation and will approach to within easily observable distance. Despite its usual shyness I once saw this bird working industriously on a fallen tree in the midst of a populous public campsite.

Throughout the Maine forests and south at higher levels to the Sandwich Range in New Hampshire, the two forms of three-toed woodpeckers occur. An exception to all well established rules for the woodpecker tribe, these queer birds have yellow crown patches instead of red, and three toes instead of four. Rather rare, usually quiet and almost noiseless in their drilling, it is only by good fortune that one occasionally encounters the species.

The omnipresent woodpecker of the forests is the yellow-bellied sapsucker. Its drilling always reminds me of random machine-gun action — a burst of rapid staccato drills, a pause, another shorter burst, another pause, and finally two or three haphazard pokes. Answer it with your fountain pen or any handy object tapped on a dead tree and bring it up to you. It may even alight on the tree you are "working." Should it find a metal road sign it will fill the world with sound just as do our southern New England woodpeckers in courting time.

An old friend in the form of the ubiquitous blue jay turns up with surprising regularity even in the deepest forest. For once, however, it has to play second-fiddle; the wilderness bird is its equally clever gray and white cousin, the Canada jay or moosebird. Usually furtive this bird comes freely to logging camps and steals articles left not too far inside the barracks. Let civilization in the form of clapboard or shingle houses push in, however, and our jay leaves for parts unknown. Resident of the lonely, deep coniferous forest, it may nevertheless be found among the spruce ridges of Whiteface and Sandwich mountains in New Hampshire. On mountain top or open elevation in the forest which may afford unobstructed long distance travel for sound waves, try squeaking on a blade of grass — the more high-pitched, varied, and uncouth the sounds the better. From far away an answer may come and draw gradually nearer. Get out of sight now and continue your discordant concert. Look sharp — the bird may circle and look you over quietly from behind. Later, as the smoke is rising from your supper fire, pound long and loudly with your knife on a saucepan and be sure to put some bread or fat on the ground outside the tent. Only, don't do as I once did, leave an entire two-week's supply of soap on a nearby rock. With a little further noisy encouragement in the morning your jay visitors may arrive — if indeed they haven't already cleaned up at crack of dawn. Kindly treated and tossed bread or soap they quickly become tame and will even come to feed out of your hand.

From Fitzwilliam northward you may hear ringing through the forest a song which would make even a canary listen in awe — the long rippling, rising, falling, silvery tinkle of the winter wren. Try to catch a glimpse of the bird. You can hardly believe that the series of irate rasping squeaks and squawks, always just beyond you, can come from the same throat. Only once have I seen the bird in song. Its wide-opened, motionless mouth reminded me of the horn of an old-fashioned victrola pouring forth a famous aria by some popular prima donna.

Throughout the river valleys of New Hampshire and southern Maine the superb indigo bunting is a not uncommon sight on a sunny day, perched on a telephone wire overhead. Its rival in color, the scarlet tanager, follows the line of second growth and is found irregularly throughout Maine and New Hampshire.

The fascinating freaks of the finch family are the crossbills — here today, there tomorrow, absent entirely one year and abundant the next, breeding as they see fit whether it be January or July, then gone no one knows where. To get a meal they quite literally shut their mouths. The crossed points of the closed bill are ideally adapted to prying open spruce cones, thus enabling the bird to extract the seeds. If a salty moose-lick is discovered the birds greedily partake, even swallowing earth in their eagerness. The red and the white-winged crossbill occur in small mixed flocks, as well as in larger individual groups. Where a number of one species appears a group of the other is apt to arrive soon after, to take a stand nearby. A sentinel perches atop the highest point of a spruce while the remainder of the flock often disappears completely from sight within the dense foliage. At a sudden note of alarm, the flock departs as a unit for points unknown, but if the food is abundant the birds may ultimately return. Not quite sure whether to be afraid or not, a crossbill will swing upside down under a bough, or perhaps hang by its bill, looking for all the world like a cone.

When winter's deep snow blankets the forest, the joyous activity and sound of innumerable breeding birds are gone. One can almost hear the silence. Except for the sapsucker and flicker, the woodpecker family remains as do the two forms of partridge, the Canada jay, both chickadees, the nuthatch and the crossbills. From the far north a few new species arrive to enjoy what they consider a mild winter — horned larks, snow buntings, a few shrikes and busy flocks of redpolls and pine grosbeaks. But distances are long and the total population small. The bird lover had best wait the cycle of another summer.

Spirit of Northern Waters/ THE LOON CALLING

SCOTT A. SUTCLIFFE/JEFFREY FAIR

1979

*T*HE EERIE CRY OF THE LOON *is, to many, the ultimate sound and symbol of the wilderness. Nature writer Sigurd Olson describes the "wild laughing tremolo of the reverberating choruses" of the loon as the "crowning symbol" of the wilderness of the northern lake country. Appropriately, the loon is highly intolerant of human activity. Lakes that encourage development — vacation homes and more boats — tend to lose their nesting loons.*

There are different perspectives on this "spirit of northern waters" in the two papers that follow. Both authors are wildlife biologists. Scott Sutcliffe writes empirically of the loon's evolutionary characteristics and problems of survival in a modern world, while Jeffrey Fair writes impressionistically of his personal encounters with the loon.

*A*NTICIPATION OF SPRINGTIME, the long wait that begins with the last of good cross-country skiing, snowshoeing, and skating, evolves into a game to guess the day of ice-out and foretell the return of many wilderness denizens. Above all, I anticipate the timely return of our lake's single pair of loons. When I was a kid, there were two pair, but now I feel lucky that one nesting couple returns to grace our lake as a welcome harbinger of spring. How naked a wild lake in the northeast would seem without the *whaaaahooooooooooooooooooaaah* plaintive wail, or the bizarre preening antics of an energetic, self-engrossed, uninhibited loon. In part, a human visitor's positive perception of our lakes is a state of mind created by the auditory and visual profundity of loons.

Loons are often referred to as possessing primitive physical and behavioral characteristics. Indeed, they are an ancient group displaying several qualities uncommon to most birds. A few obvious examples pop into mind, especially those elements adapting loons to an aquatic life. They cannot walk or take off from land, they have solid rather than "hollow" bones, and the only time they usually come on shore is to mate and nest. Their behavioral nature is marked by a preference for solitude, especially when nesting.

A question often asked is, "Shouldn't we accept the demise of loons as a natural phenomena, an evolutionary change enhanced by the loons' primitive physical and behavioral nature?"

The well-documented decline of loons in the northeast during the past 100 to 150 years is supportive of these fatalistic claims. Around the turn of the century, loons were reported to breed as far south as Pennsylvania and many records, especially those from Massachusetts, indicate their breeding range south of New Hampshire, Maine, and Vermont was quite extensive. Now there are no substantial populations breeding south of central Vermont and New Hampshire and southern Maine.

Their extirpation was due to a variety of factors. Market hunting and sport shooting was a common practice before the Migratory Bird Treaty Act of 1918. This act eliminated massive spring shootings, with hunters' boats often lined up row upon row in places like Buzzards and Manomet bays in Massachusetts. Many people thought loons were competitors with fishermen for game fish, especially trout, and it was often a common practice to rid a lake of loons, by shooting, to enhance fish populations. Finally, shooting loons was considered great sport as they were fast-moving, hard-to-hit targets.

Available data suggest that loons may have increased their range following the protection offered by the Migratory Bird Treaty Act. Recently, however, other man-related pressures have significantly decreased the loons' range. Present population figures, compared with historical records, show a decline of approximately fifty percent in the number of New Hampshire lakes used by loons during the past fifty years. Recent figures, except those for 1979, indicate a continuing decline in loon numbers as well as in the number of lakes where they nest.

I do not believe we must accept these gloomy facts as

indicators foretelling future loon population declines. These declines appear to be caused, directly or indirectly, by human activity and encroachment upon loon nesting areas, and they may be reversed. Recent studies in New Hampshire and other locales suggest three reasons accounting for most nesting failures. They are loss of suitable nesting habitat to human habitation, increased human activity around nest sites and chick rearing areas, and probable increased populations of raccoons, resulting in a disproportionate loss of loon eggs to these masked predators. Other more subtle factors such as the chronic toxicity of ubiquitous chemicals, especially DDT and its derivative, PCBs (polychlorinated biphenyls), and heavy metals (possibly lead, mercury, zinc, or selenium), may be affecting embryo development. However, recent tests suggest that the latter are probably not among the loon's major problems.

So far, we've been able to tackle many problems contributing to the loons' demise and are optimistic that, at least on the loon's summering grounds, we can help ensure their successful reproduction. But summers only constitute a portion of every year and, for about five months, our lakes are sealed over and loons must head for ice-free, oceanic wintering grounds. As early as late July, nonbreeding loons and those that have been unsuccessful in nesting will begin flocking on many lakes. Unrestrained by their own territorial boundaries, these flocks will roam freely until late fall, when their urge to migrate prompts their departure. They do not fly off in Vs, like Canada Geese, but in loose flocks — often a long string of loons, each separated by a great distance from another. Little is known about their migratory routes, and not much more is understood about their distribution on the wintering grounds. They have been observed wintering along the coast from the Gulf of Maine to the Gulf of Mexico, but where loons from individual regions congregate is unknown.

Also, before a picture of the loon's life cycle is complete, we need to answer other questions. What effect do oil spills, chemical deposits, or fisheries practices have upon wintering loons? What other characteristics of the oceans may predispose loons to disease or other cause of death? Are juvenile loons more susceptible to these factors than adults? All of these questions need to be eventually pursued if we are to understand the loon's habits and habitat requirements.

OUR DOG SAGE is the unwitting medium in a wild seance. When twilight is close by to unleash the wolf in her hollow up-straightened throat, and the distant town fire siren is persistent enough to conjure in her the spirit, she answers with an ancestral howl too rapturous for a Brittany spaniel. I never scold her for this — who am I to punish instinct? Besides, I enjoy this wild timbre so thoroughly that often I encourage the spirit with my own voice. And if the blur of her tail is reliable indication, Sage quite enjoys the ceremony herself. Afterwards, she descends to drowsy doglife none the worse for wear and perhaps the better. If we lived in the wild country farther north, I am certain she would answer the real thing. I entertain no doubt that, left to her own volition, she would forsake her warm bed by the wood stove and the yellow enameled dish she carries to me at suppertime to search out and overture the lusty lupine chorus. Although I would never wittingly allow that, I would most certainly understand the urge.

All this brings a provoking question to my mind. As my own species weaned itself from early instinctiveness and onto the hard regimen of intellect, did it become insulated from its wild callings? Has our upper level of consciousness overshadowed a deeper one which once turned our ancestors' ears to subtler sounds? Or, can we still hear our own sirens?

Perhaps so. I have a memory.

Not so long ago my wife Kathy and I invested a summer in the study of common loons on the mountain-gleaned waters of northern New Hampshire. One season is certainly too brief a stay to study any wild species, especially one so primitive and inspiring as the great northern diver. However, we began in the winter with our books and papers, readying a fact-and-figure framework on which to shingle our summer observations. In May we migrated north just behind the loons and moved lock, stock, and binocular into a trailer which Kathy described tearfully (and with distressing accuracy) as fully four feet shorter than our canoe. I had no parry, save to note that an airy lodge would have seemed confining there among the cerulean waters and spruce forest. We were soon busy with our boats and notes and maps, waxing familiar with the furtive loons, with their pristine haunts and haunting music — hysterical yodels, mournful wails, and tintinnabulous tremolos which whelm the upcountry listener with a paradox of wild comfort. Full days passed like leaves through rapids, allowing us little time to be crowded except in cozy sleep where crowding is a luxury on those northern nights. Summer seemed to quit without quite beginning. The black flies had passed and the mosquitoes were upon us and then the stinging notion that it was fast coming time to leave. We had accomplished the data collection expected of us, but within me something remained missing — the experience was crucially incomplete.

Ever since those faded summers when my best friend and I were explorers in our treehouse fantasies, Saturday mornings have rarely failed to release within me a boyish magic. The final one of this northing proved no exception. Pending the expression of an urgent visceral excitement, breakfast was abbreviated to a mug of boiled coffee and poring over an inspired Friday-night late entry in my journal. Kathy understood when whatever was calling led me out alone.

Free of my usual bedecking of daypack, camera, and field books (my only burden was a pair of binoculars which tugged at my neck, and had I intuited that I would neglect to use them, they too would have remained behind), I wandered straight to the head of a nameless but familiar trail. A relatively short path which subtly intrudes on three reticent ponds, this route had on previous excursions offered up a running commentary rich in the pedal evidence of coyote, moose, deer, grouse, and only rarely a human Bean's boot. It had always been alive with the phrases and glimpses of boreal songbirds and garnished with the warm aromas of a summering forest. Though reconnoitering loons was my employ, to have used that excuse for my rove this particular morning would have favored outright rationalization. A farewell in one of my vast cathedrals might have been a more apt description.

In the air, barely falling, was a vestige of the nocturnal downpour which had scoured and sopped the trail and driven all the wild things to their snuggest niches. The still-life was heavily dabbed with watercolor grays, rendering the spruces into misty shadows, cardboard cutouts fading in the distance. The silence was inspiring, as an empty church is to prayer, and with a whirl of piquancy I drifted into the deserted wood. On the knob where the path bent northward, a handful of thin-fingered snags tore at the pall of falling dew. But only the moccasin flowers could penetrate it, contrasting warmly along my way like flames on pallid candles.

I found the first two ponds still, in perfect agreement with the morning's mood. At the trail's end, in a shallow basin incidental to the random roll and pitch of these low mountains, lay the third. From the unwrinkled and unbroken gray of its surface and from the firry circumvallate slopes rose slender stacks of vapor to blend with and replenish the low sky.

No telling exactly what hijacked my motor control, flexing the muscles I believed were voluntary, but in a fluid and unassumed motion my hands clasped and rose thumbs first to my lips. Many times before had I tried to imitate the hollow flute-notes of the mourning dove or the barred owl in this manner, always unable to manufacture any sound other than a rush of poorly handled air. But this morning my wind streamed through my hands as though a waiting world were drawing it.

*Whaaah*ooooooooooooooooooOOOOOOOOOOooooooo*aah* — the stirring plangency of a loon's wail broke the spell of silence. It rang for a standstill in time, the benign mountain acoustics pooling echoes from a thousand distances and directions to absorb the blemishes to tone and timing and lend a full shade of authenticity. For that moment I was no more than one of the spruces, except for my wonder.

To a religious man, I have heard it said, only the joy of an answered prayer is superlative to the comfort of prayer itself. It was a similar joy which swelled in me when, just as the echoes died, I received an unreckoned-for answer. Infusing the morning with the excitement of their wavering tremolos, a pair of loons dipped into my gray bowl from some tramontane lake to the north. Three times they called, perhaps sounding for the one that had wailed; three times I heard the airy-whistled rhythm of their rushing wings before they lifted over the treetops that guarded the direction of their approach.

The world decrescendoed to gray silence, but within me another spell had been broken. On my way back to Kathy, camp, and the few remaining hours of work, I no longer dreaded my approaching departure. The emotional requirements I had somewhere set for this special summer had been met by a voice on the wind — a voice that would carry through the work remaining here and later echo between distant walls as I finished by book and pen. Oh, I am too much the scientist ever to say that the great northern divers spoke with me, or I with them, or to claim even a moment of their acceptance, for these things are just not so. But I am too human ever to forget the day I followed a trail of impulses to find the calling of the wild loons — the voice-spirit of the North Country eternal — in my hands and ears and all about me. And I shall cherish it forever, as a memory to tide me across the times when my calling fades, as a chunk of evidence to be heavily drawn upon whenever I ponder my relation to the wild.

THE WORST WEATHER IN THE WORLD
CHARLES F. BROOKS
1940

To MANY VISITORS, the first and perhaps the most lasting impression of the White Mountains is extreme weather. The temperature at the base of Mount Washington may be a pleasant 75° F when it is a frosty 30° F on the summit. Winds are severe and nearly constant. The highest wind velocity recorded on earth — 231 miles per hour — was measured on Mount Washington in 1934. Charles F. Brooks describes some of the readings taken at the Mount Washington observatory that contribute to the mountain's claim of having the worst weather in the world.

Meteorological observations upon the mountain and establishing the observatory were early interests of the Club. In 1870 Charles H. Hitchcock, later a charter member of the Club, organized a scientific expedition that maintained the first winter-long observatory on the mountain. The party's official report, Mount Washington in Winter, *provided the first details on the severity of summit conditions. Lighter reading was their "burlesque" journal, surely conjured up during long periods of isolation. In it a Professor Jones was reported to have become lost during a hailstorm and when finally discovered "he was covered with a coating of ice three inches in thickness" and had to be released with boiling water. A Professor Smith made the mistake of standing on the windward side of the observatory in a high gale and "was instantly flattened against the building. He was spread out over an area of eighteen square feet; and experienced considerable inconvenience from the disarrangement of his hair. Toward evening the wind lulled, and he was carefully dispatched by knives, and laid upon the shelf until means for his compression could be devised." Later on, "He was laid upon the floor and hammered, chiefly on his edges, by large sledge hammers. After six hours of continuous hammering he had regained nearly his former shape."*

This original observatory was not maintained, but Club members started regular collection of meteorological data in the mountains in the late 1880s as part of the AMC's natural history program. The present observatory was established in 1932 with direct and continued assistance from the Club; it is specified that two positions on the observatory's Board of Directors be filled by AMC members.

E|VERYONE KNOWS THAT THE CLIMATE on Mount Washington is severe. The severity of cold climate is described in terms of (1) the penetrating qualities of the wind, (2) the lowness of temperature, (3) the amount of snow, and (4) the occurrence of freezing fog. The first three are present, in varying degrees, in our familiar New England blizzards. All are found on Mount Washington.

The most extreme feature of the climate on Mount Washington is the velocity of the wind. Figure 1 shows the three-year average of the hourly wind velocity on the summit. This diagram, which shows average wind velocity of around 55 m.p.h. from December to March, and more than 20 m.p.h. in the summer months, may not, at first blush, give the impression of the windiness which visitors to the summit have experienced. At lowland stations, however, the average wind velocities are generally in the neighborhood of 10 m.p.h., with higher values, up to 14 m.p.h. or more, only at exposed points on the coast, such as Cape Cod, Nantucket, and Cape Hatteras. Thus, the wind on Mount Washington averages something like four times the ve-

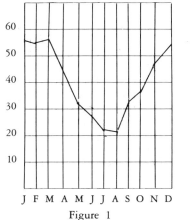

Figure 1

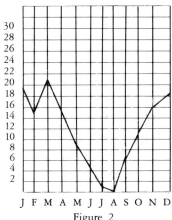

Figure 2

locity of the lowland stations. This greater velocity, however, is not the measure of relative windiness. From a personal standpoint, we feel the wind as the pressure of the air upon us. The four times greater velocity on Mount Washington, allowing for the three-fourths density of the air at that level, gives Mount Washington a wind pressure of about twelve times that at the lowland stations.

As with any other meteorological element, it is not so much the average that counts, as the extreme conditions. Figure 2 shows the number of days per month on which the wind reached hurricane force (75 m.p.h.) in the years 1938 and 1939. From November to April the wind of this velocity occurred, on the average, at least every second day. In March, the windiest month, the wind reached hurricane force as often as two days out of every three.

The greatest extremes of wind velocity, measured for periods of less than an hour, have reached the neighborhood of 200 m.p.h. During the last eight years the heated rotation anemometer has shown an extreme maximum, in a fraction of a second, of 231 m.p.h. on April 12, 1934, and 163 m.p.h. on September 21, 1938, during the hurricane. The latter figure occurred some hour and a half before the maximum velocity of the wind, which could not be recorded owing to the vibration of the anemometer and the anemometer tower. Other comparisons, however, led to an estimate of 189 m.p.h. as the true maximum velocity during the hurricane. There is a false impression of accuracy given by the precise numbers 231, 163, or 189, for in winds of such severity no apparatus can record the air-flow more than approximately. Although the actual velocity of these extremes may be in error by 10 to 40 m.p.h., there is no question but that the severest winds of Mount Washington, which are the strongest yet recorded by any rotation anemometer, reach the neighborhood of 200 m.p.h.

The low temperature on Mount Washington, the second of the four elements of a severely cold climate, is a marvel to visitors ascending the mountain at any time of the year. The average temperature on the summit is some 25 degrees lower than it is in the surrounding valleys. Occasionally, it is 40 or even 45 degrees colder. The mean temperature runs from about 5° F. in January and February to a maximum of 45° F. or a little higher in the summer months. The highest temperature in summer has reached 71° F.; the highest in winter, 45° F. The highest of the monthly minimum temperatures is below freezing. The lowest temperature in the last eight years is 46° below zero, a figure which was reached twice in the winter of 1933–34. In 1872 a temperature of 49° F. below zero was recorded.

High winds and low temperatures frequently attack together. Whereas in the lowlands the lowest temperatures occur in the calm after a cold wind has blown, the coldest periods on Mount Washington are brought by the strongest northerly winds of winter. On both occasions when the temperature was below 40° below, in the winter of 1933–34, the wind reached velocities in excess of 100 m.p.h.

Snow, the third characteristic of a cold climate, occurs on Mount Washington in all months of the year. In the winter months it is the chief form of precipitation. The water content of the snow, however, averages only about a third of the total annual precipitation. The snowfall on the summit averages over 200 inches per year. This measured value is rather uncertain, because the snow that falls is usually quickly blown away, and other snow that has fallen elsewhere is blown over the summit. The snow plume from Mount Washington may be seen for many miles. Much of the "snowfall" of Tuckerman Ravine and even Pinkham Notch, several miles away, is second-hand snow that has been blown off the mountain by the violent winds.

Freezing fog, the last in our list of considerations to determine severity of a cold climate, is one of the most remarkable features of Mount Washington weather. When it is realized that the summit is in the fog more than half of the time in winter, and that the temperature is almost invariably below freezing, the importance of freezing fog as a phase of the climate can be appreciated. Even at the lowest temperature, an appreciable portion of the fog, which is in reality a cloud enveloping the summit, is still in the liquid-droplet form. At a temperature as low as 46° below zero, the formation of rime, the ice deposit which comes from the freezing of these liquid drops as they strike cold objects, has been observed. These rime formations form an impressive feature of the winter landscape on the summit. Every object is coated with the firm, white covering, often beautifully feathered in appearance. After several days of freezing fog and high wind, the deposit of rime reaches several feet in length. Rime three feet long formed on the Yankee Network radio tower during two days late in August this year. Five or six feet have been formed in a single night.

❧ *Looking out over Androscoggin Valley, 1914* ❧

4

MEANING OF
MOUNTAINS

Prose and Poetry

WHAT IS IT ABOUT MOUNTAINS that draws
us to explore and climb them? The reasons are varied and personal
— escape from the confines of urban life, and aesthetic pleasure,
or physical and mental challenge. For some, mountains are the
medium for strengthening family bonds through shared outdoor
activity. For others, mountains have religious significance.

Psychologists have recently suggested another meaning
that mountains may have. When the constraints and distractions
of society are removed, human creativity is released to an unusual
degree; under such circumstances, an individual may achieve his
ultimate potential for cognition, insight, and perception.

Preliminary evidence to support this hypothesis comes
largely from writings and experiences of the "literary natural-
ists." George Catlin, for example, who is credited with the
original idea for national parks, described an incident that occurred on a journey he made in 1832 to study the Indian tribes of the
Upper Missouri River. Resting in the shade of a tree, he con-
centrated intensely on a small map of North America, excluding
all other thoughts. In the process he had a "vision" of the savage
destruction of the great North American buffalo herd and subsequently proposed a "nation's park" as a solution. John Muir
details another incident, his well-known experience of riding out
a Sierra windstorm in the crown of a tall Douglas spruce, clinging

to it like a "bobolink on a reed." Muir reports heightened sensitivity, intense feeling, and enhanced intellectual insight. Similarly, it is reported that Aldo Leopold, during his extensive travels in the Sierra Madre Mountains of Mexico, first envisioned the land and its inhabitants as one organism.

Several of the nation's most creative thinkers and artists have had a special relationship with New England's mountains, including Ralph Waldo Emerson, Henry David Thoreau, Robert Frost, and Frederick Church. We are fortunate that the mountains inspired them and that they are there to inspire us to reach our own creative potential.

EMERSON'S TRANSCENDENTAL MOUNTAIN
PAUL F. JAMIESON
1957

RALPH WALDO EMERSON, *American poet, essayist, and philosopher, was architect and chief spokesman for transcendentalism. A complex philosophy dominated by a sense of religious naturalism, transcendentalism sought to link humanity, nature, and God. Full of optimism, the transcendentalists suggested that although human existence was rooted in the material world, the soul had the power to go beyond materiality to reach higher spiritual truth, and that — since God spoke most clearly through His own creations — nature was the prime source of higher reality. To Emerson, "nature is the symbol of the spirit."*

Though he traveled extensively, Emerson's own search for knowledge was most often satisfied within sight of Concord, Massachusetts, his home during adult life. Visions and visits to Mount Monadnock inspired his prose and poetry. On a climb of Monadnock in 1845, Emerson rose at sunrise on an early May morning and improvised a few lines of his epic poem "Monadnoc." Perhaps the following verse from that poem best conveys his feelings for his " transcendental mountain":

To far eyes, an aerial isle
Unploughed, which finer spirits pile,
Which morn and crimson evening paint
For bard, for lover and for saint;
An eyemark and the country's core,
Inspirer, prophet evermore.

At the time that this article was written Paul F. Jamieson was a teacher of English and American literature at St. Lawrence University. He has a special interest in "the point where poets and mountains converge." Jamieson also contributed an article on Robert Frost, which is included as the third selection in this chapter.

PROBABLY NO OTHER MOUNTAIN in America has meant so much to so many as Monadnock. Rising purposefully from the plain in central New England, it is "the country's core" and the magnet that draws all eyes for scores of miles around. If looked at long enough in the summer haze, its outlines take on the likeness of a dream, a Platonic original of mountain. The temptation to climb is almost irresistible, and tens of thousands do so every year.

Such a mountain naturally has a past. Its history is partly told in the selections in prose and verse, by writers from colonial times to recent years. The richest section of these concerns the give-and-take relations between the mountain and the transcendentalists of Concord. For them Monadnock was an inspiration, a challenge, and a gauge. It hinted at great secrets. It put them on their mettle to be up to the universe. It served as a thermometer of their spiritual life. For Emerson the mountain was a friend and collaborator throughout the adult years of his life.

The distant view of the mountain never failed to move him. The cloudrack which Monadnock often unfurled from its cone seemed to him like a banner of friendly greeting. He loved the "ethereal tints" of the mountain. It was like a great opal in the western sky, pleasing in both color and form. As he says in an epigram of two lines:

> *A score of airy miles will smooth*
> *Rough Monadnoc to a gem.*

This transformation which air and distance made in the appearance of the mountain, smoothing out the rough irregular surfaces known to the climber into a broad-based pyramid, was noted also by his friend Thoreau, who wrote in his journals: "When you are on the mountain, the different peaks and ridges appear more independent; indeed, there is a bewildering variety of ridge and valley and peak, but when you have withdrawn a few miles, you are surprised at the more or less pyramidal outline of the mountain and that the lower spurs and peaks are all subordinated to the central and principal one." This power of drawing together the many into the one gave the mountain a glorious mythic character to the Concord transcendentalists, who were forever seeking the one purpose behind the varied appearances of the world. The mountain seemed to share their demand for unity and became for Emerson the type of "the old building Intellect" or World-soul.

The sight of Monadnock in the distance made him cheerful and optimistic. He had, to be sure, moments of doubt, when the lofty land seemed to him taunted by little men, but he could not long feel discouraged in the face of horizons so grand and exhilarating. Looking westward toward the mountain, he saw an endless vista of opportunity for thinker and doer in America. Beyond Monadnock were other great ranges. The land must have a great destiny. "Who shall dare think he has come late into nature, or has missed anything excellent in the past, who seeth the admirable stars of possibility, and the yet untouched continent of hope glittering with all its mountains in the vast West?"

Emerson was not overawed by mountains. His association with them was that of an equal, with as much to give as to receive. "Not less," he said, "is there a relation of beauty between my soul and the dim crags of Agiocochook up there in the clouds." He was even capable of Yankee impudence now and then. In his poem "Fable" the mountain and the squirrel have a quarrel, the latter having the last word:

*"If I'm not so large as you,
You are not so small as I,
And not half so spry.
I'll not deny you make
A very pretty squirrel track;
Talents differ; all is well and wisely put;
If I cannot carry forests on my back,
Neither can you crack a nut."*

Well, the mind of man has its sufficiency, too; it can crack all sorts of nuts.

Although the mountains did not overawe him, they did not make him complacent either. They were rather a perpetual challenge, "Nature stretches out her arms to embrace man, only let his thoughts be of equal greatness." The universe is a riddle wrapped up in a bewildering variety of forms. In the poem entitled "The Sphinx" one of the incarnations of this mystery is "Monadnoc's head". And the challenge that the mountain presents to mind is the theme of the short poem "Monadnoc from Afar":

*Dark flower of Cheshire garden,
Red evening duly dyes
Thy sombre head with rosy hues
To fix far-gazing eyes.
Well the Planter knew how strongly
Works thy form on human thought;
I muse what secret purpose had he
To draw all fancies to this spot.*

The distant view was not enough for the man to whom walking was a necessity and an inspiration. He once said that all his thoughts were foresters with the breath of the pines on them. His poems, according to his son Edward, were often conceived and at least partly composed out-of-doors. The rough surface of a woodland path helped this philosopher of the infinite to keep in salutary touch with the finite. Stubbing his toe on a rock helped to remind him that nature is something more (or less) than the insubstantial veil of a thought. He was a little condescending toward matter, but appreciative too. It had a steadying effect.

"The rock seemed good to me. I think we can never afford to part
with matter. How dear and beautiful it is to us. As water to our
thirst so is this rock to our eyes and hands and feet . . . . Comes in
this honest face, whilst we prattle with men, and takes a grave
liberty with us and shames us out of our nonsense." One could, of
course, have too much matter. Emerson did not often go into the
wilderness, for, as he once said, a man is not a woodchuck. Most
of his walks were among the woods, meadows and hills about
Concord, where he found the most fruitful mixture of society and
solitude, mind and matter. "Caesar of his leafy Rome,/There the
poet is at home." Still, he was something of a mountain climber
on the more familiar peaks and trails. Before the mountains to the
north and west quite dissolved away under the pressure of his
thought, he stubbed his toes on their granite crags to find them
real, for the moment at least. He could not afford to miss, as poet,
"each joy the mountain dales impart" or, as moralist, "the lessons
which a country muse taught a stout pedestrian climbing a
mountain."

He was more at home on mountaintops than most men,
though the test, as he saw it, was rigorous:

> *Hark! in thy ear I will tell the sign*
> *By which thy hurt thou may'st divine.*
> *When thou shalt climb the mountain cliff,*
> *Or see the wide shore from thy skiff,*
> *To thee the horizon shall express*
> *But emptiness on emptiness.*

The whole world is hidden in man's heart, he held. What one sees
from a mountaintop depends on how much of this hidden wealth
he can avail himself of. A mountaintop is a fine place to make test
of one's resources.

Monadnock speaks like a transcendentalist in its reply to
the poet's questionings, as if the prevailing winds sweeping its
cone had come straight from Concord. Emerson had said: "Nature is the incarnation of a thought, and turns to a thought again,
as ice becomes water and gas." "A profound thought will lift
Olympus." Monadnock agrees. It is so firmly convinced of the
superior reality of mind that it argues itself out of material
existence. It foretells the coming of the "cheerful troubadour"

who will free the thought and the melody now imprisoned in its granite walls. Then its rocks will dissolve, its cone spin.

> *"Monadnoc is a mountain strong,*
> *Tall and good my kind among;*
> *But well I know, no mountain can,*
> *Zion or Meru, measure with man.*
> *For it is on zodiacs writ,*
> *Adamant is soft to wit:*
> *And when the greater comes again*
> *With my secret in his brain,*
> *I shall pass, as glides my shadow*
> *Daily over hill and meadow."*

Adamant is soft to wit. This thought has many echoes in Emerson's essays and other poems. "Nature is the immense shadow of man." "Nature always wears the colors of the spirit." "The light, skies, and mountains are but the painted vicissitudes of the soul." What is the mountain without the man? As a mountain-lover of today puts it, "What is Everest without the eye that sees it? It is the hearts of men that make it big or small." The Sherpa Tenzing and the Concord idealist would have understood each other. Monadnock or Everest, it is all the same. Either is as big as a man can make it.

To Emerson, Monadnock was big enough. It was the projection on the sunset sky, not only of his ideal self, but of the ideal America. It was the Transcendental Mountain.

THOREAU AND WILDERNESS
RICHARD FLECK
1964

*E*MERSON'S *YOUNGER COLLEAGUE in the*
literary circle at Concord was Henry David Thoreau, the most politically
astute and fiery of the transcendentalists. Thoreau's classic statement
before the Concord Lyceum "In Wildness is the Preservation of the World"
characterizes his philosophy. Thoreau craved more intense contact with
the wilderness than Emerson's regular visits. He retreated to Walden
Pond for two years where he produced his best-known work.

Before and after his hiatus at Walden Pond, Thoreau made visits
to the White Mountains. The first, in 1839 when he was twenty-two
years old, was a side trip during the boating excursion described in A
Week on the Concord and Merrimac Rivers. *Frederick Kilbourne,*
writing in Appalachia *in 1919, reports that the "week" of which*
Thoreau wrote was actually more than that because it was interrupted by
this visit to the White Mountains. The northernmost point of the boat
voyage was reached on a Wednesday night, and the journey was not
resumed until Thursday of the following week. Thoreau spent the
intervening period exploring Franconia Notch and the Mount Washing-
ton area.

Thoreau's second visit to the White Mountains, in 1858, was to
botanize the New Hampshire peaks. He found the going a little rough.
Descending Mount Washington toward the head of Tuckerman Ravine,
he traversed a patch of crusted snow and "tore up" his fingernails to save
himself from sliding down too rapidly. "It is unwise," he recorded in his
journal, "for one to ramble over these mountains at any time, unless he is
prepared to move with as much certainty as if he were solving a geometrical
problem." Later on in the six-day visit he sprained his ankle so badly
that he could not sleep that night nor walk the following day. Neverthe-
less, he completed his visit collecting forty-two of the forty-six species of
plants he had hoped to find.

While nature held deep philosophical meaning for the trans-
cendentalists, Thoreau's interest in wilderness included other aspects as

well. He was an accomplished naturalist and an acute observer of society around him. Richard Fleck examines the extensive writing of Thoreau and identifies his "four needs" for wilderness.

THE PROBLEM OF THE VANISHING wilderness faced Thoreau, as it faces us. "Kataadn," written over one hundred years ago, is remarkably similar to today's pleas for saving the Allagash country of Maine. Whether we read about the need of saving the Dinosaur National Monument or read Thoreau's "Chesuncook," the basic expression is the same. Indeed, "In Wilderness is the Preservation of the World," Thoreau states it well; we have need of space and the wilds, but to explain why to the indifferent may cause us to seem mawkish and unrealistic.

Thoreau can hardly be thought of as a logician. Instead, the writings of this New England mystic are an amalgamation from a vast ocean of thought. From his voluminous works I have pieced together his "four needs" for the wilderness: practical, therapeutic, spiritual, and literary.

In "The Succession of Forest Trees," Thoreau concerns himself with the fundamentals of forestry and the necessity of proper forest growth for future use. Conservation practices of raising pine forests as nurses for oak forests and the transplanting of saplings for the amelioration of soil are discussed at length. He realizes the necessity of protecting animal life, the squirrel and the jay, in order that the natural dissemination of seeds be continued. Woodland preserves with their ecological relationships must be understood and maintained. This appreciation of wilderness as a conservatory for food, fuel, and shelter is easily understood, except by those to whom spruce or maple trees appear as dollar bills. The three other needs for the wilderness that Thoreau presents are far more subtle.

Where there is continual tension and ultra-mechanization some catharsis is sought. Thoreau found what many seek today — the inner retreat where the mind can relax and divert to the aesthetically pleasing. The town and city dweller can be revived in the wilderness. As Thoreau puts it, "There is no scent . . . so wholesome as that of the pines, nor any fragrance so penetrating and restorative as the life-everlasting in high pastures." This statement rings true as shown by the continually increasing flow to our National Parks. Since we are natural creatures ourselves, we have a continuing need to be reminded that the artificial world of man is only part of life. Thoreau, in *A Week on the Concord and Merrimac Rivers*, states, "There is something indescribably inspiring and beautiful in the aspect of the forest skirting and occasionally jutting into the midst of new towns, which, like the sandheaps of fresh foxburrows, have sprung up in their midst. The very uprightness of the pines and maples asserts the ancient rectitude and vigor of nature. Our lives need the relief of such a background, where the pine flourishes and the jay still screams."

A balance of natural with artificial is essential for the mind as well as the spirit. When one roves the woods, climbs mountains, or walks along the seashore, his soul gains a proper perspective of the world and human experience. "In passing over these heights of land, through their thin atmosphere, the follies of the plain are refined and purified . . ." The very hills act as a catalyst. Thoreau feels that colleges should be near nature and the mountains. "Some will remember, no doubt, not only that they went to college, but that they went to the mountain. Every visit to its summit would, as it were, generalize the particular information gained below, and subject it to more catholic tests." Does the wilderness, then, not only relax us, but also broaden us? Anyone who has stood on the rim of the Grand Canyon, a mountain summit, a cliff of the Maine coast knows that something happens to thought. Is it "refining"?

Both the form and content of literature are affected by the wild. Thoreau writes, "In literature it is only the wild that attracts us. Dullness is only another name for tameness. It is the untamed, uncivilized, free, and wild thing in *Hamlet*, in the *Iliad*, and in all the scriptures and mythologies that delights us — not learned in the schools, not refined and polished by art. A truly good book is something as wildly natural and primitive, mysterious and marvelous, ambrosial and fertile, as a fungus or lichen." The wild sea coasts, mountain forests, and choppy rivers are for the writer as well as the painter. As the cosmic Yankee states, "It is remarkable that the autumnal change of our woods has left no deeper impression on our literature yet." His works as well as those of such greats as John Muir, John Burroughs, and

Stewart Edward White reflect it well.

Thoreau is no sentimentalist. He writes, "The surliness with which the woodchopper speaks of his woods, handling them as indifferently as his axe, is better than the mealy-mouthed enthusiasm of the lover of nature." One extreme is as bad as the other. He realizes that what the wilderness stands for is what man should stand for. It is upon this strength that our nation depends.

In his essay "Walking" he speaks of America and her wilderness when he says: "If the moon looks larger here than in Europe, probably the sun looks larger also. If the heavens of America appear infinitely higher, and the stars brighter, I trust that these facts are symbolical of the height to which the philosophy and poetry and religion of her inhabitants may one day soar." One hundred years of time separating Thoreau from today has had no effect upon the meaning of what he has to say to us and to those who come after us.

ROBERT FROST:
POET OF MOUNTAIN LAND
PAUL F. JAMIESON
1959

CERTAINLY ONE UNIFYING ELEMENT in Robert Frost's work is mountains. Throughout his poems there is recognition of nature's supreme separateness from humankind. To Frost, mountains were a challenge to the resourceful: he delighted in the trials of the New England hill farmer, whose ranks he once joined. Upon returning from England in 1915, he purchased a small farm in the New Hampshire hills near Franconia. He made few serious attempts to work the land, however, commenting that he couldn't raise much on his farm — it was only good for cattle, and he hadn't any. But the land produced poems.

Mountains are a refuge for the harried, and Frost retreated to them often to build reserves of strength. In his youth he reportedly spent three months alone on Ossipee Mountain thinking things over. Like the drumlin woodchuck, Frost retired to the security of his burrow:

We allow some time for guile
And don't come out for a while
Either to eat or drink.
We take occasion to think.

Paul Jamieson illustrates the meaning of mountains to Frost, and in turn of Frost's poems to us: "the slope it gives the head" as we pause now and again in our daily routines.

MOUNTAIN LAND NORTH OF BOSTON is geographical and spritual home to Robert Frost. A house is hardly a home to him unless its back door looks uphill and its front door overlooks a mountain range across the interval. Even the family colt and cow take naturally to a tilted pasture full of rocks and Christmas trees. On a fall night Orion comes up sideways "throwing a leg up over our fence of mountains." In spring a frozen peak sends a chill wind down into the valley to vie with the sun for the heart of an April day. Even where mountains are not specifically mentioned in his poems, we sense their presence in the crisp atmosphere and in the slope the poet's head has taken from so much looking up.

After a three-year absence in England, where Frost won his earliest fame, his Franconian farm renewed an old association with the people and the mountains of New Hampshire. "Not a poem, I believe, in all my six books . . .," he wrote in his early sixties, "but has something in it of New Hampshire . . . I lived, somewhat brokenly to be sure, in Salem, Derry, Plymouth, and Franconia, New Hampshire, from my tenth to my forty-fifth year. Most of my time out of it I lived in Lawrence, Massachusetts, on the edge of New Hampshire, where my walks and vacations could be in New Hampshire . . . . So you see it has been New Hampshire, New Hampshire with me all the way. You will find my poems show it, I think." Since 1920 he has lived much in Vermont, but the difference is negligible. Yokefellows as they appear on the map, Vermont and New Hampshire pull together as "the two best states in the Union." In one the mountains stretch out straight, in the other they "curl up in a coil"; otherwise, what you say about either state serves almost as well for its fellow. And whichever one you are living in at the time leaves only the other as a rational direction of escape. It's "restful just to think about New Hampshire. At present I am living in Vermont."

Diversity, confusion and risk stimulate him. In a wilderness of words he sees a challenge to make a well-ordered little poem. In a wilderness of mountain slope he sees a chance to set up a snug little farm. His characteristic image of the human condition is the isolated farm nudged up against woods on a mountainside. This is his symbol of our rather precarious hold on the planet. Boulders lie in the pasture "as touching as a basket full of eggs." The hill wife is lonely and fearful — too glad when birds return in spring, too sad when they leave in the fall. On a winter night the snow creeps up the windowpane, and the comforting barn grows far away. In summer a cloudburst washes the topsoil of the garden a little nearer the sea. Even Farmer Brown himself has a precarious hold on his mountain slope. Caught by a gale on the beaten path betwen house and barn one winter evening, he slides two miles down over the icy crust of steep pastureland. Almost as familiar in Frost's poems as the farmhouse on the slope are the cellar holes along the back roads up the mountainside. Starkly gaping or belilacked and closing in "like a dent in dough", they mark the enterprises that have failed, the round of land cleared, settled and abandoned:

> *Here further up the mountain slope*
> *Than there was ever any hope,*
> *My father built, enclosed a spring,*
> *Strung chains of wall round everything,*
> *Subdued the growth of earth to grass,*
> *And brought our various lives to pass.*
> *A dozen girls and boys we were.*
> *The mountain seemed to like the stir,*
> *And made of us a little while —*
> *With always something in her smile.*
> *Today she wouldn't know our name.*
> *(No girl's, of course, has stayed the same.)*
> *The mountain pushed us off her knees.*
> *And now her lap is full of trees.*

Yet the experiment goes on. There are always some to accept the challenge to pit their resourcefulness against the maximum risk. Frost admires these descendants of the pioneer who have the manifold handiness and the daring to make their stand on the edge of an untamed mountain slope. "It's knowing what to do with things that counts." The character his poems praise is the resourceful man, not morose or resentful when nature turns antagonist, but ready to turn with grace and a kind of gaiety to the problem of survival. It is the character of his fable, "A Drumlin Woodchuck," a poem that begins in delight and ends in wisdom, as Frost says a good poem should. It is the story of Homer's *Odyssey*, Defoe's *Robinson Crusoe*, and Thoreau's *Walden*. Frost once said of the last two that they are old favorites of his because they show "how the limited can make snug in the limitless." What the sea with its perils is to Odysseus, the uninhabited island to Crusoe, and Walden Pond to Thoreau, the mountain farm is to Frost — an outpost of human enterprise on the edge of the limitless, a snug defense "between too much and me."

Frost's best profile of a mountain is found in the poem called "The Mountain" in *North of Boston*. This is in the form of a dialogue, between the poet as visitor in the region and a native farmer driving a team of oxen on a road at the base of the peak. Attracted by the great shape that shadows the town where he is lodging, the poet has walked forth at dawn "to see new things." By question and answer a picture of the mountain is built up bit by bit until the reader comes to share the poet's desire to explore it. The mountain is so massive that the township it fills is never likely to have more than its present sixty voters. The mountain takes up all the room within boundary lines except for the few farmhouses clinging to its lower slopes like boulders broken off the upper cliffs. Pastures run up the sides a little way and end in a wall of trees. Above, in sun and shadow, are great terraced cliffs, some dropping sheer for a hundred feet. A climber, resting on the granite shelves with ferns in the crevices at his elbow, could have serial lookouts all the way up. A dry ravine, looking like a path, emerges invitingly from the woods into a nearby pasture. Right on the summit, according to local report, there is a spring, almost a fountain, the source of a brook whose water is warm in winter, cold in summer, relatively speaking. If the summit is not wooded, the poet speculates, there ought to be a view round the world. At any rate, the farmer replies, the spring at or a shade below the summit ought to be worth seeing. He has never seen it himself. Though he has worked around the foot of the mountain all his life, he has never climbed it; only been on the sides deer-hunting and trout-fishing. He has always meant to climb, but there never seemed to be a proper reason. He could not picture himself doing it. Would he go in overalls with a big stick as if to fetch the cows? Or with a shotgun as if after a stray black bear? " 'Twouldn't seem real to climb for climbing it," he concludes.

This exposure of enslavement to a sterile routine comes as a shock to the reader, now thoroughly convinced that a mountain of such individuality is worth climbing. The poet, however, nods assent — "I shouldn't climb it if I didn't want to" — and changes the subject. But he can't withhold one last question, to make sure that this specimen of native incuriosity is all that it seems. "You've lived here all your life?"

The real reason for climbing mountains is the subject of a sonnet entitled "Time Out" — time out from the routine to which the farmer is bound, time out from "all this now too much for us." Here is the poem in full:

> *It took that pause to make him realize*
> *The mountain he was climbing had the slant*
> *As of a book held up before his eyes*
> *(And was a text albeit done in plant).*
> *Dwarf cornel, goldthread, and* Maianthemum,
> *He followingly fingered as he read,*
> *The flowers fading on the seed to come;*
> *But the thing was the slope it gave his head;*
> *The same for reading as it was for thought,*
> *So different from the hard and level stare*
> *Of enemies defied and battles fought.*
> *It was the obstinately gently air*
> *That may be clamored at by cause and sect*
> *But it will have its moment to reflect.*

THE ARTIST OF KATAHDIN
MYRON H. AVERY
1944

THE ARTISTS of the American Landscape school added bold illustration to the prose and poetry that glorified mountain wilderness. Searching for identity in the early nineteenth century, American painters struggled with the young nation's lack of history and cultural tradition. What was to be America's contribution to the arts?

Influenced by the trend toward romanticism of nature emanating from Europe, landscapes became the focus of American artistic endeavor. American landscape painters quickly moved beyond the pastoral images of England, however, and seized upon the wilderness of the American continent as its distinctive feature. This, combined with the notion of religious naturalism borrowed from the transcendentalists, led American landscapists to accentuate the sublime in nature.

Beginning in the late 1820s, Thomas Cole, a young immigrant from England, sought out the wildest regions of northern New York and New England as the subject of his paintings. His remarkable talent and the popularity of his work led to his being recognized as founder of the Hudson River school of painting.

Frederick Church, an early student of Cole, ranged even further to the wilderness of Maine's Mount Katahdin. On his first trip in 1856, Church painted "Sunset," which focuses on a lake and surrounding mountains. The only reminder of civilization is a rough country road along which a few grazing sheep are shown. On a return visit to the Katahdin region four years later, Church painted his seminal "Twilight in the Wilderness." Here, all visions of the pastoral have vanished, and the artist concentrates his attention on the power and sublimity of nature.

In this article Myron Avery briefly explores the relationship between Church and Mount Katahdin. The article is one of a twelve-part series on American mountain painters that appeared in Appalachia *from 1936 to 1966.*

BOTH THE NUMBER OF ARTISTS and the extent of their paintings of Katahdin are indeed surprising. It is a gratifying record, not only in the pictorial representation, but in the impressions sought to be created. The wildness, the ruggedness of the area, the unbroken forest expanse, the complete absence of human invasion, and that which still fascinates today — the varying aspects of the sheer-walled cirques with the play of light and shadow from the moon, the rising and setting sun — brought to this area many distinguished painters. Katahdin is indelibly associated with the great American Landscape School of the last century.

Frederick Edwin Church, perhaps the outstanding genius of the American Landscape School, is the master painter of Katahdin. His works number close to fifty. He was the first pupil of Thomas Cole, the founder of the American Landscape School, and it may have been his association with Cole in the latter's Catskill home that led to the love for the mountain regions which is so evident in Church's paintings.

It is, indeed, a tribute to the appeal of the sheer granite walls of Katahdin that Church should have made so many studies of this region alone. In the *Catalogue of the Paintings by Frederick E. Church* of the Metropolitan Museum of Art Exhibit in 1900, there is reproduced a photograph of "Twilight in the Wilderness," signed and dated 1860, on a canvas 64″ x 40″. At first glance it is perhaps difficult to orient this painting and one might be disposed to query the accuracy of the statement that this "was painted in 1860 by Church and represents the wilderness about Katahdin." Closer study, however, will identify the area. In the central background is a portion of the ridge of the Katahdinauguoh, showing Barren and the Owl, and the long ridge which the Appalachian Trail follows to the highest point of the mountain, known in those days as Monument Peak. The locality may well have been some outlying pond, close to the Penobscot West Branch, which was, on a number of occasions, the route of Church's approach to the mountain.

On Church and his associates this solitary peak in Maine created such an impression that to it he returned again and again. With this group, Katahdin was the American representation of the world's master scenes. Perhaps to Church it symbolized the wilderness in the form of a towering mountain mass rising above an illimitable forested land.

MOUNTAIN MONTAGE
SELECTED AUTHORS
1922–1974

PREPARING FOR HIS FIRST ATTEMPT to ascend Mount Everest, George Malloy was asked the insightful question "Why?" Ever since, the genus homo ascendens has struggled to uncover what are often deeply personal answers. Over the years, a number have committed their thoughts to the pages of Appalachia. *The following is a montage of their reflections.*

Norma Hart Anderson, an active rock-climber prior to her serious accident on the Grand Teton, begins the series by equating climbing mountains with an art form. Like painting, music, and literature, time spent with mountains provides rare moments of heightened sensitivity.

In the next excerpt, Maynard M. Miller, a scientist whose studies of geology and glaciology have taken him to the glaciers of Alaska, looks to the mountains for answers "beyond human consciousness." Perhaps personal experiences with the enormity of nature and with the unsolved riddles of the earth sciences brought him to that point.

Perceval Sayward focuses on the vicarious pleasures mountains offer: remembrances of mountains climbed and daydreams of those not yet climbed provide enjoyable diversion from the day-to-day world. Mountains bring a sense of hope and optimism into our lives: they are sanctuaries, there when we need them.

Finally, George DeWolfe dispels the notion that the object of mountaineering is conquest. Mountains are to be climbed, not conquered. Growing preoccupation with technique, endurance, and competition reduces the mountaineer to climber, and robs him of the opportunity to

*develop a personal realtionship with nature, whatever form this relation-
ship might take.*

THE MOUNTAINS' GIFT
NORMA HART ANDERSON
1955

WHEN YOU TELL PEOPLE that you climb mountains, they are wont to react, "But why? They're so
dangerous." Too often the mountaineer's answer is the lazy
cliché, "Because they are there."

That phrase is a mere suggestion from which the inquirer's
imagination builds a picture of a huge, solid-set object, an
obstacle on the frontiers of Man's collective and individual accomplishments. Mankind has not triumphed over this mass of
snow and wind. The climber has not borne some glacier with
endurance, this cornice has not been pierced by his skill, his
courage has not tamed that cliff.

So to the man who does not climb it appears that climbing
constitutes a challenge and the climber will risk his life to subdue
a mountain; that if the mountain resists, the climber is capable of
failing with a shout, "We'll get you yet," and a vehement
shaking of his fist. It would be reasonable to let this sole picture
stand; men with such will and disregard for security and comfort
are needed in the soft society of today, they keep a certain portion
of Man's spirit alive. Nor are other men to be condemned who are
pictured as climbing, less commendably, for reasons of self-
assertion. Life has its needs; everyone seeks fulfillment, according
to his own psychological make-up, and mountains absorb such
self-assertion much better than a human or even a nation against
which it might be turned.

However, this picture does not do justice to the mountains. They are not men's enemies, ultimately dealers in death.
Indeed, it is because they bestow what is most precious in life that
we love them. Though the challenging aspects of mountains were
worn smooth, even the men who try to tame them and those who
use them as bulwarks for their egos would still climb mountains
for this same love.

The provocation to climb is still the mountains' "being there." We can't change that. What should be changed, to bring out Mallory's true meaning, are the connotations of "what" is there; and the "what" should be made more concrete. The mountains are not felt as blocking but as enveloping presences. The demand on a climber is to absorb rather than to attack, and that which he absorbs is felt as a wondrous experience of living. This life of the mountains is accepted by the climber as their intrinsic quality, dominating, encompassing their other attributes. As it is felt, not seen and touched, the mountains assume a metaphysical bulk which makes them loom large in a man's heart and spirit, instead of in his pathway. Rather than shake his fist at such a life, a man wants to kneel, almost, for being allowed to share it.

To describe how the mountains move a climber through this life, this essential "being" of the mountains is one thing, and to render it substantial to those who do not climb, another. Feelings are concrete enough, but only to those who experience them. Can we find a similar experience in all lives?

T. S. Eliot provides the clue. In describing ceramics he says, "They are life itself. To be among such things if it's an escape, it's an escape into living." Moreover he describes this living as "an agonizing ecstasy." Here is a parallel! The equivalent of the mountain experience, the life we find in climbing, is to be found in the enlightenment wrought on so many lives by art. The subject matter of Man's artistic endeavors is everyday life. When an art gets far from the values of everyday life, that art loses its potency. The scenes of painting, the feelings of music, the ideas in literature are all prevalent outside the arts. So likewise the values making up this mountain experience are met with every day: the elementary physical aspects of nature such as the sun, trees, and the combinations of these which form our sunsets, mists, raindrops on leaves, and moonlight on snow — certainly nothing unusual in these occurrences, nor in the similar physical aspects of the human body, muscle strength, sweat, grace and freedom of movement, the workings of the seven senses. Even the interaction of these qualities noticed in climbing: the warmth of the sun on a shoulder and the chill of air in the lungs, solid rock resisting the foot, cold water on thirst, leg muscles pulling against steepness, even these are sometimes felt in everyday life. There are spiritual values too, human ones of love, compassion, unselfishness, tolerance, and cooperation and values produced upon men's interaction with both other men and with nature: faith, humility, peace, the freedom of mind which comes from peace. Only a few, the forces of immutability, infinitude, remoteness from baseness are common in the mountains, hard-found in daily living.

So why are the joys of climbing and of art so seldom a part of everyday living? The reason points to another similarity of the two. Human beings that we are, rushed, blinded by habit and drives, our moments of sensitivity are rare in ratio to the total moments of a lifetime. The mountains and art force us into cognizance of these joys by increasing their intensity; they are multiplied or exaggerated beyond the unobtrusive aspect habit places on them in daily living, or simplified by separation from the clutter of surrounding non-essentialities in which we wallow each day. They are separated, too, from their own innate non-essentialities. Van Gogh did not give stars their usual dimensions in the sky, but exaggerated them until looking at the picture we are caught up in their convolutions. A writer will emphasize the traits of a character by repeated innuendoes. Just so Wagner brought home the meaning of "redemption through grace" by repeating the theme throughout "Tannhauser." Rembrandt showed the beauty of suffering in a man by lighting his lined beneficent forehead and keeping the rest of the face in shadow.

So the mountains are a realm of beauty. And inasmuch as the aesthetic and philosophic are coexistences, the mountains are a region of truth. (Beauty is corporeal truth, truth abstract beauty.) In them, as in great music, painting, any great art, we touch the marrow of living's glory. We know we live, we know why we live.

ON REACHING UPWARD
MAYNARD M. MILLER
1950

IN THE MOUNTAINS, man is especially close to the earth. There, where the inner conflicts of his soul tend to resolve themselves, can he find aid in his search for truth. With this he senses even more emphatically his insecurity in the unfathomable depths of nature and perhaps as a result is more willing to look for strength and help beyond human consciousness. Perhaps this is why Christ's greatest visions and most powerful teachings were delivered on a mountain height. The poet of the Psalms long, long ago summed it all up, "I will lift up mine eyes unto the hills from whence cometh my help."

SANCTUARY
PERCEVAL SAYWARD
1922

THE MOUNTAINS AND THE OPEN country are the "land of the heart's desire" all too often to individuals so closely held by circumstance within the walls of great cities. For this overwhelming majority, the breathing space of short vacations and holidays furnishes but the foundation upon which to build constantly plans and schemes for future holidays and ampler leisure; — some of which are happily to become realities and some of which are only to perform the important function of relief from the immediate burden of the "thick world of men," and escape into the "world of blue!"

Various indeed are these thoughts! Some consist mainly of fond recollections of old, well-known and beloved fields of delight, so well-known and beloved that it is pleasure enough just to bask again in the warm sunshine pouring down over some favorite landscape, or to linger in the cool shadows of some mountain glen, with the perpetual music of its rushing stream to lull the senses to blissful forgetfulness of present surroundings.

Then again our minds may ramble on to the most unusual, the grandest and most glorious of prospects that we may ever have been fortunate enough to look upon, once more to visualize these inspirations to the sublimest emotions, these challenges, which demand our kinship with the Red Gods as an essential to admit us fully into such Elysian Fields. Some there are, alas, who look but see not, who are called but hear not, who return to the haunts of men to report nothing but that which profiteth not — but to the credit of the breed of trampers, of those who have taken pains to "go and find it," there are few such hopeless ones.

Also we have the pleasures of pure imagination to console us in the long "winters of our discontent." Dreams have we of the places not yet visited and, sweetest of all, of those places "discovered" by our own ingenuity of reading, correspondence, questioning of "natives," poring over of maps, or by our cleverness of intuition (in our own opinion!) — places not known to fame but reported as very choice, or probably so, or at least, highly promising prospects. What joy to keep a mental catalogue of such spots, to be ever on the alert for opportunities to learn more of them, to light on some reference to one of them in a book (from the stalls of a second-hand shop preferably) or in a stray magazine article, to secure maps and railroad schedules in order to plan out a possible, unexpected flying trip, if events should happen to take one at all that way! It may be years, you know, but yet, but yet, — well, if you are all ready you can act on a moment's notice and who can tell, perhaps it will be tomorrow!

These are all sanctuaries for the labouring soul, but the most precious of all is the region or district of which we know something, the fringes of it possibly, yet over which the light of the imagination has full play. We know its character well enough to love it positively and assuredly in advance, and because it contains no railroads, or "good" roads by the maps, except on the edges, if it contains roads at all, and because no one refers to it, we know it is unspoilt by the ways (wise or unwise) of the city bred. It is just as it is — a wilderness, a semi-wilderness, an abandoned farm section, or whatever your fancy may have lighted on for *your* sanctuary.

DEATH OF A CLIMBER
GEORGE DEWOLFE
1974

THERE ARE FEW THINGS on the face of the earth more egotistical and vain than the idea that one can conquer a mountain. Among the adherents to this idea are many individuals who have lost their initial perceptions and feelings for the mountains amidst technical and competitive considerations. And here, with the technically and athletically adept, but spiritually stagnant climber, the rift between men and mountains sets in and begins to widen. Limited by a set of conditioned techniques and expectations, the sensory experience becomes stifled.

Preoccupied with this game, many climbers see little, if any, of the mountains. The climber, in this sense, is no visionary at all, as someone has recently written, no matter what distant ranges he has visited or dizzy cliffs he has scaled. His awareness is concerned only with getting up and the way in which that is to be achieved. His many successful conquests convince him of his invincibility and disguise his endeavors as one of the higher pursuits of the human spirit. "It is a lack," a friend of mine once told me, "of an understanding of the frailty of the human design." The end product of such nearsightedness is a sensory and intellectual death, an atrophy of that obscure process which molds a broader human consciousness towards the mountains. It is, in the final analysis, the death of a climber.

There is a story going about in climbers' camps now that illustrates this narrow, egocentric attitude. It seems that a very famous climber went out late one night to a boulder. He took his wife and a flashlight. Everyone else was asleep. Besides, it was a problem only he could solve for himself. Well, the tale runs that his wife sat by the rock holding the light on a certain move he had been unable to follow that day. Two others had already made it, but he had failed. He tried again, now, at midnight. No one would see his failure now. In the darkness he clutched at the small circle of light illuminating the difficult bulge. No sunlit vistas. His entire vision was contained within that pale circle. He went up many times. In a last desperate attempt, he lunged. Not good style at all, it must have occurred to him. He failed. Caught up in the climbing drama he had helped to create, he was himself a victim of the same play, an actor who could no longer recite his lines. Refuge in the climbing game had replaced climbing the mountains. Lost in competition and techniques, he had some-where misplaced the real meaning of being on and moving with a mountain.

Rather than encourage the idea that man wages war against the peaks, it might be well for us to consider, in this age of dizzy routes and competitive moods, a more human way into the mountains. We might consider, for example, how it is to be at one with the mountain environment, an idea which begins to take hold in the mind only when we discard the game of conquering and wish simply to be high up there with the sun. We might consider also the effect of the long historical experience of men in the mountains, that mysterious union of man and nature.

Infrequently now I will remove my box of slides from the shelf and, one by one, hold them up to the light. There, where only long familiarity can dispel disbelief, is the remembrance of experience. There's Pete, fourteen years ago on the Grand Teton. A bit faded. And here's Hugh, making one of his famous breakfasts at Seneca. Whew! There's the place we turned back on the Wetterhorn. What a storm that was! "Mount Blanc, sunrise," reads the inscription on the slide. I handle it reverently and think back. We had been crossing a flat snowfield high on the mountain and I remember Fletcher trying to move me faster. I was very slow, however, and besides, my feet were terribly cold. I had just reached the top of a small outcrop when a pull came on the rope. He had stopped and was looking intently towards the faint glow of morning.

"Come on, Fletch, let's get up this death-walk," I muttered, my words evaporating as they hit the air.

He just stood there.

"Let's sit and watch the sunrise," he ventured without moving. "It'll be a good one today."

We squatted in the snow together, like a couple of buddhas, and for half an hour looked eastward as light spilled over the Alps. I can remember few things as moving in my life. The experience comes even now and brings a faint swell inside. He had helped me then, unknowingly, to understand that mountains are not just for conquering. The sunrise landscape has ushered in a feeling that cannot be found on a battery-lit boulder at midnight, where, troubled with some last ditch effort, one feels his resources fail. "Climb the mountains and get their good tidings." We have heard this many times. John Muir knew — he knew better than all of us. He meant, I think now, not just to climb, but to climb the mountains.

SELECTED POEMS
1974-1981

THERE IS A SPECIAL RECIPROCAL relation-
ship between nature and poetry: nature inspires the poet to make verses,
and poems, through the power of their images, heighten our appreciation
of nature.

Nearly from the Club's beginning — as early as 1879 — time
was set aside during meetings for members to read poetry aloud. The first
poem to be featured as such appeared in Appalachia *in 1929, a*
whimsical verse entitled "Lament of the Soft Boiled Egg" (which the
author suggested be read to the tune of "The Man Who Has Plenty of
Good Peanuts").

Recently, published poetry has become more serious, especially with
establishment in 1973 of the annual Appalachia *Poetry Prize. The*
following selections are taken from this recent period. Those marked with
an asterisk were Poetry Prize winners.

CONVERSING WITH KATAHDIN*
RICHARD ALDRIDGE
1977

It's true that at your peak I mostly felt
I'd done it then at last — I'd conquered you;
the fact that twice I'd nearly turned back down,
that my whole body seethed with ache and strain —
these things were lost beneath the spread of joy
that came like spreading rain across parched earth.

I revelled in the thought that everything
to see necessitated looking down —
far down the northern steeps to Chimney Pond,

or just down to the Knife Edge running east —
but even as I did so I began
to feel my burgeoned sense of triumph wane.

And what this had to do with was your vast
indifference to terms like this of mine —
that I and others reached your highest point
was even less the point than was the fear
that kept the Abenaki Indians
in olden days from climbing you at all.

For these same Indians chose legend as
the way to meet on truthful terms with you,
and even as I made my slow descent
the reason for this started coming clear
in that I knew your reach down into me
was no whit less than mine upward to you.

As mists swirled by across the tableland
I realized suddenly the white-blazed trail
was now a lifeline of the frailest kind;
as thunder snarled and boomed I tried to hear
just vacuum-filling air, but knew as well
I somehow heard Pamola voicing ire.

So I know now that I will always think
of you whenever I shall take stock of
the scope of my own dreams, the limits of
my strength, the kind of life in legend I
and my own people have, or do not have —
and thus our conversation, endless into time.

THE RAVENS OF BONDCLIFF
SUSAN DAVIS
1974

back at dusk
shafts of red light
edge raw ridges
getting late
in empty country
weathered cubes above the rim
coming over Bondcliff

the fissured rock here
hides a heart
center of the Pemigewasset
cwms and slides
cut off sight

no men
nor any trace
this crack of granite cliff
wedges it all still
locked in place

tomb of a range's ancient throws
columnar ruin
slanted light
the rupture shows a deeper movement
under stone

sun's setting light
enclosed the summit
in scrub pine below

a sharp unyielding cry
filled us
many of them
sky swoop drowning

eye of evening slit
by dark wide wings
wild voices echoing off the stone

"the ravens are back"
left this country years ago

now centered on their death dark rocks
their far wild sound

BREAKING TRAIL
CAROL VARNER
1978

The snow is deepest near the top.
Night catches her with its early
drop in temperature.
She knows to push on.
She knows this path; she sweats,
breaking snow like weighted sleep.
Such spiked cold in moonlight
is a danger she must embrace
like being hurt, like waking.
She divides the snow, leaving
a wake of clenched water
from some ocean of herself.
She spreads herself foaming
behind like a fan.
To do away with
constant deference, her chopped
apologies like gasps for breath,
she has started up this ridge,
a plow through waiting.
She stamps and breathes
the cold as power,
a dry muscle she must warm
inside herself.

HIKING CARDIGAN
ELIZABETH GALLOWAY
1978

*trails of exposed roots lead
to the rock face of the mountain,
I carry a humid sadness.
The mountain is a sure thing
to be moving on.*

*I turn from the stand of beech,
shift my pack, face the great boulders.
I am good tired, walking out again
the boundary that was marriage,
the repetitions of children,
the small steps called work,
the mending of my life.*

*Beyond, the fern moss, pale as a moon,
froths up. I think of sphagnum
gathered from the bogs of Britain,
absorbing the burst lives of the Great War.*

*I am bleeding, too. This gathering reservoir
has given back life. Now it leaves me.
Burden of months and births,
cloths of seclusions, ancient mothers
walk with me.
I tuck in my small bundle, saturated, dark,
warm as my body,
beneath the gray moss quilts,
tidy,
leaving part of myself close to the earth
for now.*

END TO END*
JAMES W. PROVENCHER
1976

After Constantine Cavafy's "Ithaca"

When you set your course for Maine
Pray the route be long:
That it be filled with adventure filled with learning
Do not fear the Cherokee
The Pisgah or the Nantahala
Such you will not find
Unless you carry them in your mind
Unless your mind sets them up before you
they will not harm you.

Pray the route be long:
That on many a dew-lit morning
you ply the mountain seas
The Blues and Whites and Greens
From Shenandoah to Pocono
That you pitch your tent in lush hollows
And call at fine valley-bounded towns
For shelter and food and trading tales
To share the frightening intimacy there
To learn and learn from the instructed.

Pray the route be long:
That you arrive in Maine
An old man wise with all
You gained along the way.
And though you find Katahdin's
peak brooding cold and barren
The mountain did not cheat you
You understand now what
They mean: these Appalachians.

KROPOTKIN MEETS MARX ON THE SUMMIT OF MOUNT HOOD*
ALLAN SAFARIK
1975

> *Morning Star,*
> *the fire in the snow*
> *the orange silk tent*
>> *is a glacier*
>
> *Your eyes will meet*
> *and wander the rock*
> *you have hiked*
> *from idea to reality*
> *as elusive as the breath*
> *that turns the fabric of cloth*
> *to ice*
> *on the mountain*
> *the power is the mountain*
> *the man is a footstep*
> *and either the ledge is there*
> *or it isn't*
> *who can explain the dust*
> *on the snow*
> *except to say*
> *that it's lunar*
> *and best left*
> *for the wind*
> *to ponder with hands*
> *that twist trees into human limbs*
> *trees that bleed*
> *trees that give off a yellow human odour*
> *and those eyes*
> *intense and liquid*
> *are flowers*
> *I saw*
> *you standing* there
> *when morning stopped for me.*

*Edward Charles Pickering,
the AMC's first president*

Madison Hut, 1889

Madison Hut over seventy years later, in the early 1960s

Liberty Spring Shelter, 1922

August Camp's nomad tents at Pinkham Notch, 1905

*Snowshoeing
in long skirts*

*Women dressed for
"tramping" on AMC
excursion to
Mt. Desert Island,
1915*

Formal afternoon tea on the Profile House porch

Skiing in the 1920s — no poles, just hands

Three-legged snowshoe race

Slides used for AMC rock climbing instruction, 1920s: "too close to the rock" (L) and "about right" (R)

Skating on the Wildcat River, 1919

Early AMC trail "crew" at work on a bridge

Ready for Carrigain, 1906 (L to R) Paul Jenks, George Blaney,
C. W. Blood, Albert Kent, and Hubert Goodrich)

Pinkham Notch Camp, 1922

Joe Dodge at the wheel of Azma, the mountain-going Ford

Inside Madison Hut

On Three Mile dock, 1900

Joe Dodge

Three Mile Island, 1912

Rosewell B. Lawrence

Canoeists at Three Mile, 1900

Taking August Camp baggage over the Mt. Washington Carriage Road, 1910

August Camp cook, Charles Learned

Allen Chamberlain (R) and Francis Chamberlain (L) prior to 1920

Among the Carlisle pines, an early example of land reserved for public use

Railroad trestle on Mt. Washington after a frost storm, September 1915

The worst weather in the world, 1926 (?)

Above, Charles E. Fay, first editor of Appalachia
Left, a rest on Mt. Jackson

Mt. Webster looking toward Mt. Jackson, 1896

Right, AMC group in front of Old Summit House, July 1894 Below, on Cherry Mountain, 1917

Down the Bridle Path between Big and Little Monroe

Clambering up
Six Husbands Trails,
1910

A rest on the way up
Whiteface, 1911

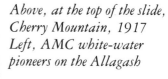

*Above, at the top of the slide,
Cherry Mountain, 1917
Left, AMC white-water
pioneers on the Allagash*

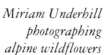

*Miriam Underhill
photographing
alpine wildflowers*

AMC women hikers pause along Sawyer River on the road to Livermore, 1892

OUT OUT*
ANNE FESSENDEN
1975

Mountains climbed for you
rise above me
clouds banking them.
At dawn in Alpine glow
they stood out.
Sun hitting trees at the base
cast long shadows.
They seem to point below
and draw me under.

The navel orange, my present
after long absence, broken and dumped
in the ladies room wastebasket.

Words addressed to you torn up
their edge unravels.
Land in the Sky left in the chapel
I took out Being and Nothingness.

A small orange — like a tangerine
but rounder — and a grapefruit
yet smaller than your broken orange
and with no navel, froze last
night beside the dark mountains.
How to describe them? They were themselves
yet petrified of life
             Pure Stone

Let them come to your den,
my brother says.
I shall go there now, draw in
the strings of shattered places,
recompose latches.

PAUL AND JUDY*
JONATHAN SISSON
1980

Twenty years: I remember their names, Paul and Judy.
Reading a novel of "growing menace and terror,"
Crawlspace, *wherein the poor fellow writes GOD in his blood*
on the Graves' cellar door, his Sherlockian RACHE,
whereas Paul or Judy scratched DARK on Mount Washington,
in a defile a third of a mile from the summit,
on the Crawford Path, a gentle trail made for horses
a century ago, I paused, looked out the window,
musing on the careless time lapses in this creeper.

In a mild summer they arrived at the Base Station
at noon, were told the weather might change, it was too late.
But they started, apparently up the Jewell Trail,
in jerseys and shorts. They must have read the yellow sign:
"Stop. The area ahead has the worst weather in
America. Many have died there from exposure,
even in the summer. Turn back now *if the weather*
is bad. White Mountain National Forest." They pushed on.
By this sign, posted at the first ridge of the Rockpile,
sometimes by the air on your bare legs you distinguish
the essences of north temperate, taiga, and tundra.
The huge cairns are placed so close together, fifteen yards,
toweringly, that smiles must have been brought to their lips.
And they who worked there packing food, oranges and eggs,
to the Lakes of the Clouds Hut, who knew every rock there,
who had all the hurricanes of the eastern seaboard,
and who when gusts exceeded seventy miles an hour
found the foot land a foot from where it was expected,
in sudden fog out of a cloudless sky were puzzled
often. Paul and Judy sought shelter eventually.
Next morning a hiker alone mentioned having passed
two hikers on the trail. Were they coming or going?
He couldn't tell. Well, if they're coming, we'll prepare lunch.
He couldn't tell, probably they wouldn't need any lunch.
Well, why wouldn't they need any lunch. He couldn't tell.
He wandered about the hut, abstracted, distrait, dark.

POEM*
JUSTIN ASKINS
1980

When you come to where
the trail ends
and stones begin
to be placed one upon the other
crowding into a wall
that splits the land,
and stumps break
the elegant curve of birch
angling to the emptiness,
when a light mist
turns to cold
drenching rain
and you crawl
into your own
sense of outside;
do you walk into the cleared field
expecting no worse than a gentle admonishing
that your muddy tracks have disturbed
the rows of seed waiting to join
the inevitable harvest,
do you draw back and fold
those earlier steps into a neat deck
of snapshots certain to please
the vicarious roamer
emptying your blood on the path
even as you struggle to alert him
of your intimate presence,
or do you draw open your hood
to the icy rain,
laugh at believing in anything
other than the cold
wet soft murmur of rills
threading the shadowy edge of forest,
and turn again to the darkening trail
as a child to the wind of night.

LEGEND OF THE DEATH OF PASSACONAWAY, CHIEF OF THE PENACOOK INDIANS, 1665*
HELEN HOWE
1981

We bury you
at Namaoskeag,

> white falls
> thunder,

gilled waters
salmon-eyed

> where Merremake river
> runs to the sea.

A sled, drawn
by twenty-four
huge wolves,

> circles the sky,
> descends

in cloud-flame
to fetch you,

> we hear howls
> over river spate.

Your bear robe
fills the sled.

> Child Of The Bear
> beast-driven

north,
to Wambecket
Methna,

Mountain of the
Snowy Forehead

You are
your legend
now,

> *arrow*
> *of memory,*

a people lost
from a place.

I climb
the spine of loss,

> *cling*
> *to granite,*

watch
for fire,

> *wolves*
> *in whirlwind.*

Take me
from myself.

SOLO
PHILIP D. LEVIN
1975

solar wavering gold
his urine flashes in the wind
arcing on the gusts
like the cries of girls on summer nights
far out from the ridge
rainfalling
five thousand feet
to firs
river valleys
unmeditated seas
stripped to his boots
his shadow-hurling flesh
momentarily
encompasses the sun
and starts the long glissade
the slide down home
crystals flashing from his boots
his damp hair combed out
in the uprushing air

and become

a moving shadow point

in the vast snowfield
shining

WIND AND THE SCENT OF SNOW*
SUSAN COONS
1977

I have not met
the bones of old philosophers
but if they speak
it will be a night
wind laden
with a coming storm,
stars out
no moon behind the clouds
spruce hung back in blue shadows
darkness with no feature
save the scent of snow.

🌿 *Backpacking in 1905* 🌿

✳ 5

EXPLORING THE MOUNTAINS

Adventures of the AMC

THE FOUNDING OF the Appalachian Mountain Club marks the beginning of organized mountaineering in America. The Club's principal objective was to explore the mountains of New England and adjacent regions. Focusing first on the White Mountains of New Hampshire, the early members of the Club ascended all the unclimbed and lesser-known peaks and prepared detailed descriptions of their adventures that were read at regular Club meetings, often illustrated lavishly with "lantern and stereopticon views." Many of these papers were later published in *Appalachia*.

Exhausting the supply of first ascents in New England, the more adventurous among the membership turned westward, first to the mountains of Colorado, then, with the opening of the Canadian Pacific Railway, to the newly opened Canadian Rockies and Selkirks. Here Club climbers distinguished themselves, logging over fifty first ascents of mountains over 10,000 feet high. During this period, through its publications and the western trips Club members made, the AMC was influential in introducing modern rock climbing to the newer climbing clubs in the West: several joint outings were held with the Sierra Club and the Mazamas.

But all activity had not ceased in New England. The trails and camps that the Club and others had developed attracted many newcomers to the mountains, first for simple mountain tramping, then for other activities, all pioneered by the Club — snowshoeing, nordic and alpine skiing, white-water canoeing, and modern backpacking. Taken together the papers in this chapter present a capsule history of outdoor recreation in New England and, by extension, the nation.

A DAY ON TRIPYRAMID

PROF. CHARLES E. FAY

1876

IN THE VERY FIRST ISSUE OF APPALACHIA,
Professor Charles Fay describes the beginning of what nearly became an obsession for the Club in its first decade — climbing the higher peaks of New England which had no previous recorded ascent. With tremendous energy, Club members stripped away the veils which shrouded the northern Appalachian wilderness. As early as 1880, just four years after the Club was founded, the Councillor of Exploration reported that the White Mountain region had been so fully explored "that the Department feels the scope of its work very rapidly diminishing." He went on, however, to list thirty-five less visited peaks of the White Mountains, eighteen of which had at that time been described in Appalachia. *By 1885 the Councillor was able to report, with ill-concealed glee, that all of these mountains had now been described in* Appalachia.*

Fay, a charter AMC member who had chaired the preliminary meeting to organize the Club, served as president four times, and as Councillor of Art, Councillor of Exploration, Corresponding Secretary, Trustee of Real Estate, and editor of Appalachia *over a record span of forty years. In addition to these administrative duties, he was one of the most ambitious and adventuresome mountain climbers and explorers in America. After numerous trips among the White Mountains and Adirondacks, he was among the first climbers to explore the Canadian Rockies and the Selkirks, making many notable first ascents. The Canadian government named Mount Fay, one of Canada's prominent peaks, in his honor. He served ten years as president of the American Alpine Club and was an honorary member of the British, French, Italian, and Canadian Alpine clubs.*

 RIPYRAMID STANDS IN THE SOUTHERN limits of the woody wilderness that stretches from Greeley's in Waterville to the Ammonoosuc valley. Above a range of wooded hills immediately at its foot, and which seems to form a part of it, rises the symmetrical range of Tripyramid — clothed at the apex of each of its three members completely in its closely woven garment of dark spruces, save where it is rent from top to bottom by the great landslide of 1869.

For several successive years my companion and myself had been content to enjoy Tripyramid from a distance, but having at length been seized with a decided attack of what a European climber has called the "cacoethes scandenci", and having made ourselves familiar with the other peaks and ranges in view, we determined to unveil its mysteries, to ascend the path of the slide to the summit of the south mountain, and, passing along the ridge over the intermediate spire, find out on what the remoter northern peak was looking down so calmly. When an appropriate day offered we found two other gentlemen, novices as yet in mountain excursions, but, as the sequel showed, of good fibre, who were ready to undertake the enterprise with us. And thus one moderately clear morning in August, 1874, we set out from Campton Village at a little after six o'clock, behind a stout farm horse that should carry us to Greeley's Hotel, twelve miles distant. We reached Mr. Greeley's hostelry — the *ultima thule* of civilization and travelled roads in this direction — at half past eight, gave our rustic conveyance into the hands of the hostler, and prepared ourselves in marching order.

From Greeley's, the writer and his party set off along a trail some four miles carrying them first through a swampy pastureland and then up through the forest at the base of the mountain. We join them again as they reach the debris at the foot of the great landslide.

Standing at this point one is in a fine position to comprehend the extent of the mass that on that rainy night slipped its century-long moorings. Some twenty-four acres of the mountain side with its added tons of forest, must have descended into the ravine — a surface more than half that of Boston Common. How thoroughly the work was done is testified by the fact that, as far as I saw, not a single trunk or branch of a tree, or even a patch of the original vegetable mould appears on all this surface.

We had reached this point after numerous brief halts, at half past ten o'clock. At quarter to eleven we attacked the acclivity. Not as in the ascent of many mountains does one here have to regret time and strength lost by having to surmount a knoll merely to descend on the other side and begin anew, nor is one subjected to the disappointment of attaining some pseudo-summit only to find the true one still beyond. The top of the slide, which is but a few hundred feet below the summit of the peak, is constantly in view up a slope inclined in one place at full 45°, and usually at nearly 35°. The footing is treacherous, large stones being continually loosened and rolling down in one's wake, so that we found it advisable to choose different paths.

At its upper extremity we made a long halt, and beside the aesthetic enjoyment of the lovely prospect, we indulged in the boyish pastime of disengaging small boulders and sending them leaping and ricocheting down the incline. At noon we found ourselves at the head of the slide. A few minutes more among the trees and tangle of the underbrush and we stood upon the summit, 4100 feet above the sea. As we anticipated, we found it covered with a dense forest growth, and we were debtors to some party that had preceded us for what of view we obtained. They had kindly cut away the trees for a little space on the southeasterly side, granting a good outlook in this quarter.

After our lunch and noon rest we proceeded to our pioneer work — to make our way through the wilderness to the north peak, perhaps a mile and a half distant. But such a mile and a half!

Those whose acquaintance with the forest has been made on lower and more civilized levels, have a very inadequate conception of what the work may mean when transported a few thousand feet above the sea on a New Hampshire hill. It is not enough that you have to burst your way with bowed head through the irritating screen of dwarf spruces, or even to assimilate yourself to the indigenous bear, hedgehog, and even serpent, and crawl or writhe humbly under them, content to escape the whip of their insolent, fretful branches, but you must make your way among trees of honest size that rise from treacherous foundations, where the plausible, thick mosses artfully conceal the interstices of the rocks, into which the incautious pedestrian plunges, now ankle, now knee keep, or even, as we have sometimes experienced it, so that a whole limb parts company with its competitor, and you stand transfixed like an ungraceful ballet-dancer. Such was the character of the region through which we now began to make our way.

Crossing the woody area of the south summit we directly came in full view of its neighbor, the central and highest of the trio. There it rose dark and forbidding, in shape like the upper part of a sugar loaf, just across a ravine two hundred feet deep. Cautioning each other to beware of sprained ankles and worse, we began to descend the precipitous northern side of our peak, holding on by the trunks of small trees, yet now and then taking a generous step, and soon we had reached the yoke that connected the two, anon had crossed it, and commenced the ascent of the other slope.

As we began to approach its precipitous summit a new source of emotion was opened to us. We knew that we were invading a region sacred from time immemorial to the shaggy friend of solitude, *Ursus americanus.* As we made our way in single file along the steep — and directly at the summit the crest is so narrow that two persons can hardly walk abreast through the small trees with which it is beset — we thought we discovered traces of the recent proximity of Ursus. We agreed to unite in one astounding yell in case we should intrude upon his privacy, that should give him a worse idea of human nature than had his imaginary European cousin, Heine's misanthropic Atta Troll, and without doubt send him careering down his native mountain side with a velocity equal to that with which our desire would fain bear us in a contrary direction. That excitement and expenditure of breath we were spared.

We obtained no view of any consequence from this peak, though it is the highest by about a hundred feet. The small growth formed a dense screen and the trees were not large enough to scale.

Again we descended to the level of the crest that connects the three peaks with each other. The distance from the middle to the northernmost is much greater than that between the other two, and the rise is much more gradual. For quite a long stretch we found comparatively good walking. The crest here has considerable width and is level right and left. The trees border but do not infringe upon this portion, and one makes his way rapidly through the tall ferns and the bright green of other delicate plant life. Towards the end, however, the north peak showed its kinship with the others.

At three o'clock we found out on what it was looking down so calmly. To unveil the secret, however, we were obliged to climb a withered tree on the easterly side of the summit. The view was far more enchanting than that from the south peak, at least it had the charm of greater novelty. And why should not this peak seem more restful than its fellows? It catches but the faintest glimpse of the civilization of restless, anxious, careful humanity. It gazes down upon the unbroken wilderness of evergreen stretching northward far as the eye can reach, and is lulled by the "hush" of their murmuring. It looks upon that Prince of the Wilderness, Mount Carrigain, and, with it and Osceola, worships, looking northward to the throne of the Great Spirit on cloud-capped Agioochook. And then that gem upon its train, the peep eastward into the pretty upper valley of the Swift River, where it flows brightly, yet silently, along through the green meadows of its intervale! I scarcely know a more lovely picture.

But soon it was time to think of our descent. We did not propose to retrace our steps, but, taking a course by our compass, strike directly for the lower part of the stream we had followed up in the forenoon. In due season we intersected the brook and from this point retracing our morning's course with rapid steps, reached Greeley's at about half past four and Campton Village at about half past six, or little more than twelve hours from our time of starting.

A few days later we met Mr. Greeley driving the red wagon, and delayed him to recount the story in an abbreviated form. What Mr. Greeley does not know about this region is generally considered as being unworthy of any inquiry. Looking down upon us with something which we interpreted as admiration, he said: "You are probably the first persons that ever stood on that north peak." We feel confident that Mr. Greeley meant what he said. We find ourselves therefore forced to a conclusion similar to that adopted by certain argumentative theologicans not so very long ago, when they opposed the "testimony of the rocks," and said that it was as easy to create fossils ready made in rocks as it was to make rocks themselves; and until some man shall come forward and say that he did it or saw it done, we shall steadfastly maintain that a certain tree on that summit grew up with the old mark of an axe upon it. Even then we will maintain that we were the first to make the tour of Tripyramid.

THE FIRST ASCENT OF MOUNT HECTOR
PHILLIP S. ABBOT
1896

TWENTY YEARS AFTER THE ADVENTURE on Tripyramid, we climb again with Professor Fay, this time in the "Canadian Alps." Fay's first visit to this region was in 1890 when he and fellow Appalachian J. Rayner Edmands were returning from a summer in southern California. With a mere twenty-four-hour layover at the Glacier House near Lake Louise, Fay explored the lower portion of the Illecellevaet Glacier and attempted a frantic ascent of 10,000-foot Mount Sir Donald. Charmed by the boundless opportunities of "America's Switzerland," Fay returned to this region, often with a party of Appalachians, each summer for many years.

The ascent of Mount Hector described by Phillip Abbot was the first major first ascent of an alpine peak by Appalachian climbers. Abbot was only twenty-seven years old at the time, but he was already an experienced and knowledgeable climber, having participated in expeditions to the mountains of Yosemite, Mexico, and Norway and spent two summers in Switzerland to study in the "very university of mountaineering." Following their success on Mount Hector, Abbot and the other members of the party returned to the Canadian Rockies the following season. This time, however, triumph turned to tragedy.

Mount Lefroy was one of the major peaks Abbot had reconnoitered in his ascent of Mount Hector. Attempted but not yet ascended, Lefroy consumed Abbot's attention. It was his principal objective in the expedition of 1896. Climbing with Fay and two other Club members, Abbot chose the direct but dangerous route to the summit — through the

"Death-Trap Col" rather than the previously tried couloir. After a long and difficult day of climbing, the party reached its last obstacle, an immense bastion possibly seventy-five feet in height, beyond which lay the summit. The mountain was nearly within grasp. Desperately seeking a route past this obstacle, for it was now 5:30 P.M., Abbott was unroped from the party to explore the rock wall. Following an apparent lead, he was momentarily lost to the sight of the party, then, inexplicably, fell to his death.

Abbot's loss had a profound effect on the Club. Fay published a lengthy paper in Appalachia *later that year recounting the circumstances of the climb. He concludes; "Thus closed the saddest episode in the history of our Club, for this is the first fatal accident in its twenty years of existence. It occurs at the very dawn of a new era of genuine alpine climbing, for the extension of which among our young countrymen Abbot was so earnest an advocate. That a man like Phillip Abbot should love this form of recreation — and to him it was an education as well — argues for its nobility. Let his death, then, point no moral against it."*

S O FAR AS THE CLUB IS CONCERNED, Mount Hector is the first alpine peak which has been conquered for the first time by an Appalachian party, as such, climbing without guides. We do not claim to have achieved greatness, but we do expect to have greatness thrust upon us, as being the first parents of a very long and illustrious line to come. The Expedition was an interesting one to ourselves, because it was so fair and even a tussle with Nature — and with Nature in no accommodating mood. We did our own work, and fairly earned for ourselves what measure of success we had.

We left our train at Banff on the morning of Sunday, the 28th of July last. The sight of the gray mountains encircling us on every side made our hearts leap like grasshoppers. How daft we became, the sequel will show. Our first step was to get hold of Wilson, the best guide and outfitter for that region, and to hold a council of war. Many plans were proposed, but none hit our fancy. Finally, for about the tenth time since he joined us, Thompson brought forward his fixed idea. Mount Hector was reasonably near to Laggan, the next stopping-place of the main party, but not too near; it had never been climbed; better still, it had been attempted without success; and it was high, because the Canadian surveyors, when they turned back, had already reached 10,400 feet. It further appeared that Wilson himself had been with that party; and he said he believed the peak could be climbed. He also told us of an enormous snow-field, lying to the west of Hector on the main watershed, and stretching away to the north for fifty miles, which was absolutely unexplored, and which might perhaps be crossed so as to bring us down into the valley of the Wapta by a new col over the backbone of the continent itself; and not only this, but there was a great snow-peak by the foot of which such a col would have to pass. What more could one ask? We brushed aside the reflection that this was a four or five days' trip; that no horses could be obtained; that we must carry our bedding and food on our backs, and that we had not begun to get into condition; in short, that the plan was absurd. We voted to start forthwith, and separated to make ready.

The climbing party — the three Appalachians, the local guide Wilson, who twice led the party astray, and a porter, "a taciturn and admirably patient individual named Hiland" — was off at six the next morning, boarding the train from Banff to Laggan, the closest approach to Mount Hector. From Laggan, they hiked the twelve-to-fifteen-mile plateau to the foot of the mountain, making camp that night around eight-thirty. After a nearly sleepless night plagued by clouds of mosquitoes, the party rose at three in the morning to make ready for the climb. Reconnaissance of the mountain the previous day had revealed a number of parallel ribs or buttresses ascending to a point at which several sheer limestone strata encircled the mountains. The strata presented an insurmountable barrier, except at one point, above the largest and most southerly of the buttresses, where they appeared to be broken down and reduced to a slope of shale. The party of Appalachians chose this route for the climb, leaving the guide and porter to return to Laggan.

In a general way, we knew that we had gone too far up the valley the day before, and must bear to the south; we hoped, however, that we had not passed the northern end of the slopes which led up to our buttress. Fortunately we were right, but by a very narrow margin. We bore to the right through pleasant open woods, each member of the party taking the lead in turn; and when the trees thinned out, about six o'clock, we were relieved to see above us what we knew from our observation of the day before to be the beginning of the buttress proper, — a great rounded shoulder, almost a mountain in itself, which we had picked out from the valley as a landmark.

This part of the climb was encouraging. The footing was good, we kept to our work steadily, and every step told. Soon the steep grass began to give place to gentler shale slopes, and these in their turn became steeper and more fatiguing. The pace began to tell a little. Out of a sense of duty, we stopped at half past seven for a brief and rather shivery second breakfast, but the inclination was wanting to eat what we really needed.

The passage of the limestone strata — elsewhere, as we now saw, a perfect barrier — proved even easier on our buttress than we expected. The cliffs were broken down so completely that we scarcely needed the help of our hands. Above the strata we were glad to exchange the wearisome shale, which now was very steep, for two or three long patches of winter snow, up which we zigzagged, kicking our steps and keeping guard with our ice-axes against slips, with an excess of caution rather ridiculous to look back on. None of us had our alpine legs as yet. The snow grew thin and petered out, and we were forced back on the slopes of shale, steeper than ever, and apparently endless. By and by the distance began manifestly to decrease between us and the edge of the cliffs, and by nine o'clock we were almost there, — still in the shadow, with nothing in sight more alpine than the steep rock slopes and precipices up and between which we had come, and with the real difficulties and problems of the ascent as unknown as when we started.

The same step which brought us over the edge of the plateau created a new world. In front, almost blinding from the reflected rays of the morning sun, there stretched a broad and almost level expanse of dazzling white, sinking very gradually to the northeast, rising as gradually to the southeast, and toward the south first rising slowly, and then suddenly lifting itself up in a splendid snow-peak, nobly proportioned and very steep. Except for two or three dark lines which indicated crevasses, and except for a few rocks outcropping along the two aretes and just below the summit, it was as pure and perfect an alpine picture as can be found anywhere. I do not know any other mountain so completely deceptive.

Our first impulse was one of pure admiration; our second, after a careful scrutiny of the details, was to say to one another that if we were careful and took our time, the game ought to be in our own hands, but that it was no mere holiday excursion — to us, at least, for one member of the party had never climbed with the other two, and one had never had occasion to use axe and rope. There was little to fear from crevasses in themselves; but on the upper part of the peak the snow lay at as high an angle as snow ever lies except in couloirs, and there was enough of a berg-schrund below to make a slip very undesirable. The climb was worth coming for, at all events. We ate another light lunch, disburdened ourselves of one rucksack, put on the rope — I ahead, then Thompson, and then Professor Fay — and were off again at 9:30.

So far as choosing our way was concerned, there could not be a simpler problem in mountaineering than the one before us. To the south, along the edge of the valley cliffs, the plateau was level for a distance, and then for a while rose gently; but about a third of a mile away, where it merged into the northern arete of the peak, it sprung up in a succession of perpendicular steps which effectually barred all progress in that direction. The other arete, the eastern, was similarly broken at more than one point, and was too far away. The face between, on the other hand, was virtually uncrevassed except by a single good-sized bergschrund, and this was well bridged a little to the right of its middle point. Our cue, therefore, after following the edge of the valley wall to the foot of the first great step, was to cut adrift from the arete, strike off to the left, and zigzag to and fro up the snow-slope.

We went along merrily, for the snow was in perfect condition. Then, as the angle increased, we planted our feet with greater deliberation. Then I had to kick footholds, — first mere notches, then full-sized steps, — and finally we brought into play the holding powers of our ice-axes, not only for balance while kicking, but for actual support and distribution of weight. From the member of the party who had never used an ice-axe before, there became audible a steady paean of thanksgiving to the inventor of that admirable implement, which beguiled the monotony of our way until the speaker's breath was required for other purposes as the slope grew steeper.

By the time we had passed the bergschrund, the angle was one of at least 40°. Above the schrund, however, certain natural stopping-places developed themselves. The first was a sort of level platform, far to the right above, on the edge of the northern arete. This enabled us to rest a moment. Some distance above this platform, the arete was notched more deeply than usual, and a sort of funnel-shaped gully ran back a little way into the face of the mountain. Above this gully the arete seemed to turn a little to the right, so that it formed a sort of promontory projecting farther toward the valley than it had done below. From here up there was an uninterrupted slope to the summit; short — perhaps only one hundred and fifty feet — but as steep as snow can lie on in an unsheltered place. It was not all snow, however; the edge of the arete was of rock, and for the upper hundred feet, this broadened out so as to form a narrow face, offering — so it seemed from below — an easier passage than the snow.

We could reach these rocks by a long zigzag to the left and then back; and I calculated that we could profitably keep on as far as the eastern edge of the snow-face, and perhaps get a view there. We were so near the top now that the two aretes had converged greatly. As we approached the eastern arete, however, it looked deceitful. Nothing could be fairer to the eye, — the smooth snow easing off a trifle in its steepness a few feet this side of the edge, as though to tempt us to find a pathway there. Personally, however, I preferred not to try experiments; investigation by one of the party — still on the rope, of course — confirmed my suspicions that it was a cornice.

When we began our long zigzag back, we knew that we were on the home stretch. We were monstrously cautious! I can testify personally that the steps I kicked were as large as coal-scuttles, and I inferred from what I heard behind me that Thompson was kicking them larger still. We had a good excuse, however, after we had got far enough back toward the northern arete to be above the gully I spoke of. If we had slipped within reach of its funnel-shaped mouth, there would have been no question of rolling down a comfortable slope of snow; we should have gone down a brief chute, and then been shot out over the edge of an abyss offering an uninterrupted descent of not less than a thousand feet. Therefore we took our time. At one spot we found the snow getting thinner; and our bootnails, when we kicked, rebounded from hard ice. This, of course, meant cutting steps. Very quickly, however, the snow grew deep again, and in ten steps more we put our hands on the first of the final rocks. We scrambled up the last hundred feet in pretty good time, for we knew the mountain was won, and at precisely 12:30 stepped on the summit. This was itself a little ridge of broken rocks; the snow on the northeast came up to within a foot of it, and then stopped.

One feels great reluctance in attempting the description of a mountain view; and yet two things should be said in regard to this one from Hector. There are few summits to which the approach is so spectacular. We had been climbing for three hours with our horizon limited by the edges of a narrow field of snow. We came to the end, — and it was as though we were suspended in mid-air. For three fourths of our circumference there was nothing below us for the eye to rest upon except so far below that it did not seem part of the same world. Secondly, in its broader aspects, the view is one which in its own kind can scarcely be matched by any known peak in the Rocky Mountains of Canada, and that demonstrably cannot be matched in any other mountain system in the world except in Asia. As far as our eyes could reach — and that was about as far as the human eye can ever reach, for the day was brilliant, with no hint, from horizon to horizon, of either cloud or haze — there was nothing visible but the one unbroken wilderness of ice and snow and crag, an ocean without shores whose waves were mountain ranges.

We stayed on top for over an hour, till we were shivering with the wind. I don't think we quite enjoyed the idea of descending the first two hundred feet, chilled as we were; but two reflections helped us, — we had little choice in the matter, and the worst part came at the beginning. We roped in reverse order this time, — Professor Fay first, then Thompson, I last. Professor Fay says the rocks were simple, but that he did not wholly enjoy the traverse above the gully, and Thompson agrees with him. I maintain that the rocks were not all they should have been. They needed sweeping badly; they were steep; they offered very few good handholds; and, most objectionable of all, they tended to slope out. The latter point, especially, is appreciated by the last man on the rope. However, we took all the orthodox precautions. We moved only one at a time, the others holding the rope taut, or standing ready to help, as the case might be. We made use of all our surfaces of adhesion, our rate of speed and manner of progressing reminding one at times of the motions of the garden slug. When we left the rocks, we crept across the bit above the gully like the villains in a melodrama to commit a crime. But when we had left the gully behind, our minds relaxed, our attitudes became normal, and our spirits gradually rose. The pace quickened correspondingly, until, after passing the bergschrund, we broke into a trot, and let ourselves tumble occasionally in pure wantonness. By three o'clock we reached our impedimenta at the edge of the valley wall, rather breathless, hungry, thirsty, and very hot, but triumphant.

A CLIMB THROUGH TUCKERMAN'S RAVINE

MISS M. F. WHITMAN

1877

IN 1877, Miss M. F. Whitman stepped boldly before the group gathered at the February AMC meeting and read a paper relating her adventure the previous summer in Tuckerman Ravine. Her paper was published later that year in Appalachia. *The Club voted to admit women to membership at its second regular meeting, only a month after its formation, apparently without debating the issue. Whitman was the first of many vigorous women who were prominent in the Club, among them such mountaineering luminaries as Fanny Bullock Workman, Marjorie Hurd, Elizabeth Knowlton, and Miriam Underhill. We meet the latter two later in this chapter.*

The accomplishments of early women climbers are remarkable given the extraordinary burdens placed (literally) upon them by the fashions of the day. Writing in Appalachia *the year after Whitman, Mrs. W. G. Nowell describes the manner in which ladies' skirts would become so entangled in rocks, stumps, and undergrowth that jackknives would sometimes be required to cut their wearers loose. She cites a particular instance where a companion's skirt had been reduced to such a tangle of rags that it caught fast on a large jutting rock along the trail. The hiker's next step pitched her violently over a precipice where she dangled — caught by her skirt — over the rocks twenty-five feet below. Though she was dragged back from the abyss without harm, it was some time before the shaken lady could resume her journey. Nowell then suggests a mountain suit for women that would "be feminine and yet be adapted to exploring primeval forests." She describes the suit as " . . . made of stout gray flannel. The upper garment is a long gray sack, reaching to the knees. This is neatly buttoned and makes all the skirt that is needed. It is confined at the waist by a loose adjustable belt. The sleeves are full and are gathered into bands at the waist. The lower garments are loose, full, Turkish pants gathered into a band around the ankle. These are held up by being buttoned to the emancipation waist."*

Whitman's adventure in Tuckerman Ravine began as a pleasant side trip but, due to the vagaries of White Mountain weather, developed into a harrowing and dangerous experience. Caught suddenly by a violent storm and then by darkness, she and her companion were forced into a desperate climb to reach the shelter of the Tip Top House on the summit of Mount Washington. Near the end of their journey, the climbers are reminded of Lizzie Bourne as an inducement to push on to the top. Bourne was the second of what are now scores of climbers to perish on Mount Washington. She began to climb the mountain with her uncle and cousin, September 13, 1855. A violent gale with freezing rain struck when the party was about three miles from the summit. After darkness, Lizzie became discouraged and could climb no further, so her uncle prepared a crude rock windbreak where the group spent an agonizing night during which Lizzie perished. At first light, the uncle and cousin tragically discovered that they were camped less than forty rods from the Tip Top House and safety.

THE RETIRING ADDRESS of our late President, in its appeal to members of the Club for reports of their mountain work and experiences, even though unscientific, has emboldened me to offer you an imperfect account of a personal adventure among the White Mountains.

Our party had been camping among the mountains several weeks, our plan of operation being to select a good camp ground in an interesting locality, and with that as a base to make excursions to the various points of attraction in the neighborhood, and, in good time, to move on to another spot. In the middle of August we had reached the Glen House, and were in camp on the clearing close to the Peabody River.

From this point one of our excursions, as a matter of course, was to Crystal Cascade and Glen Ellis. The tramp down the Notch Road was delightful; light fleecy clouds slightly obscured the sun, and the freshness of Nature, clean-washed by last night's shower, made every breath a delight. Emerald Pool, with muddy waters stirred up by the rain, showed no right to its name; but Thompson's Falls had gained a beauty from the same source, and the swollen waters leaped and danced with bewitching loveliness.

The grandeur of Glen Ellis, with its unbroken leap, held us entranced so long that it was past noon when we found ourselves back at Crystal Cascade.

While discussing our lunch on the precipice above, one of the gentlemen of our little party, who had often been our leader in exploration, challenged us to follow up the stream to the snow arches in Tuckerman's Ravine. I had long desired to explore this region, and, feeling great confidence in his powers as well as my own for the work, without hesitation announced my readiness to start upon the instant. The rest not feeling inclined to join, we left our heavy wraps with them to be taken back to camp, and divested ourselves of all but the most necessary luggage, which little we carried slung to our belts.

At a little past two o'clock we started, promising to be back in camp at dark with true mountain appetites for a hot supper.

The old path is considerably overgrown, and in many places the blazes are obscure, but we rambled leisurely along, every step a revelation of beauty such as is only seen in the deep recesses of the unbroken forest. Rank beds of fern covered with a veil of loveliness the scars left by trees uprooted by the winter's storms, the beautiful Linnaea in many places bordered the path, orchids, both old friends and new, seemed to spring up in every direction luring us from our way in our eager search for floral treasures, beds of starry Oxalis temped us to stop and revel in their beauty, while our indolence was awakened by the dainty upholstery of soft green mosses on huge old logs. But amid all these temptations we did not lose sight of our object. It was a constant climb, but so filled with delight, so brimming with invigoration and excitement, that we heeded not the work or the passing hour.

Neither did we heed what afterward proved a serious matter for us.

As we came out of the forest upon the cleared space just above Hermit Lake, we observed for the first time that the sky had become clouded and a dense blackness was fast settling down upon the Ravine. The solitude of the place was awe-inspiring. But we did not tarry long, neither was there a word said about turning back. We were accustomed to accomplish whatever we attempted and the casual glimpses of the snow beyond, apparently so near, but which we found so far, encouraged us on.

We rapidly passed through the low growth of wood just beyond the lake, reached the alders and were soon utterly lost. To those who have never travelled that road it is impossible to convey any definite idea of its horrors; added to the natural difficulties of the way, we had hardly struck into the alders when the clouds shut in around us, drenching us to the skin and weighting down the bushes so as to obliterate all traces of previous footsteps.

We floundered about wildly, first on one side then on the other, the wet alders lashing us with icy boughs as if resenting our efforts to force a passage.

We were finally compelled to take to the middle of the stream. At first we jumped from rock to rock trying to keep our feet from the waters fresh from beds of ice. But we soon plunged boldly in, wading as we might, knee deep and sometimes deeper. Those who are familiar with that stream — or those streams, for it constantly divides — remember that it is filled with boulders, some of them completely blocking the way. It is not pleasant to boost another up a slippery rock in the face of an ice-cold cascade, but this I frequently did and was pulled up afterwards, having but one boast to make for my part of the work, that in no case did I require assistance where I had not also to give it.

Out of the alders the snow arches seem close at hand, but benumbed with cold, weighed down with wet clothes, and with clouds freighted with rain dashing in your face, the scramble over the rocks is neither easy nor agreeable. I fear our course from Hermit Lake to the Arches could hardly be called a pleasure walk, neither can we boast of our walking time, but at last we accomplished it and stood sheltered beneath a roof of ice and snow.

Under some circumstances it might have seemed a shelter in fairy land, and we should have lingered long, as we have since done, in examining its wonders. Above, the vaulted roof studded with a million projecting points, from each of which ran a tiny stream or hung a glistening drop; beneath, the streams dancing over the rocks, and the whole interior lighted by that strange greenish light which penetrates the roof; before the entrance, within a radius of a hundred yards, a fine procession of flowers, from the curiously folded Veratrum just piercing the frozen ground at the edge of the ice, to the Golden Rod of late summer.

But now it seemed rather an abode of demons. The Thousand Streams had become foaming torrents and rushed down the precipice above us and through the ice caverns with a deafening roar. The winds howled, the clouds thickened and thickened as the storm every moment increased, and the black walls of the Ravine seemed to be shutting us in closer and closer.

For the first time I fully realized our situation. Night was coming on, we could hardly reach the woods before darkness would be upon us, the only implement we had for building a shelter was the knife I wore in my belt, our stock of matches had become wet and dry wood was not to be found. Our provisions consisted of two hard crackers and a very small pocket-flask, with not more than a spoonful of brandy, and to increase the danger we were wet to the skin and shaking with cold. All this passed rapidly through my mind, but what was in the mind of my companion I knew not, for little had been said during the last hour and I would not by a question indicate to him that I had the slightest anxiety. At last he broke the silence. "To return is impossible; our only hope is to reach the top. Are you equal to it?" With no conception of the further difficulties before us, but reading the necessity from the tone and look of my companion, I answered, "I think I am," and without delay we started.

We knew nothing of the path from the ravine to the top and had no time to explore. All this time the clouds had been falling lower and lower, covering the tops of the cliffs and even obscuring their sides. But as we stood facing down the ravine we discovered on our left what seemed to be the bed of a spring torrent or the track of a slide. We selected this for our attempt. Up, up we went, clinging to twigs of spruce and willow, or when those failed us to the very grass and ferns; often on our hands and knees, sometimes pushing and pulling each other in turn; carefully, for every step sent loosened stones bounding down, warning us by the sound how far a misstep might send us; often finding our way blocked by some steep cliff or huge rock whose vertical face offered us no hold for foot or hand, then a climb around to one side and then the other to find a way, but always up, till, at last, a climb which I cannot now look back upon without a shudder and which later examination convinces me we never could have accomplished had not our haste prevented our looking back and the darkness obscured the danger of the way, was ended.

But our perils were not yet over. As soon as we were above the protecting walls of the ravine the storm struck us with its full force, compelling us to cling to each other for support. Night was hard upon us and the clouds so dense we could hardly see a dozen rods ahead.

There was no time to be lost, and scarcely stopping to take breath we turned in what we supposed to be the direction of the carriage road. Almost immediately we were plunged into that dense sea of scrub which lies between the road and the ravine on the north-easterly side. We floundered helplessly, the wind driving us and the scrub with its Briarean arms dragging us in. At last we escaped and hastily retraced our steps to the edge of the ravine. Again we started — this time following around the head of the ravine and striking off in a north-westerly direction, as nearly as we could guess, for the old Crawford Bridle Path, with which we were somewhat familiar, having passed over it but a few days before.

Occasionally fierce gusts laden with sleet would strike us, compelling us to crouch and cling to the very rocks.

Bareheaded and with skirts close reefed, on we went, not daring to stop a moment in our chilled condition, knowing the necessity of speed, yet realizing the dangers of bewilderment and that a single misstep on those icy rocks might end in disaster, hardly daring to hope we were steering in the right direction, when suddenly, as our courage was at its utmost tension, and our helplessness in the face of the furious elements, and our loneliness on that mountain waste more and more drear in the gathering blackness, had become almost appalling, the clouds parted for a moment, revealing directly ahead of us the unmistakable outline of the summit of Mount Munroe.

With a cheery "We are all right," on we went with

renewed courage, changing our course as much as we dared toward the summit but with slower and more careful steps in the increasing darkness until at last we came to a ridge of stones apparently thrown up by human hand, over which we stumbled and found ourselves in the Bridle Path. We were not a moment too soon, for our strength was nearly exhausted, and it was now so dark we could hardly distinguish each other's faces.

For the first time I knew where we were, and though remembering the difficulties yet before us felt that we were safe. A sigh of relief was the only outward expression of feeling from a heart too grateful for speech.

Many of you are familiar with that last mile up the cone, and will appreciate the difficulties of travelling it by night in the blackness of a furious storm. How we did it I cannot tell. I only remember that we felt every step of the way — sometimes on foot, often on hands and knees — and that somehow we reached the old corral, the end of the Bridle Path. Here sheltered slightly from the force of the storm we rested for a moment and I was at last allowed the spoonful of brandy which to this time had remained untouched in our flask — my companion dryly remarking that Lizzie Bourne perished even nearer the summit than we were. We soon left the corral and slowly dragged ourselves over those huge boulders which surround the immediate summit, with nothing to guide us save the sense of feeling and the knowledge that we must go up.

So thick was the night that we struck the platform which surrounds the house before we discerned a gleam of light. We hesitated a moment with a realizing sense of our ludicrous appearance, but finally opened the door and stood, — hatless, with remnants only of shoes, stockings, and skirts, before the wondering crowd which surrounded the blazing fire.

Our kind host came at once to our relief, furnished us with dry clothes, hot food and drinks; and after a telegram had relieved our anxious friends and stopped a party of men from the Glen House who had started out with guides and lanterns to search for us, we were soon oblivious of our perils in that slumber which only comes to mountain climbers.

A DAY ON FLUME MOUNTAIN AND A NIGHT IN THE WILDERNESS
J. RAYNER EDMANDS
1886

*D*ESPITE HIS ULTIMATE MISADVENTURE
*requiring a "night in the wilderness," the trip on Flume Mountain in
1886 described by J. Rayner Edmands typifies many of the outings
undertaken by the Club's early members who had a scientific bent. While
enjoying the outdoors was important, the overriding purpose of these
outings was to carry on the Club's "business," that is, systematically
exploring, measuring, and generally opening the White Mountain wilderness. Marking and constructing trails, measuring mountain heights,
clearing summits for their views, building cairns, placing record bottles,
and preparing detailed descriptions and maps of the mountains were often
the major part of the outing. This work led to the early publications of the
Club and ultimately, in 1907, to the first* AMC White Mountain
Guide, *now in its twenty-second edition. The accuracy of the early
members' mapping is remarkable given the relatively primitive technology
of the day. The Mount Washington Range Map, for example, which
Louis F. Cutter prepared in part as early as 1898, has appeared in every
edition of the* AMC White Mountain Guide. *In 1960 using aerial
photography and other sophisticated techniques, those revising the original map found no substantial errors.*

*The night that Edmands became disoriented in the mountains
there was an unsuccessful search. At a subsequent meeting of the Club,
Edmands read a short paper titled "What should be done by or for persons
detained (possibly lost or injured) among woods and mountains?" The
paper generated a lively and interesting discussion, but the only conclusion
was that "many more questions were asked than were answered."
Mountain safety has continued to be an important issue for the Club,
which plays a prominent role in mountain search and rescue.*

*Edmands is remembered for many activities with the Club,
including a term as president, but he was concerned chiefly with trail*

building. His wife had died at an early age, and to assist others who, like her, loved the mountains but found the "rude blazed trails" beyond their capacity, Edmands developed a system of carefully constructed trails with easy gradients. The construction of these trails was an imposing task and required considerable engineering talent as well as much time and effort.

I N STARTING FOR AN ACTIVE VACATION among these hills, there are a number of little things which should enter one's baggage, but which might easily be forgotten because they are not used at home. For example, who starts "down town" or "out shopping" armed with a drinking-cup? It is well to keep these things all together at home between trips, in order that none may be left behind; but woe be to the man who packs so hurriedly as to forget all of them! In this condition your humble servant found himself, a few weeks ago. Flume Mountain was to be ascended, and the top prepared for observation. Accordingly, an axe-man was needed. Our trusty man, Sargent, had been engaged by a friend for the northern part of the same range, but there was available a man who was ready to undertake to conduct parties through these woods; and so, contrary to rule, the forest was entered without a compass.

After pleasant good-byes at the Flume House, at a quarter before eight we took a leisurely pace to and through the Flume. Flume Brook, which had been curving somewhat to the left as we ascended, here bends a little the other way, and a small brook comes in at the left, forming a fork. From this point we took to the woods on the right until we reached the mass of gravel lying below the broad slide that is so conspicuous on Flume Mountain. We now ascended an avenue from one to two hundred feet broad, of gravel and boulders, which, as we afterwards saw, has a narrow companion on the right, the broad avenue forming a bow for which the narrow would be the string. Above the upper limit of the trees, on the narrow belt that separates these avenues, we travelled on the gravel ridge which still divides the two gullies, and thus reached the steep, outcropping ledges. Frequent rests for breath are here necessary; but how the view broadens with each short pull! There is more or less loose stuff intermingled with the ledges here, and still farther up is reached an area of very treacherous ledge. Once I had to spring from one footing to the next while holding on to a certain piece of the ledge. It is sometimes pleasant to be met half-way in any movement; but I should not have chosen the ready response which this rock gave, as it moved ponderously to the spot from which my foot had just been hurried away, and then bounded down the ledges with such a noise that I had to wait for it to stop before assuring my companion that all was well. Still higher are very steep banks of fine gravel, stones, and small boulders. After reaching the middle of one of these, the whole mass showed a tendency to move slowly down, like tar. It was necessary to lie on the back and dig one heel into the gravel, to keep one's position while digging a similar socket for the other heel. Interchanging heels then freed the foot on the advancing side to make another socket. Thus, crab-fashion, the edge of the bank was reached and the ascent resumed. As there seemed to be nothing further to see by keeping upon the slide, we took an easier and safer course in the woods on the left.

A very short climb from the top of the slide brings one to the crest south of, but near, the summit of Flume Mountain. Following this crest over two of the knobs, helped by a hedgehog trail, we reached the highest point of the mountain. The slope eastward from the crest bears fair-sized trees, but the westward slope is steep and scrubby. The gnarled growth looks as if it had been continually blown up hill by prevailing westerly winds.

Of the view from Flume Mountain I can say nothing, thanks to rain and cloud. The time was spent directing the clearing of the summit, to fit it for occupation with a theodolite.

Mention has been made of a friend. He was upon the northern part of the range, but his lunch was in my basket. So I started early in the afternoon to meet him on Mount Liberty, lying northeasterly from Flume Mountain. It was admitted that if one descended the ridge to the lowest point between Liberty and Flume Mountains, and then desired to go direct to the Flume House, he must descend to the left. The axe-man, who was to stay and finish his work on Flume, had added the caution that if I went up Liberty and returned upon my course, it would be necessary to descend from the ridge toward the right instead of the left. With advice whose correctness was so indisputable, with one lunch eaten and another in my basket, but without a compass, I started northward down the ridge, light of heart but fairly well loaded with instrument, lunch-basket, and wet clothes. The crest of the ridge was kept; but time went on very mysteriously, without any ascending toward the summit of Liberty. Deciding that I should be too late to catch and feed the hungry, I descended on the left of the ridge, in order to reach the Flume House as soon as possible. The fact is that the ridge broadens out and forks, so that I was descending into a ravine between the forks, and lying behind Mount Liberty. The water in this ravine runs a dozen miles through the wilderness on its way to civilized parts near North Woodstock. My first shock was on reaching the water, and finding it not a handful of water running from me, but a goodly stream flowing from left to right. Then the fact that I had travelled so long on the ridge without meeting any ascent toward Liberty became significant; and the question arose, How was I to gain my liberty from the imprisonment of these woods and ridges?

With a compass, or with a clear air which would allow glimpses of surrounding summits, it would have been a simple matter to follow up the stream, cross the mountain ridge between me and the Flume House, and descend to the road before dark. Without such means, the only safe way to attempt it would have been to retrace my steps to the summit of Flume Mountain, and then descend with greater care and more knowledge of the lay of the land. For this course there were not hours enough of daylight left. The other and more prudent way was to keep on down stream, and follow successively the Lincoln Branch, the Franconia Branch, and the East Branch of the Pemigewasset to Pollard's, whence a half-dozen miles of open road would lead to the Flume House. To reach Pollard's before dark was impossible; to get out of the woods before daylight was improbable: but I tore on with a vigor born only of thoughts of anxious ones at the hotel, and as the hours flew by, encouraged hopeful reflections about the probability of bark shelters left by some of the fishing-parties which frequent the flatter regions toward which I was hurrying with all my might. The stream soon became too large to follow without wading, and the water was too cold to make wading prudent, as I found by taking an involuntary seat in mid-stream. The banks sloped toward the stream with inconvenient steepness for a long distance, but finally the country flatted out, the stream merely occupying a gorge. Then I took the more level walking above the bank on the right of the stream, and soon after struck a welcome trail, partly by accident, but partly by beating to and from the bank in hope of finding one. At length this trail descended a little slope overlooking a flat near a bend in the stream. On this flat stood a couple of bark shelters. But more! A murkiness in the air above, a little thread of smoke below, a camp-fire, and some forlorn-looking pleasure-seekers moving about in rubber coats preparing camp for the night. On inquiry, I found myself on the Franconia Branch, a quarter of a mile from the East Branch of the Pemigewasset. It proved to be still eight miles to Pollard's, six miles to the point where the broad logging-road of the East Branch begins to follow the northern bank of the river, and four miles to the burnt place, so called, a point beyond which the path might possibly be followed in the dark. It was after half-past six. To reach the burnt place seemed hopeless; but I pressed ahead before they could advise stopping. The minutes flew, the daylight weakened, my pace slackened, the trail grew blind. I could not get out in time to relieve anxiety at the hotel. So I turned back, and again found the camp, with its hospitable inmates conscience-stricken at having let me go.

If you wish to appreciate a fire, and a cup of hot coffee and camp-fare generally, first take a ducking. Let it suffice to say that after wringing out his clothes your adventurer had a warm night of it, left camp a little after half-past three o'clock in the morning, after a good breakfast, took a few glasses of milk at Pollard's at a quarter-past six, and reached the Flume House shortly after eight o'clock, in time for another breakfast.

Meanwhile, how did all this look at the hotel? A man accustomed to find his way about mountain ridges and through woods had failed to appear. But stop! The day and the night mentioned in our title are over.

ON SNOW-SHOES AT JACKSON
JOHN RITCHIE, JR.
1888

IN THIS ARTICLE, John Ritchie, Jr. describes an early outing of the Club's Snowshoe Section in 1888. The very first winter outing of the Club had taken place just six years earlier when a party of sixteen venturesome Appalachians spent four days, also at Jackson, in February of 1882. So novel was this first trip that other passengers on the train from Boston were heard to make a number of uncomplimentary remarks about people so foolish as to take a pleasure trip into the mountains in the dead of winter. A principal focus of this trip was snowshoeing and the trip was wholly successful with a "difficult" ascent of Thorne Mountain attained, even though the party owned among them only a single pair of snowshoes. Annual outings continued for thirty-six years. By 1886 snowshoeing had become so popular that a Snowshoe Section was organized with membership eventually growing to over five hundred.

Ritchie notes the discovery by the party of a pair of "skees," the first mention of such in Appalachia. *Their novelty is evident in his description of "these foreign shoes." Though no one was able to furnish instructions about their use, at least one member of the party was so intrigued that through repeated trial and error, he was eventually able to use the skis to negotiate the toboggan chute.*

Ironically, it was skiing, first nordic, then alpine, that came into vogue as interest in snowshoeing subsided. The techniques of downhill skiing began filtering into New England from Switzerland and Austria in the 1920s aided by several AMC members who had skied in Europe. In 1929 the Club's subcommittee on Skiing Excursions was formed, similar to the Snowshoe Section of the previous generation. The Club was instrumental in popularizing skiing, holding the first proficiency tests in alpine skiing, sponsoring and participating in races, and developing the Cardigan Ski Reservation. In 1931 Club members persuaded the Boston and Maine Railroad to run the first Snow Train, which proved successful far beyond the original sponsors' intentions. Looking back at the Club activities that popularized skiing in New England and also set the stage for its popularization in the West, one observer — one of the "old men" of the Snowshoe Section — notes that the Club has "helped to foster a child which has not only outgrown its clothes but will no longer stay home at night."

A FLOURISHING SECTION OF THE CLUB had been formed, including some forty members; and quite a number of trips had been taken about Boston, even in snow unsuitable for the sport. Having thus acquired some familiarity with the demands of snow-shoeing, and some notion of the exercise and fun connected with it, we hailed with delight the opportunity afforded by the winter excursion of the Club.

The journey northward, familiar enough to Appalachians, presented little more than a succession of superheated cars, a series of ten-minute waits presumably for refreshments, and a country giving evidence on every hand of the fall of heavy snows. Chocorua seemed more a junior Matterhorn than ever; its rugged, crooked form made more striking by the contrast of its snowy ravines. At North Conway our sleigh was in waiting, and we sped up from the station, through the pine woods to the east of the railroad, past cold, bleak Intervale, through Lower Bartlett, across the whitened plains where the fences barely peeped above the level now, by Glen Station, through Jackson City, to Mr. Gale's home, — our way ever a series of delights realized and delights anticipated; for snow, snow-shoe snow, was everywhere, and we were all "old men."

"Old men" and "snow-shoers" have come to be synonyms with us, and for this reason. A number of us, mostly young bearded men, were snow-shoeing together one bitter day last winter, and through the freezing of the breath to our beards, we became, in face at least, counterparts of the conventional Saint Nicholas. As a sleigh passed the road at a little distance from us, it became evident that we were the subject of remark. A turn in the road exposed our faces to the gaze of the sleighers, and we caught the one remark, in a high feminine voice, "And they're all

old men." The application was evident. Since that day we have
been "all old men."

The day after our arrival at Jackson was devoted to Mount
Willard. The carriage-road up Mount Willard was filled with
snow, — a fact which became the more evident when branches
which in summer must clear the wagon tops swept off our hats or
punched us amidships. Another evidence was given when a
snow-shoe came off, and the liberated foot sought mother earth to
the fullest extent that its limiting circumstances permitted. One
of the party notes that during a quick descent of the mountain, —
with a record, by the way, fully equal to that of a summer
showering party over the same course, — he twice inadvertently
performed the feat technically termed a "dive," but neither time
could he touch bottom. The summit of Mount Willard was warm
and comfortable, and we stayed on the top upwards of an hour.
The view was extended, fully as much so as in summer; and for a
time, while the clouds lifted, the Presidential Range, so far as
visible from this point, was clear.

Next day our goal was Tin Mountain, one of the three
summits across the valley from Mr. Gale's. Here was illustrated
another particular wherein mountaineering in winter is widely
different from that in summer, — the ascents are, if anything,
easier. This may not be strictly true on steep slopes; but the
streams being sealed, the gullies filled, and slopes made more
sloping, a direct attack may be made upon the desired strong-
hold, without preliminary skirmishes with woods and courtesies
with brooks. From the river at Mr. Gale's to the peak of Tin, we
hardly diverged from a straight line; there were no detours to
make, no fence gaps to seek.

I do not think that any of us knew just what the back of Tin
was like; so there was a spice of adventure in the descent. A series
of inclines, down which we coasted, became more and more steep
until we scuttled from tree to tree like children at their games,
with a dash of uncertainty of issue pervading the whole proceeding. Sometimes the tables were turned, and it was the tree which
caught the man. I know that I picked the Engineer out of a tree,
where he was hanging turkey-like by his feet, with his head down
the slope; and before long I found the Skee-man hung up in a tree
to dry, and by a slight detour was able to save him. From the base
of Tin we ascended the hill between it and Thorn, and in a

driving snow-storm, cut across the country by the straightest line for the Eagle Mountain House.

Speaking of the Skee-man reminds me of the skees. A party which visits Mr. Gale's once or twice each winter has a decidedly Norwegian flavor, and a pair a skees are among the legacies to which he has fallen heir. These add additional picturesqueness to his front snow-bank, and raise it above the ordinary level of the neighboring ones, which sprout only common hunter's shoes. If you imagine a hogshead stave eight feet long, turned up a little at the toe, flat and polished on the bottom, and furnished with a little leather toehold about the middle of the top side, you have a notion of the skee.

We did not have the leisure to master these foreign shoes, nor was there any one handy, familiar with their use, to instruct us; but we did experiment enough to learn that there is a great deal of fun to be had with them, while they afford ample opportunity to study the principles of mathematics and physics. When the skees mark out for themselves divergent tracks, and are permitted to follow their divided purposes, the resultant force is always in the vertical and downward. When this fact had been proven experimentally, the skees, freed from their limiting tendencies, skim like birds over the snow to the lowest possible level, each after its own fancy, forming in a twinkling an isosceles triangle with the late passenger at the apex. Then again on rises there come places where the shoes barely hold, where to move forward is to invite a slip backward to the point of beginning, and to turn is not easy. At Jackson the feat of feats was to skee down the toboggan slide. Our Skee-man tackled the chute early in the trip, and after three or four trials had mastered it. To him afterwards the toboggan seemed but a tame affair.

A logging company is at work in Carter Notch, and camps and mills are here located. These were interesting to visit. The route by which the Notch is reached in winter is widely different from that of the summer. From the camp, we kept directly up the stream. The snow was many feet deep, and the river was pretty much like all the rest of the country, the air-holes being the only evidence of its presence. These holes — veritable wells with snowy walls — were ten or twelve feet deep; the sides were smooth and vertical, the form rounded, and at the bottom prettily fringed with icicles. Upward we went, with just such variation from a straight course as was needed to avoid these wells, for more than half the distance. Then came the steep slopes of the head wall. The steep part of Pulpit Rock was accomplished, and there remained only the long slope of the Dome itself; but the time that would have been necessary to traverse this was wholly lacking. We were easily back at the logging-camp at the hour agreed upon, and found Mr. Gale awaiting us. The ride down to the hotel in the early dusk — a race with the darkness, as it were — was a race indeed.

The fourth day of our stay was devoted to Double-head, which for a low mountain is a good climb on a summer's day. Here were the most glorious views of our stay. Everything was clear, excepting Washington; and this was fringed with light vapors which softened but did not obscure its outlines. These clouds, white as the driven snow, peered above the ravine walls in ever-shifting forms. The houses, the gulfs, — all the details were clear, but fringed and flecked with spots of flying mist.

To sum up the results of our experience, winter is well adapted for mountain excursions. The air is clear and the views surpassingly fine. Mountain forms, relieved of the masking of the trees, are more prominent, and can be studied to better advantage. It seems as if winter should afford a more advantageous time than summer for those seeking the best paths to mountain summits. The gullies filled with snow mark the watercourses, while the trend of the principal ridges is evident upon casual inspection. Then again winter weather is suitable for climbing; the violent exercise, which causes much discomfort on sultry days, is little more than is needed for comfort in cold weather. Snow-shoeing has, it is true, some disadvantages as compared with walking on the ground; but the directness of the path, as a rule, more than compensates for these. In the light of our experience at Jackson, it is safe to say that the lower mountains and the ascent into Carter Notch were as easily accomplished as if it were summer, while our novel sensations in the woods in winter went far towards making our expedition a success.

Down the Piscataquog
ELIZABETH KNOWLTON
1929

*W*HITE-WATER CANOEING IS ANOTHER *of
the outdoor activities pioneered by the AMC. The Club began running
organized trips on rivers around Boston in the late 1920s. Elizabeth
Knowlton describes her first experience with white water on the popular
Piscataquog River in 1929. She notes that the white-water season at
that time was confined to a single trip in the spring of the year. These
early white-water outings were undertakings: few sturdy automobiles
and paved roads required that canoes be rented and trucked in near the
river in the fall, since all but the few main roads were clogged with mud
in the spring. The canoeing party traveled north by train and horse team.
The trips were also expensive — the fragile wood-and-canvas canoes of
the day often sustained extensive damage from rocks and snags in the
river.*

*There were more canoe trips in the 1930s, when there were more
automobiles used to carry canoes, and the Club purchased a fleet of
more-or-less expendable boats for white-water use. Today, the Club and
its chapters offer a white-water program that lasts for weeks and ventures
to rivers far from Boston. The Piscataquog, in which Knowlton took her
first dunking, is still used for white-water instruction.*

*While Knowlton may have been a novice at white-water canoeing,
she was considerably more expert at climbing, logging a distinguished
career in North America, the British Isles, Europe, and Asia. During
her 1932 Himalayan expedition, she ascended higher than any woman
had previously reached, 26,620 feet. She is the author of* The Naked
Mountain.

THERE WERE A FEW CASUAL SPECTATORS gathered to see us tie in our packs and other belongings and embark. At the time we hardly noticed them. But we remembered them later. For Paul Revere's ride to rouse the countryside was nothing to the job they must have done. From that moment on, we moved like royalty, continually in the public eye. Every bridge was lined with spectators, the more accessible banks were lined, and over a dozen, of assorted ages and sexes, sat patiently motionless in a row for an hour, watching us eat our lunch. Whether the bulk of our audience were "repeaters," real canoeing fans, running by road from one point of vantage to another, or whether the whole population of New Hampshire actually did have a peep at us at some time during the day, we never determined.

Our stream began by rushing through narrow shallows, among willow roots and thickets, and the trip was varied by frequent tree-climbing, to haul the canoes over logs, and occasional rock-climbing, when the waves proved to be of the solid kind. This, by the way, seems to be one of the charms of swift-water canoeing: it combines so many sports and occupations — tree and rock climbing, above noted, wading, bathing, and swimming, towing, hauling, lifting, and weight-carrying, carpentering and repairing, — not to mention paddling. All of these the party were fortunate enough to enjoy at one time or another during the day.

Toward noon, an SOS from the bank summoned to the first casualty. Assistance was required in patching a canoe that had ripped a hole in its bottom on a snag. On a pleasant day, few things are more restful than giving just this kind of help, — that is, loafing about in the sun, watching in a desultory fashion the one or two real workers, and offering occasional useless advice.

Just after lunch, a stretch of swift water piling down over ledges offered the best rapids of the day. They combined pleasingly a striking effect, some real difficulty, and very good vantage points for watching. One by one the canoes shot down into the boiling torrent, among huge rock-fragments that seemed waiting to destroy them (but very kindly didn't), paddled frantically over to hug the right bank, swirled with the current around a big rock toward the left, steered sharp right down a little cascade, and shot proudly out of the rapid, — only to run aground among the spreading shallows at its foot. In the deep smooth water beyond, the boats gradually formed a neat row, each holding the gunwale of the next, as they lined up to watch the later comers. There was one spill, and a spectacular struggle took place, waist deep in full mid-current, to drag ashore a water-logged canoe before it battered itself to pieces against the rocks. Otherwise, the passage went prettily and without incident.

The afternoon passed as had the morning, with rapids and smooth stretches pleasantly alternating; and the writer was beginning to feel that she was not getting her money's worth, as her canoe had not yet had the promised spill. But the fates were kind. Ahead, the river swerved and poured narrowly between two ledges with a rock in the centre. It did not look anything special, and success had made for over-confident carelessness. Suddenly the boat gave a vivid demonstration of just what does happen when a canoe gets on a rock broadside to the current. Panting, choking, and gasping from her plunge, the writer finally emerged, to see our craft safe in the hands of her shipmate. He pointed out that her technique on the spill had been poor, as when one goes over, — and under, — it is etiquette to rise with the paddle still in one hand, and the canoe, quickly seized, in the other. She could not but feel, however, that to perfect this technique, as he had, much practise is required. It proved ideal weather for a swim, and the divers found themselves so much refreshed that they regretted only the sympathy they had wasted on earlier bathers.

The final excitement of the day was furnished by a canoe which, left a moment unoccupied, tried to commit suicide by plunging head-foremost over a twelve-foot dam. But it stuck miraculously halfway, and hung in midair, plastered perpendicular against the fall, with packs dangling by their straps and paddles falling from it like rain. Thence it was hauled on down to safety by its indignant owner.

As the sun was setting, the last of the fleet floated into a glassy millpond, and were welcomed on its banks by the complete population of New Boston. The official "white-water" canoeing season of 1929 was over.

FRIENDS, FAMILY, AND THE
FOUR-THOUSAND-FOOTERS
DANA CONVERSE BACKUS
1953

IN 1931, NATHANIEL GOODRICH published a short note in Appalachia *entitled "The Four-thousanders." In it, he noted that it had been the ambition of some European climbers for some time to bag all the sixty-seven peaks in the Alps of 4,000 meters and over. Among the climbing community of Colorado, 14,000 feet is the crucial altitude, while 4,000 feet is the magic number among climbers in the Adirondacks. Why not, he suggested, extend this game to the White Mountains. Noting that the figure four had some almost mystic significance, he prepared a list of all the mountains in New Hampshire of 4,000 feet and over — forty-six such peaks are now recognized rather than the thirty-six listed by Goodrich — and offered it as a challenge.*

Francis B. Parsons, a club member already known for his prowess on the trail, especially to those attending August Camp, was apparently the first to climb them all, describing his experiences in Appalachia *in 1949. The challenge issued by Goodrich has since interested so many climbers that the Club initiated its Four-Thousand-Footer Club in 1957. Variations have been added, such as the Four-Thousand-Footers of New England (Vermont and Maine add five and twelve peaks, respectively) and the New England Hundred Highest. The benefit of such games is that they encourage people to climb beyond the old favorites of the Presidential and Franconia ranges.*

In the following article, Dana Backus describes several of his experiences in attaining membership in the Four-Thousand-Footer Club. He got his start, without realizing it, in the early 1920s, when he spent three summers on the AMC trail crews; he finished in 1953, accompanied along the way by various friends and family.

LONGEVITY AND LONG LEGS are the two characteristics chiefly needed for climbing all the 4,000-foot mountains in New Hampshire. When a relaxed approach is adopted, longevity is the most important ingredient. After all, the same mountain will be there a decade later and perhaps it will not then be raining.

On my wedding trip, my wife and I climbed Mount Greylock (3,491 feet), the highest mountain in Massachusetts, although not over 4,000 feet. She took to the mountains from the start and they to her. On our wedding trip, we climbed the Valley Way on a damp day and ascended Mount Adams in a fog. When we reached the top the clouds broke to show a patch of sky above the peak and a great white swirling wedding ring of cloud below us completely cutting off the top from the rest of the world.

Mount Hale (4,077 feet) has a fire tower on it and lies north of North Twin. In 1936 I climbed this mountain with a three-month-old Irish setter pup who was good for about two-hours' walking a day. The rest of the time he rode in my pack basket. This quite mystified the fire warden who thought the dog and I were one — a super red fox puffing up the trail. This same dog, when he grew older, was on one of my longest trips, up Mount Cabot as far as the fire tower, down again, and up Mount Waumbek (4,020 feet). Whom should I meet coming down the woods road but Red Mac, who had run the AMC hut system during the twenties. Red Mac used all his Scotch inheritance in this job for the good of the Club. They tell the story that he gave two hitchhikers a ride into Gorham on the Club truck when they thumbed a ride, but charged them fifty cents apiece for the privilege.

But this day Red Mac was on foot followed by a beautiful young girl. I recalled to him our previous acquaintance and he introduced the young lady, his daughter. This gave me an idea which I had to defer until after my own daughters grew up.

The dog and I continued our way, bushwhacking over Mount Waumbek and down the ridge to Mount Starr King whence a trail led to the road — a total of what seemed like twenty miles of bushwhacking and trail walking in the daytime. The dog ended up on three legs which, even so, gave him one more than my two stiff ones.

So much for pre-war activity. Subsequently, I started taking daughters on trips. This can be an absorbing business. The eldest, when in her early teens, looked with me from the top of Mount Garfield (4,488 feet) down to Owl's Head. She also climbed to the fire tower on Mount Cabot when I went on to the wooded and unrewarding summit (4,190 feet) about one third of a mile beyond.

Then, another summer, she, her next sister, Mrs. Backus, and I went on a Waterville trip where everything went just a bit askew. Daughter One climbed Tecumseh with me (or so we thought) but we found ourselves perched on the top of the ski trail instead. The moral of this story is to take the *AMC White Mountain Guide* instead of casual conversaton with a well-meaning woman guest of the Waterville Inn. I took the party to the lovely Greeley Ponds where the beaver and we swam in the same lake. We started up Osceola and got over the east peak, but increasing wind, rain, and fog caused an influential member of our party to have us return to the shelter. The net score was no mountains climbed, four people well wetted, and two beavers interested in the whole proceeding.

By 1953, we had daughters One and Two working with Pinkham Notch AMC Hut Crew, so we rushed in the reserves. Daughters Three and Four went with my wife to Greeley Ponds. Daughter One joined us on days off and she and I ascended Osceola (4,236 feet) to the top, unhampered this time by weather. We got a marvelous view of Mount Hancock and mapped out a route up this trailless peak (4,430 feet).

The next day we tried our route and it worked. So did I. The trip will long stand in my memory for several events. We had deduced that the long slide on the south side of Hancock should lead into a brook draining that area. So we bushwhacked up this brook from the Cedar Brook Trail, reached by quite a hike from Greeley Ponds. As the hours went by and the brook went dry, I began to doubt our success, but suddenly the slide opened up above us, a veritable highway (albeit steep) to near the top. Then

I knew we would make it, a determination which daughter One had never once doubted. At the top of the slide are about two or three hundred yards of bushwhacking through thick, new-growth balsam. We hit upon the AMC cairn at the top, although it could easily be missed among the balsam. The earliest registration date was 1908. We were the first 1953 party to find the cairn, and there had been but one party in 1952. Another high point was the last pull of the return trip up to Greeley Ponds. I got there, stiffly but steadily, and felt that I was calling on muscular reserves dating back all the way to 1923. It was a full ten-and-a-half-hour day.

Mount Tecumseh (4,004 feet) proved to be easier to locate this time with the help of the guidebook. Mrs. Backus and I with daughters Three and Four made it with some energy to spare.

This left only Owl's Head (4,023 feet) in the Pemigewasset Wilderness to be climbed in the 4,000-foot group in New Hampshire. Owl's Head is almost everything that a mountain should not be. It is wooded at the top; it is surrounded by higher peaks; and it has suffered from fire and lumbering. I am something of an authority on not climbing Owl's Head, as I had looked at it many times from the Garfield Ridge and even sought to climb it with daughters One and Two from Galehead Hut as a base. This attempt started in the rain and ended in a thunderstorm, unsuccessfully. The eastern slope of the mountain was not the correct approach.

But this time, daughter Three and I started from a good base at Franconia Brook Shelter accompanied part way by daughter Four and Mrs. Backus. We went around to the west side and stopped walking the Lincoln Brook Trail at a junction of a side brook with Lincoln Brook where a 58° compass line (magnetic) showed the way to the top of the Owl's Head Ridge. On this side all the rubble of fire and lumbering had rotted away, another advantage of the Fabian approach to this sport, and a young birch forest provided good bushwhacking. In fact, the slowest going was in the spruce at the very top of the ridge where only an occasional outlook rewarded all the effort. The mess of bramble and blowdown on the east side occasionally topped the ridge. But we persevered along the crest until it started to descend, whereupon we took a course down the mountain parallel to our ascent. Due to our progress along the ridge, we hit Lincoln Brook a few hundred yards north of the cairn we had built on crossing it for the ascent. My clothing was ripped to ribbons. Scarcely enough was left of my shirt to flag a wheelbarrow, but I had at last reached the top of Owl's Head.

As for further trips in this decade, there can be some profitable ones near the Appalachian Trail in Maine to complete the ascent of the 4,000-foot peaks in that state. Daughters Three and Four will not both escape before this is tried, and anyway, I still have Daughter Five in reserve.

CLIMBING THE FOUR-THOUSAND-FOOTERS IN WINTER

MIRIAM UNDERHILL

1967

NOT CONTENT WITH BEING *charter members of the Four-Thousand-Footer Club, Miriam Underhill and her husband Robert started a new game, climbing the four-thousand-footers in winter. As initiators of the game, they set the rules, which chiefly concerned the definition of winter. "Snow on the ground" and other "namby-pamby" criteria were discarded; winter was to be measured exclusively by the calendar.*

Both were already experienced winter climbers, long-term members of the rugged "Bemis Crew." This informal group of AMC members met for the first time in February 1923 at Bemis, New Hampshire, to engage in more active climbing than is customary on scheduled Club excursions. In 1959, when the Underhills began their quest for all of the four-thousand-foot peaks in winter, they had already climbed half of them.

Both Underhills were among the finest climbers that this country has produced, climbing in the Alps and the American Rockies, in addition to their extensive outings in New England. Robert prepared the first and most important articles ("On Roping Down" and "Technique of Rock Climbing") on technical rock climbing to appear in Appalachia. *Miriam wrote the book* Give Me the Hills *and edited* Appalachia *for seven years. She was in her sixties and he was in his seventies when they made the climbs described in this paper.*

I T DID SEEM TO US, my husband Robert and me, Charter Members of the Four-Thousand-Footer Club, that climbing the New Hampshire four-thousand-footers in winter would present an even more sporting challenge than ambling up the well-trodden trails in summer. In winter there is no footpath visible under the snow and, particularly in open hardwoods, finding the route may be a puzzle. Winter is colder; you can take only the briefest of rests, no more of those sybaritic siestas, stretched out on the warm, soft ground. Days are shorter. The rucksack is heavier with all those extra clothes, not to mention the crampons clanking away and the ice-axe. Then there's the business of finding water, which is more of a problem than in summer, with the rills trickling around here and there. Add to this the fact that the water in your canteen, as well as sandwiches in your pack, are all too likely to be frozen rock-hard. Unless, that is, you have been careful to carry them under your outer garments, close to your body, where they will be tangled up with your camera and films. And these do not like to get too cold either. Most of all, the real work of breaking trail in deep or heavy snow, or kicking steps up steep slopes, is often considerable.

All these may sound like splendid arguments for staying home, but not to us. We were old winter climbers from way back, thanks to the good old Bemis Crew.

Osceola

Strict as our rules were on the definition of "winter" they said nothing against taking advantage of a lucky break, and our chance came on the first day of winter in December 1959. Earlier in the season snow had fallen, but in the valleys it had now pretty much melted away. Well aware of the great advantage of attacking Osceola while the Tripoli Road was still open, Merle Whitcomb, Robert and I hurried down there. The ground we had been looking at, at North Woodstock, was bare, and we felt that even though snowshoes might be needed for a short distance at the top, it was a bother to carry them. Anyway, we did not mind a little wading through snow. We got all we cared for. It never occurred to us to take crampons. It never occurred to us, either, that the trail would be so icy that we should have to bushwhack along its edges.

On the summit of Osceola we looked at our watches with consternation. But it would be only a mile to Osceola East. It turned out, however, not to be one of those rapidly-covered miles, what with hard ice on the steep slopes and deep snow wherever it could lie. I remember a particularly uninviting north sidehill slope on the approach to the summit of Osceola East where, in stamping vigorously through the crust in order to stay on the slope at all, we were rewarded by plunging into snow above our knees.

As we started down from the main peak on our return the snow under our feet glowed red from the sunset, and across the red snow the dark parallel shadows of the tall trees reached way down into the valley. Through the woods near the bottom, as we felt our way along by hand, we met many more large boulders in the trail than we had remembered. But we were buoyed up by Merle's cheerful thought: "Every day now," she observed, "the days are getting longer and longer."

Isolation

For the weekend of January 16, 1960, Bob Collin was leading a one-night camping trip up Mount Isolation by way of Rocky Branch Shelter Number 2. From the shelter to the Montalban Ridge above, with its Davis Path, was a bushwhack, but one which Robert and I had done in summer and found fairly innocuous. We were, of course, going on the trip, too. On the preceding Tuesday afternoon Robert and I broke out the trail towards the shelter for a short distance and on Thursday, after a new snowfall, Robert, Merle and I broke it out again up to the height-of-land, where we cached our tents and some other gear. On Saturday, although we drove down to see the others off, my two comrades preferred to chicken out. Their trifling excuse was merely the vicious weather. Now, in the fall of 1967, I have checked up on that weather, and I find the following in the official records: "January 16, 1960, 19° maximum, − 12° minimum, wind WNW, 79 M.P.H. average, 123 peak." This was on the summit of Mount Washington, and our friends were not too far away from there when they got up on the Montalban Ridge. A wind of 123 miles per hour, even just a gust, has considerable cooling power. The records from Pinkham Notch, in the valley only a few miles away, include the notation: "High winds, snow flurries."

The other party later reported more than scheduled frills to their trip, and I quote: "Intense cold, winds of gale force. Collapse of only one tent (this was Chris Goetze's; he continued to use the tent as a bedspread). Frostbitten cheeks were eivdent. One climber was picked up and literally blown to the summit."

That night, snuggled in our down sleeping-bags, Robert and I awoke to find a snowstorm of considerable determination raging outside. Climbing Isolation was of course out of the question, said Robert. At the first inkling of daylight he would like to start for home. Merle ought to hear about this change in the weather, and since we feel that we should look after our little friend, so much younger than we, we woke her up. "Merle," we called, "it's snowing." "It's been snowing for two hours," she called back.

Soon we heard inexplicable sounds from Merle's tent. What could she be doing in the middle of a cold, black night? Rolling up her sleeping-bag, that's what she was doing. Speechless, Robert and I crawled a little deeper down into ours. Merle was all slept out, she explained, and with her flashlight she was going to start breaking trail up the mountain. And that was that! Of course a storm is never so bad, anyway, when you are dressed for it. When we reached the summit we gave a quick glance around, in the driving snow and rushed back to the shelter, ready now, all three of us, to start home traveling light and fast. We left the heavier pieces of our equipment neatly piled (Merle must have done that) in the northeast corner of the shelter. For we lived nearby and would come back again soon. It was most unlikely that anyone else would go in there in the meantime.

As it happened, we did not come back soon and when we did it was to follow the tracks of other people. We pondered, of course, the likelihood of our finding anything still there in that corner. When we did, when everything turned up apparently untouched, I expressed my gratitude to those unknown men of integrity by doing a very thorough cleaning job around the shelter and its environs.

Zealand

Back in 1959, when I asked George Hamilton, at that time Manager of the AMC huts, if we might spend the night at Zealand, he told us cheerily just to open the back door and walk in. It took us two hours to open that door. First we had to find it. Stretching back from the ridgepole of Zealand Hut to the rocky bank on the north lay an expanse of hard, windpacked snow completely fillng in what, in summer, is a gap eight or nine feet wide at its bottom and narrowest part. As for the door, we had to guess where it might be, under all this snow. Choosing what looked like a reasonable location, we dug. Ice-axes make rather poor shovels, and snowshoes are not much better. But finally, using a small saucepan, we could get some work done. Our system worked as follows: with the ice-axe I broke up some of the underfoot snow — or, lower down, ice — as much as could be accommodated around my legs; to clear the way I handed the axe up to Robert, who passed it on to Merle; Merle passed the saucepan down to Robert, who forwarded it to me. And so on, over and over, for the major part of the two hours. Finally, all the ice around the door which could be reached by the axe, or by a jackknife blade, had been chopped or pried away, and still the door would not budge. I squirmed around to face it squarely, put my feet against the bottom, and pushed. A great rending noise filled the air; the glass window in the door had cracked all the way across. But the door was still frozen tight. I was dejected. Robert was able to drag me up out of the depths, then descended himself and put his great boots against the door. According to all the laws of common sense these should have caused even larger cracks. But no, the door opened as easily as you please. Immediately Merle, using the same saucepan, began carrying down again into the hut the snow and ice which we had worked for two hours to get out of there. She was going to make tea, a laudable activity after all.

Not long after we were in bed, so to speak, and when all was dark, we heard curious metallic clankings. Merle, it appeared, was lighting the fire to start breakfast; she was hungry.

We pointed out that it was not quite 11 P.M. and suggested that she make herself a good lunch and then go back to sleep.

To report that the next morning we reached the summit of Zealand Mountain without incident may sound like an anticlimax. But when we left the hut and started home we discovered that the Zealand rabbits had got into the act, too. To pull our equipment into Zealand on our arrival we had used a light fiberglass toboggan which I had bought in the toy department. We had left this at the foot of the steep little pitch leading to the hut and carried the loads up the short distance on our backs. The rabbits, however, had found the toboggan rope just delicious and had chewed it into small pieces.

Galehead

The next time we visited an AMC hut, Galehead, George came along with Robert and me on a reconnaissance. We wanted to take up some supplies as well as find out if we could get into the hut. Alas! all too easily. Some earlier visitor had left the back door ajar and snow had filled the kitchen. How George worked, and Robert, too, with shovels and brooms, to get that snow outdoors! Some snow remained, however, which, with all the hard ice layer on the floor, never melted during the whole time when we were in the hut. The snow came in handy to pack against the cracks around the door. It kept out quite a lot of the furious wind which day after day was attacking the hut.

The Forest Service usually knew about our plans, chiefly because we told them. Many of the rangers were friends anyway. They liked to know what was going on. After all, if they find a car standing on the edge of the wilderness day after day in winter, they may indeed wonder if all is well.

Hutch (District Ranger C. W. Hutchinson) told me that he could see the roof of Galehead Hut from his window down in Bethlehem, nine air miles away. If we got into any trouble, or even if we "just wanted something, build a fire and we'll be right up." Then Hutch went off to Detroit. But he left two younger rangers with the job of watching Galehead. Did they see it, with or without signal fire, even once? No. For the day we moved to Galehead was the day before the start of some winter weather.

Twenty-one inches of snow came down that next day on Mount Washington, and Galehead was near enough to have about the same. Actually it seemed to us like a great deal more! The following day some additional snow appeared; the day after that, only a small amount, but there were clouds enough to keep everything covered.

For untold hours of our incarceration we sat around in our cramped quarters, now and then venturing out to find and cut up a few more dead trees for the stove. Fortunately we discovered a group of these at a little distance from the hut.

All this time our thoughts kept reaching out ahead. We had plans for those post-storm days and they all started with South Twin. If we could keep the trail broken out for those first 1,126 feet of elevation, and that certainly does not sound like much of a job, it would be a help on the start of our projected walk. Though the deep snow was working against us, and the wind as we got higher, at least we kept track of where the trail lay.

Late afternoon Merle and I, who happened to be outdoors, noticed a glimmer of clearing. Off we dashed to make a final check of our job. As I cowered behind the summit cairn of South Twin, most ornately decorated with enormous frost feathers, I looked down on a new, fresh immaculate world. But a chilly one.

The following morning all of us were off well before sunrise. Every twig of every bush and tree was coated thick with snow and frost feathers. And standing around were a few of those fantastic gnomes, small trees completely covered with snow, in sparkling white like everything else. As we neared the summit of South Twin, climbing over the hard, moulded and windpacked ripples, ridges and small dykes, we had to rely strongly on the crampons attached underneath our snowshoes.

One glance over to the east of the Twin Range and I realized that not everyone was considering this the glorious day that we were finding it. The summits of the Presidential Range stood out strongly but the intervening valley regions were filled with thick masses of clouds. On these clouds, way off to the northeast, floated a firetower on a tiny island of snow. Cherry Mountain.

I cherish the memory of that day's walk from Galehead to South Twin to Guyot, to West Bond, to Bond, and then back to Galehead. The sunshine on the snow, the sparkling air, the chance to stretch our legs after sitting still so long gave me a fine feeling of exhilaration. And I liked knowing that for some many miles nobody had stepped on that new layer of snow except a large wildcat, who paced us for most of the way between South Twin and Guyot.

Jefferson

You'd think that Jefferson, practically in our own front yard, would have been one of the earliest climbed instead of the very last. We did make gestures toward it. Between December 30, 1959, and March 21, 1960, accompanied sometimes by Merle, we four times got well above timberline, only to become enveloped in clouds or battered by wind. I am not counting a couple of times when we merely spent the night at the Log Cabin (with little ermines dashing around in the dark), ready, to no avail, to storm up the peak the next morning. The worst defeat was one when Robert and I, alone, got to Edmands Col, whereupon clouds came in. Too small a party, we thought, to go higher, when we couldn't see. And suppose one of us had broken a leg? All this time we kept our crampons at timberline, hidden between two rocks in a gray, rock-colored bag which we had great trouble finding again ourselves. We were a little surprised and chagrined to reach the end of winter in March 1960, with every peak over 4,000 feet climbed except Jefferson.

But winter rolled around again the following December and in the meantime Bill Baird had made some plans for us. The Log Cabin, said Bill, was too low. Crag Camp, although farther away from our goal, was higher and should be our base, to take quick advantage of any spot of good weather. We ought to live there. They would see that Crag was kept stocked with provisions and gasoline for the whole winter if necessary. And they would come up to bring us fresh food every weekend! Although I am not sure that the entire program would have been carried out as sketched, we at least started in on schedule. In October we cached a large stock of supplies, between two large boulders near certain trees on the trail just below Crag Camp.

December 22 was the starting day. Our son, Bob, was going to leave college a day early in order to be present at this historic event: the Fall of the Last Winter Four-Thousander. In

Harvard Square he ran into Chris Goetze, who came along too. George Hamilton also joined the party, with instructions from Brud Warren of the Berlin *Reporter* not to come home without pictures. These were powerful reinforcements.

We all went up to Crag on December 22. Along the trail where we thought we had left our cache there were no boulders at all in sight or anywhere within reach. Nobody could recognize the trees. I lay on my stomach on the snow and plunged my mittens in here and there. Finally I brought up a branch which had been cut. Although I couldn't remember having cut any, it proved that human beings had been there, and gave me new strength and longer arms to burrow farther. Finally, of course, we found everything.

We left Crag Camp the next morning with a gorgeous red sunrise over Gorham. It was lovely, but "Red in the morning, sailors take warning." Sure enough, as we approached Edmands Col wisps of cloud started blowing rapidly by. What did we care? We sat for a minute or two, for a bite to eat, in the lee of the emergency shelter on the Col. George had been having trouble that winter with the coffee in his canteen freezing. He didn't like that. This time he was going to outsmart the elements; he would leave the coffee at home and put in something which would stay liquid — namely, sherry. On opening the canteen at Edmands Col he found a solid block of ice in the middle and, sloshing around outside of it, pure alcohol.

We did not stay long. The official weather records for that day on the summit of Mount Washington, and Jefferson is close enough to use the same, were: high $-7°$; low $-18°$; wind, 72 miles per hour. When somebody wanted a string tied I removed a mitten for not more than a couple of seconds and felt a little crackling in two fingertips. Frostbite. I was interested to learn that it would take place so quickly. We left our snowshoes at the Col and traveled up the cone on crampons. Chris, who had recently been up Jefferson, recommended that we avoid the summer route, now pretty icy. Chris led by a good route: a snow slope, traverse left, then straight up hard snow again. In an hour or less we were all on top, now in thick clouds. And such wind! Nobody stayed any longer than was necessary to climb, or just touch, the summit cairn.

GEORGIA TO MAINE, MARCH TO NOVEMBER
MURRAY S. CHISM AND EDWARD N. LITTLE
1960

*T*HE APPALACHIAN TRAIL, *completed in 1937, runs some 2,000 miles from the mountains in Georgia to Katahdin in Maine. The trail traverses fourteen states, running roughly along the spine of the Appalachian Mountain chain. Approximately 154 miles are within New Hampshire, traversing most of the major peaks and ranges of the White Mountains.*

Over the years, a number of people have found, with some recollection, that they have hiked many sections of the trail on a variety of scattered holidays. With some systematic effort the missing links can be filled in to enable the climber to join the select ranks of the end-to-enders. It seems only natural to do so. Probably the first to set foot over the entire trail was Myron Avery who, for many years, was chairman of the Appalachian Trail Conference. Close behind was George Outerbridge who described his adventures in Appalachia *in 1939.*

With the trail completely traversed in a series of hikes, the next logical accomplishment was to hike the trail continuously from end-to-end in a single season. This proves a difficult task given the length of the Appalachian Trail and the constraints brought by severe winter weather. It was not until 1947 that this feat was accomplished by Earl Shaffer. He reported his story in the June 1948 issue of Appalachia.

Since Shaffer's story appeared, Appalachia *has published a number of accounts of end-to-end journeys over the Appalachian Trail, among them the paper by Murray Chism and Edward Little. These gentlemen, both in their sixties, were members of the Club, close friends since their school days at Yale, class of 1916. Both finished the journey in good physical condition, though each lost twenty to twenty-five pounds and wore out six pairs of boots.*

FOR MANY YEARS, we had dreamed about walking the entire Appalachian Trail, but we were forced to wait for retirement days to obtain our chance. That retirement gave one of us sufficient time, while a generous leave of absence from semi-retirement work made the trip possible for the other. Fortunately, at the time both of us were in very good physical condition.

One thing is certain: we had not set our goal years ago and then stuck to it through thick and thin. For long periods it was merely a smoldering idea. On occasion it would burst into flame for discussion, when in recent years we took one-day walks almost weekly or made backpacking trips of three to five days in our vacations. Some of these longer trips were over sections of the AT — in the Smokies, the Blue Ridge, the White Mountains and around Katahdin — and their beauty and variety appealed to us greatly.

There were some basic decisions to make. After many discussions pro and con we decided to make the trip from south to north. We could get an earlier start that way, and we thought we might be able to get through much of the hottest part of the trip before summer drought dried up too many of the sources of water supply. We might be able to keep ahead of the worst of the summer growth in the southern states, instead of heading into it after it had reached its peak. We might keep ahead of the worst of the insects, especially chiggers and ticks. With the early start we should miss many of the poisonous snakes in the southern part.

We decided to make the trip a backpacking expedition and to carry in our packs everything we needed to sustain ourselves on the trail from the time we started one "hitch" in our journey until we made contact again with our supplies. We planned to use lean-to shelters along the trail wherever they were available, but we would carry light nylon, one-man tents for use where there were no shelters or when shelters were already occupied.

We knew we were in for a lot of hard physical effort and a long steady grind, but we made up our minds that we would enjoy the trail and the experience to the utmost. We were not out to set any records for speed or endurance, and we wanted to be in better physical condition when we finished than we were at the start. We agreed that if the trip ever began to get us down, it was time to stop. There were rough days, of course, but things never quite came to the point of getting us down although, because of weather, the last couple of weeks in Maine were rugged enough. By that time, however, we were so close to our goal we could not quit!

Our biggest problem was to figure out how to replenish our food supplies, provide clean clothes, and replace or repair equipment which might fail or wear out. We thought of depending on the towns we passed through, or near, for the common items and mailing to ourselves the special things we might need. But maps showed that the trail actually passed through towns at only infrequent intervals. The better part of the day might be lost getting to a nearby town or even store. Long stretches of trail ran through wilderness areas with no towns around and, as we learned, no houses in sight.

The maps also showed, however, that the trail crossed highways or roads passable by automobiles at fairly frequent intervals. If we could only arrange to have a car at such crossings! Luckily for us, Mrs. Little was enthusiastic about the idea of chauffeuring the family car as a supply car (she later dubbed it the "chuck wagon"). Our biggest problem was solved.

There is something especially healthful about walking and living in the open. Frequently our feet were wet for days at a time, especially in Maine. Wet or dry, often they got pretty cold while we stood around preparing and eating supper and breakfast. Yet neither of us had to stay off the trail for a day on account of illness. One slight stomach upset apiece (at different times), a couple of days with scratchy throats, and a tooth which had to be extracted because of a serious root infection were the extent of our ailments.

All our preparations took what seemed like an endless amount of time. We had camping and fire permits to get, and maps and mimeograph sheets to supplement guidebooks where there were relocations. We could have used even more time, but cut it short and made our start from Mount Oglethorpe, Georgia, on March 10, 1959.

The early spring cold in the mountains of Georgia, North Carolina and Tennessee made us wish we had started at least three weeks later. We had some light snow there. In April we had a four-inch snowfall in the Smokies, following a couple days of drenching rain. In Virginia we ran into three weeks or so of some of the hottest weather they had had in years. Our nearly five weeks in Maine gave us an abnormal total rainfall, which meant bad going, and it was very cold at times. There was snow there, too, but fortunately it was not heavy enough to block further walking. The final ascent of Katahdin, on November 8, was in a light snowstorm. The boulders and many trail paintmarks above timberline were glazed with half an inch of ice and covered with an inch of snow. The cylinder at the summit was so encased with ice that we did not take time to open it and register. However, taken all in all, the weather probably should not be considered to have been abnormal.

We had backpacked our way something over 2000 miles. We were amazed to find the trail through Georgia, North Carolina, and Tennessee so very rugged. The mountains rise so steeply from the deep gaps between them that footing on the dry oak-leaf carpet of the trail was often very slippery. In the Smokies, especially, the slopes of the mountains are deeply scored, with sharp fins between the low, sloping ravines. All about, in these parts, the mountains lie in a wild jumble. But not all are of this character; there are many balds. Practically devoid of trees, these rounded domes are interspersed among the more rugged peaks. The balds and many lookout points on the high-timberline peaks afford grand scenic vistas.

In Virginia there are broader valleys between the mountains, which gradually diminish in height until the last of the 4000-footers is passed, Hawksbill Mountain in the Shenandoah National Park. In fact, the trail does not again traverse a 4000-foot peak until Killington is reached, in Vermont. In Maryland, Pennsylvania and New Jersey there is much rocky trail. Especially in Pennsylvania there are so many of these rocks, close together and on end, that it is hard on footwear and feet.

We passed through majestic forest, cool and moist even at high noon; through park-like woods, sunny and friendly; through woods with such dense undergrowth that they were almost impassable except along the trail. There were always mountains, either right under our feet or in the distant blue haze.

Sometimes they overlooked long, winding river valleys with their endless charm — the Nantahala, the New, the James, the Shenandoah melding with the Potomac, the Juniata and muddy Sherman Creek flowing into the broad Susquehanna, the Lehigh, the Delaware, the familiar Hudson, the placid Housatonic, and the lovely Connecticut.

We stepped where heroes had marched in bygone wars. We followed paths used by the early pioneers and were humbled by the thought of the hardships they had endured as compared with our slight inconveniences. We labored wearily along jeep roads that had been pushed through incredibly rough terrain to bring quick fire-protection in emergency; along old stage-coach roads; on abandoned railroad rights of way; along canals now clogged with trees and vegetation; through muddy manganese diggings.

The walkers we met on the trail, and the cordial fire towermen we always stopped in to visit were always interesting. We were impressed with the homely wisdom of those on and off the trail whom we met, their sense of humor and friendliness, and the independent spirit of those who live close to the mountains and wrest their livelihood from reluctant nature.

It was an unforgettable experience, and it leaves one with a new appreciation of this land of ours and with the fervent hope that the AT will long remain, unbroken and unspoiled, essentially a wilderness footpath for the enjoyment of walkers.

WHITE MOUNTAIN SUMMER

JAY JOHNSON

1978

IN 1975 JAY JOHNSON GRADUATED from high school and made his first venture to the White Mountains. Like a young chick eagerly testing its wings while its parents perch nervously on the edge of the nest, Johnson stepped down the dirt road leading away from his family's cottage in Maine. He spent that summer hiking alone among the mountains.

On the surface, Johnson's is a simple, almost naive story. Yet between the lines of his modest prose lie profound lessons. He pursues the beauty and joy of nature as well as its harsh realities. He experiences self-sufficiency by learning to make do with the limited resources at his command. And he vividly encounters the contrasts between civilization and wildlands, both of which seem necessary to personal fulfillment. Johnson's journal of his summer in the Appalachians suggests several lessons to be learned in the mountains.

THE AIR WAS CRISP AND COOL. The sun rose above the tree tops, its rays filtering down through the tangle of branches to where I stood with my parents. We were at the edge of the dirt road that led away from their cottage in southern Maine, on which I would take the first steps of my journey. They were obviously not anxious to have me depart on what they imagined to be a hazardous trek. To preserve my image forever, should I fall prey to some beast, my mother took a number of photographs of me with her old box camera. Then, after repeated handshakes and kisses (and warnings to watch out for bears), I headed away, down the dirt road toward the White Mountains.

The first week I spent walking on easy terrain in southern Maine and New Hampshire. Then, on June 16, I reached White Ledge. With thick fog and ninety-degree temperatures it was a poor day to greet the mountains. That night, when I was camped on the Three Sisters Ridge, a thunderstorm cooled me off, but also threatened to cook me with bolts of lightening that sizzled all around. For the next few days it continued to be cloudy and cool as I climbed Mounts Chocorua, Paugus, Passaconaway (my first 4,000 footer), Whiteface, Tripyramid, Osceola, Tecumseh, and Sandwich. As I descended from Sandwich Mountain, the clouds lifted and a full fledged heat wave set in. On the summit of Mount Israel I laid everything out to dry on the ledges. In a matter of minutes my soaked dungarees were stiff and dry. I had imagined during the winter that I would get a deep tan and be soaked with sunshine, but, as I would find out, Mother Nature had other plans.

My parents had sent packages of food to the post office in Plymouth, so when I reached that town after two weeks of hiking, I was able to resupply my pack with food. The next day I had an interesting time climbing Stinson Mountain. Instead of taking the trail to the summit, I bushwhacked. The walking was easy enough most of the way, but then I came to a place where blackberry bushes grew head-high and the young maple tree saplings grew only a foot apart. My nerves were shredded as I fought and struggled through the hideous entanglement of vegetation. Soon I was swearing and cursing the rotting plants as if they understood what I said. Someone high on the ridge above looking down might have found it comical to hear all sorts of profanity as some figure thrashed about in the bushes below.

Up on the summit ridge were extremely dense spruce trees. As I was crashing through these only twenty feet from the summit I heard someone yell. When I finally broke into the open I was greeted by two somewhat frightened people. They had thought a bear was making all that racket.

From Stinson Mountain I went past Hubbard Brook Experimental Forest to Mount Moosilauke and the Kinsman Ridge. The trails along Kinsman Ridge had been transformed into streams and cascades by the seemingly never-ending rain. With a few more inches of water I could have rowed up the trail in a boat.

At the summit of Cannon Mountain I did my wash in the men's room of the tramway station. From there I headed for the beautiful, rocky ride between Mounts Lafayette and Lincoln, and on to Liberty, Flume, Owls Head, Garfield, South Twin and North Twin. To break up the monotony of hiking along trails I bushwhacked up Mount Hale. The open, park-like birch forest on that side of Hale was particularly beautiful. Back on the trails again, I trotted over North and South Twin, Mount Guyot, and Mount Zealand. When I reached Zealand Falls Hut I was so famished that I downed several large bowls of chocolate bread pudding. Over Mounts Tom, Field, and Willey I flew until I came to my second food pickup. On the wooded ridge above Willey House in Crawford Notch State Park I had buried a cache of food during the spring. I found it easily.

Ripley and Arethusa Falls were impressive for their height (100 and 200 ft.), if not for their volume of water. Spring would be the best time to see them, when the melt water is rushing down the streams in a roaring torrent. Another falls nearby, Nancy Cascades, is just as impressive.

Along a trail in the beautiful Stillwater flatlands of the Pemigewasset River, one of the highlights of the trip took place when I discovered a young flying squirrel squatting at the edge of the path. He was munching on a delicate young mushroom and didn't seem to notice me. I took out my camera and inched up to the little fellow until the tip of my nose was only two feet away from the tip of his.

I was so close that I could see the twinkle in his large, dark eyes. His gray fur was fluffy and clean. His little fingers grabbed the mushroom firmly. Along his side was a stripe of black hairs, which marked the location of the folded skin flap he uses to glide from tree to tree. The belly and throat were both snow white. I was surprised at how clean he was. It almost seemed as if he was someone's pet which had just been let loose in the wild woods.

The little scamp didn't sit there quietly. He would look up with a sudden jerk every once in a while to make sure no predators were sneaking up on him. Everything he did was done in a quick, jerking manner. When he had eaten all of the mushroom above ground he started tugging on the roots. With all his strength he yanked and pulled on them. When he finally managed to pull them out of the ground, he dragged the dirty mass over to the tree trunk and up to a branch twenty feet above the ground. There he sat for the rest of the time I watched him.

I walked quietly back to my pack, slipped it on, and walked back to the squirrel's tree. "Goodbye," I said under my breath. Trying not to disturb him, I continued on past the tree and the small hole where the mushroom used to be.

During the next few days I climbed Carrigain and Hancock. Despite their superior height, I found Mount Tremont, the next mountain that I climbed, to be far more interesting. From its summit I could see the Sawyer Ponds glistening in the sun, and in the distance, the distinctive outline of Mount Chocorua. The sound of distant trains added a special touch to this mountain. Two days of bushwhacking over Bear Mountain and along the ridge to the Moat Mountains gave me my last taste of the wilds before I reached Cathedral Ledge on July 23rd, my birthday.

Here I camped at the edge of a side cliff while I waited for my parents to arrive in their car the next morning. The following two days were spent in paradise at my parents' cottage in Maine. On the third day we drove back to the mountains and I started my trek somewhat reluctantly again at the trail leading to Mount Langdon on the Montalban Ridge, only a few miles from Cathedral Ledge.

The next several days were by far the most rigorous of the entire trip. From Resolution Shelter I trucked, in just one day, to Isolation Shelter, then down Dry River to Route 302, which I followed to Webster Cliff Trail. The next two days I devoted to hiking from Crawford Notch to Pinkham via the Presidential Range. Despite the hard walking, things went fine until I neared Pinkham Notch. As I was hoisting the heavy pack up on my back, one of the shoulder straps broke. By some miracle I was able to carry it down into the notch with just one strap. There I purchased a piece of old rope for fifty cents and lashed it on the pack to replace the broken strap. The rope was by no means as good as the original strap. While climbing up a steep cliff on Mount Wildcat I had my closest brush with death. As I switched my balance the pack swung back because of the loose rope and I was almost pulled off the cliff. If I had fallen, I would have landed thirty feet below on jagged rocks.

The rest of that day and the next I walked in cold, wet conditions. Finally, I couldn't take it any longer and I pitched camp at Zeta Pass.

A day later the sky cleared, things dried out, and I felt a lot better. From Zeta Pass I walked north along the Carter-Moriah Range to the Androscoggin River, where I was greeted by the pungent odor of pulpwood. Following the Appalachian Trail I climbed up the Mahoosuc Range past numerous beautiful peaks. My longest day of the trek came as I left the ridge near South Peak in the Mahoosucs, descended into Mahoosuc Notch, climbed Old Speck Mountain and walked along highway Route 26 to Grafton-Upton town line. The next day I continued along old Route 26 past Umbagog Lake to the quaint town of Errol, where I made my last food pickup.

On the lawn across from the post office I unpacked and repacked all the food. It was a bizarre scene as I had newspapers, food packages, and boxes scattered all over the place. It's a wonder someone didn't have a car accident driving along the road as he took a second glance at the nut on the lawn.

Route 26 took me up through Dixville Notch during the next few days. The Balsams Hotel on the other side of Lake Gloriette in the notch was a sight to behold. The fields of Columbia filled with cows and horses were equally interesting. When I reached the site of the old Cleveland School I left the main, tarred roads and returned to the wild woodlands once again. Several miles of bushwhacking brought me to Nash Bog Pond.

From Nash Bog I climbed Sugarloaf Mountain and North Percy Peak. Then I walked along more roads past Devil's Slide to Devil's Hopyard, fine names for fine places. From here I bush-whacked to Roger's Ledge.

On August 17th at the base of Mount Waumbek, I stashed my pack in some bushes and began to run to the top of my last 4000-footer. Without any weight on my back to keep me down, I flew up the mountainside. Dreary spruce trees covered the summit and made a poor location to end my quest for the 4000-footers. But, coming down again I was so pleased with myself that I sang this tune as I went, "Praise the Lord, raise the flag, Jay climbed Waumbek, without a snag." During my last few days I hiked over the King's Ravine where I explored boulder caves for hours on end. Then, crossing the range, I walked up through Great Gulf and climbed the headwall to the summit of Mount Washington, the end point of my summer-long hike in the White Mountains.

✿ *In the North Country, Dixville Notch area, 1889* ✿

GUARDIAN OF THE MOUNTAINS:

The Club and Conservation

Conservation Crusade

THOUGH THE WORD CONSERVATION did not come into popular usage until around 1900, the Club had an inherent sense of its meaning even in its formative years. At a meeting of the membership in 1879, the president called attention to the "common disfigurement of natural scenery by advertisements" and formed a special committee to represent the Club in such matters. In 1882, the Councillor of Improvements published an extended report discussing the Club's concern for protection of the unique New Hampshire geologic formation known as the Old Man of the Mountains.

It was not until 1893, however, that the Club began consciously to recognize its political power in matters of conservation. During a series of meetings that year on forest preservation, Professor Charles Fay suggested that "perhaps it might not be fully appreciated how great a power the Club had become in such movements," adding that he hoped "that members would fully realize that the Club, besides being a source of pleasure, was an instrument of public good." Forestry was formally added to the duties of the Department of Exploration in 1900, and the

Club became committed to a system of forest reserves in the eastern United States, as described in the first article in this section.

Reports published in *Appalachia* over the years read like a conservation history of the country. The Club has maintained interest and activity in public-land and natural-resource issues such as Hetch Hetchy, the Adirondack Forest Preserve, Niagara Falls, Baxter State Park, the Grand Canyon, Echo Park, North Cascades, and the Appalachian Trail.

More recently, the Club has been part of the environmental activism of the 1970s. It has proven folly, time and again, to enjoy wild places without the constant vigilance needed to preserve those places. The second article in this section serves to drive this lesson home.

It has been the Club's conscious policy, however, to avoid the "battle" mentality of some sister environmental organizations. The Club's traditional stand has been to separate facts from propaganda and principles from expedients in order to develop and support the reasoned positions of its membership. The twenty-year controversy surrounding Franconia Notch, the subject of the third paper in this section, perhaps best illustrates this approach.

THE PROPOSED EASTERN FOREST RESERVES
GIFFORD PINCHOT
1906

ON JANUARY 20, 1906, *Gifford Pinchot, the nation's chief forester, was the featured speaker at the thirtieth annual meeting of the AMC. The previous year Pinchot had convinced Congress to place the nation's forest reserves under his control and to establish a bureau later known as the U.S. Forest Service. Flushed with enthusiasm from these successes, Pinchot would now involve himself in a new objective: creation of national forests in the East. His address to the AMC was, in effect, an invited pep talk to this end.*

The move to create public lands in the East was a turning point in the conservation movement. Management of the nation's public land had been marked by three succeeding eras prior to that time. The first, of course, was wide-scale acquisition in the early 1800s as the new nation moved quickly to control the central band of the North American continent. Cessions by the original states, purchases of vast tracts such as the Louisiana Territory, and treaties with neighboring countries eventually brought over eighty percent of the land area of the United States into federal ownership. Nearly concurrent was the second era, dominated by disposal of these lands, eventually into private hands. To stimulate economic development under the democratic principles of the republic, public domain lands were transferred by sale or gift to private citizens, businesses, or the states.

By the late 1800s, however, it became evident that wholesale and haphazard disposal of the public domain had, in some cases, fostered a wasteful attitude toward land and its natural resources. The prime example was the cut-and-move-on practices of the timber industry. These abuses eventually led to the reservation era of public lands. For certain public purposes, such as national parks and future reserves of timber, selected tracts of the public domain were federally owned, held in reserve for the common good. Under this policy, vast areas of the western United States were retained and are now the heart of our national forest and park systems. Unfortunately, by the time reservation became an accepted public land policy, nearly all of the land in the eastern third of the United States had passed into private ownership and much had been subjected to indiscriminate logging and abandoned to the ravages of unchecked fire and erosion.

In answer to this problem, Pinchot suggested to the AMC audience that public land policy come full circle — that the federal government repurchase certain lands along the Appalachians to establish a system of eastern forest reserves. The Club heartily agreed with Pinchot's proposal, and made it its paramount conservation objective. The Club sent representatives to testify at hearings in Washington, sponsored lectures on the issue, and worked closely with other organizations. Pinchot's optimism at the conclusion of his address was justified — eastern forest reserves were authorized in 1911 with passage of the Weeks Act, which for the first time permitted land acquisition to expand the national forest system. The act was named after Massachusetts Senator John W. Weeks. The White Mountain National Forest was created shortly after its passage. The Weeks Act and succeeding legislation have brought over twenty million acres of national forest land east of the hundredth meridian into existence.

A NUMBER OF YEARS AGO it was first suggested that forests should be preserved in the Southern Appalachian Mountains. The attention of thoughtful men had been drawn to the fact that great injury was being done to the streams, great damage was accruing from floods, and great forest destruction was going on in the Southern Appalachians, and agitation began to interfere with the progress of destruction. Then far-sighted men at this end of the great chain took up the matter; and now coming from North and South these two movements have met.

The reasons why these forests should be preserved, different as the conditions are in different parts of the Appalachian chain, north and south practically meet. We have got first the fact that it is wise policy to have these lands preserved, and for many different reasons. For example, we are now using, incredible as it may seem, ten times as much timber, valued in dollars, as we were in 1850, while the population of the United States has only increased three times. In other words, the census of 1850 gave us $60,000,000 as the value of the produce of the forests, while the census of 1900 gives $566,000,000, and during the same period the population has only increased from 23,000,000 to 76,000,000.

The timber question is far more than a business question, in the sense that it is utterly impossible for us to repair the damage of forest destruction in any reasonable time. You may start a mine which has been stopped, and there is little damage; you may let a farm lie fallow and take up the cultivation of it again, and the farm is better than it was; you may begin once more fisheries that have been abandoned, when the fish have returned; but the destruction of the forests means the destruction of the growth, the productive capacity of the land, through a long series of years.

The shortest possible time in which the damage of a timber famine can be repaired is fifty years. And all the signs point to the fact that unless the people of the United States, especially the

Government of the United States, wake up to the present condition, we shall have a famine in that material, which stands at the bottom of the productive industry of this country. Therefore, since forest destruction is going on in the Southern Appalachians and in the Northern Appalachians, the White Mountains, it is a wise policy for us to stop that destruction, and to let the lands that are better capable of producing timber than anything else produce that timber crop.

Now, secondly, it is wise policy from a buiness point of view. For example, when this movement first started for a reserve in the Southern Appalachians, it was very conservatively estimated that we could get all the land that we wanted, including the timber, for $2.50 per acre. Now I happen to know of one large tract in the Southern Appalachians which was bought for $2.50 an acre at about the time that this movement began, and the owner of it, within the last year, has given an option on the timber alone, without the land, of many tens of thousands of acres. That timber can be cut under the rules of conservative forestry, just as it would be by the Government, at $15 an acre; and much of the land has sold at higher prices. That is to say, through delay we have reached a point throughout the South where we can get only the land, without the best of the standing timber.

Now let us consider it for a moment from the point of view of water supply; and here is the nub of the question, North and South. It is estimated that there are 2,700,000 horse-power used for manufacturing in New England; and in the Southern States more than half a million horse-power (of which 180,000 are produced by water) are already in use, and not less than a million horse-power are capable of being developed. Now what happens, of course, in any region rich by nature, is that men coming in first of all use the natural resources, cut the forests, open the mines, over-crop the farms, skim the cream. Whatever the virtues of our race may be, and they are very many, it is a fact that wherever the white man, and especially the Anglo-Saxon, sets his foot, the first thing he does is to take the cream off the country, and after that he settles down definitely and quietly to develop it along more rational lines. Now we have taken the cream from our forests North and South, from our rich agricultural lands in the West, from our mines, from all the other natural resources that we have, as fast as possible.

But following the destruction of natural resources comes the era of manufactures. Now that era is wonderfully well developed here in Massachusetts, and is just about at its most rapid growth in the South; and it would be nothing less than suicide, from the commercial and manufacturing point of view, for you here, and for those in the South, to allow the destruction of the forests from which comes the water that turns your wheels. Not only is it necessary for you to protect yourselves against floods, but it is fair for you and for the South to look forward to the maintenance and the increase of the means of wealth which you have at hand. It is a direct question of self-preservation in business for you, whether or not you are to allow the destruction of the sources from which so much of your wealth has sprung in the past, and from which, under proper conservation, still more will spring in the future.

Now if I am right in thinking, then why is not the thing (creation of forest reserves) done? The answer is a perfectly simple one: that the people who are interested in this matter have not made themselves heard. I have lived in Washington long enough to know that, whatever any other government on the earth may be, this Government of ours is a representative one, and that what the people ask for and mean to have they will get, be it right or wrong — for no man has lived in Washington long without seeing mistaken demands enforced on congressmen and senators, as well as demands that were right. It is simply a question of how much and how earnestly the people of the New England States desire the White Mountain reserve, and how much and how earnestly the people of the Southern States desire the Southern Appalachian reserve; and nothing else will secure them. The matter is purely one which rests with you.

Now you have a body of men in Congress from New England who are simply irresistible when they go after something. The Southern members united on this subject would be equally so. These two bodies of men asking for an appropriation of three millions of dollars out of a total budget of six or seven hundred millions would, of course, get it without the slightest difficulty; and they will get it whenever you ladies and gentlemen in this State, in New Hampshire, in Vermont, and Connecticut and Maine, make up your minds that you really want it. And until you impress upon your representatives in Washington the fact that you really want it, I think I am perfectly safe in giving you my word that it never will be done.

Finally, if I have given you the impression that this movement does not look hopeful, I should like to correct that impression. I have been engaged in this fight since it began, and I have never seen the day when the chance of success in both these directions was anything like as bright as it is tonight.

To kill a mountain
ROBERT McCONNELL HATCH
1971

*F*OR MOST OF US, *most of the time, the battle over conservation is abstract. We sense that it is right that certain areas remain free of development. Yet the places at issue are often little more than names on the map, places we personally know little about but would like the opportunity to know better. We may care very much that such places be preserved, but the outcome does not affect our daily lives directly.*

There are occasions, however, when, to our horror, proposed development threatens our own backyard, and then conservation becomes a personal battle. So it was with Robert McConnell Hatch in 1971. Hatch was an AMC member and frequent contributor to Appalachia *on conservation topics. Developers were talking about Canaan Mountain in Connecticut, where he had spent years of Saturdays exploring the woods in all their seasons.*

Canaan Mountain is remarkable in many ways. It has uncommon diversity of plant and animal life, and such an extensive undeveloped area in a highly urbanized state is even more exceptional. For these and other reasons it is worthy of preservation. But to Hatch there was more. Canaan Mountain was his personal sanctuary and of major significance to the quality of his life. The passion and depth of feeling for the mountain and what it represents show clearly between the lines of his description of the area and his travels through it.

IN THE CLOSING PARAGRAPH of his book *Round River* Aldo Leopold pondered on what he might bequeath to his three sons. He expressed the hope that he might leave them in good health, with an education and perhaps a competence. Yet for a full enjoyment of life he knew that they would require something more — something that could be supplied only by the world of nature where it has not been devastated by the human race. As he considered this he was chilled by the thought that the time might be at hand when all of nature would be devastated.

What good, he asked, would be such things as health, an education and a competence "if there be no more deer in the hills, and no more quail in the coverts? No more snipe whistling in the meadow, no more piping of widgeons and chattering of teal as darkness covers the marshes; no more whistling of swift wings when the morning star pales in the east! And when the dawn-wind stirs through the ancient cottonwoods, and the gray light steals down from the hills over the old river sliding softly past its wide brown sandbars — what if there be no more goose music?"

Aldo Leopold died in 1948. Since then we have seen his fears steadily substantiated. Bulldozers have devoured more and more of the earth. Air and water have been poisoned to a level where they are a menace to human health. Our last bits of wilderness have shrunk to a mere remnant. Some of the most beautiful forms of wildlife, like the American eagle, have been pushed to the edge of extinction. Hardly an acre of earth is safe any more. What today is relatively unmolested, tomorrow may be engulfed by a multilane superhighway or by industrial sprawl.

It took no clairvoyant to detect this in 1948, and even the most unobservant cannot fail to be aware of it today. But until the spreading devastation threatens to swallow up a place that has some personal significance for us, most of us remain rather casual about it all, regretting the trends we read about but seldom getting excited enough to lose a night's sleep or fire off a telegram to a congressman. The whole threatening process is apt to remain in the realm of theory until it suddenly invades our own lives.

Then we are jabbed awake — and often find that we are too late to do anything about it.

So it was with me and my attachment to Canaan Mountain. For years I had gone there on Saturdays with my friend Jack Farr to explore the mountain and hike through the surrounding forest. For both of us it was an opportunity to enter a world of immense natural beauty each week, freed from the pressures of our work and from the clatter and turmoil of the cities where we lived. We became very dependent on these Saturdays in the woods. If we missed one, the following week dragged insufferably. Indeed, regular visits became an imperative and we went throughout the year, snowshoeing in the winter months. It was like repairing to a fountain of youth every Saturday morning and driving home that night after a 10- or 12-mile hike feeling positively young again, recharged in body and spirit. The mountain and its environs became one of the focal points in our lives.

The mountain is located in the town of Canaan in northwestern Connecticut. It is in a forest that reaches for several miles both east and south, extending well into the town of Norfolk. Part of the forest belongs to the state but much of it is privately owned by conservation-minded people who are anxious to preserve it and who have allowed it to be used by the Yale School of Forestry for study and research. The result is a phenomenon in a crowded northeastern state like Connecticut — a forest occasionally thinned but never clear-cut, containing some trees more than a century old, rich in its variety of trees and shrubs and wildflowers, retaining in many of its swamps and hemlock-shaded valleys a primeval quality that gives one the illusion that few human beings have passed this way before. I have seen more deer in this forest than in any comparable area. I have observed a larger concentration of northern water-thrushes and Canada warblers than I have found anywhere else in the northeast.

Canaan Mountain and its surrounding forest comprise the most extensive remnant of wilderness that is left in Connecticut. In addition to Canaan Mountain itself there are several lower ridges and outcrops that are nameless, but one bears the name of Crissey Mountain and has the distinction of being the highest point in the town of Norfolk. A number of ponds are scattered through the forest, none of them large, some supporting families of beaver and muskrat, one inhabited by otters, all occupied in summer by Canadian geese, wood ducks, and black ducks. In the valleys and sometimes even on the shoulders of the ridges are extensive swamps rich in ferns and alders, sometimes sprinkled with pink azaleas and usually a nesting place for the northern water-thrush. A few streams thread rather sluggishly through the forest. They tend to dry up in summer but support frogs and attract raccoons and mink.

The summits and shoulders of the ridges are matted with hair grass (Deschampsia), resembling the grassy balds on summits in the southern Appalachians. They are fringed with scrub oak and afford far-reaching views. By way of contrast, Canaan Mountain is the southern terminal for several northern species, like the red spruce and red pine. Oaks and maples and birch, beech and hemlock predominate on the slopes and in the valleys. In some spots the hemlocks reach massive proportions, having stood unmolested for more than a century. Throughout the forest are tangles of mountain laurel. A favorite nesting place for the black-throated blue warbler, the laurel flowers in late June, turning the ridges white and gleaming like snow in every sunlit opening. Indeed, when the laurel blossoms the forest is at its best. The whole year is a preparation for that enchanted fortnight.

The forest harbors a few reminders of human history. In its recesses one stumbles across occasional tree-choked cellar holes and tumbled-down stone walls. On one November afternoon Jack and I discovered three graves in a stand of ancient pines and maples, all sunken nearly a foot below ground level, one about six feet long, the others shorter. Only the long grave was marked — with a flat-faced but uninscribed rock. We believed the graves belonged to an adult and two children. Near them was a small cluster of cellar holes.

There are some excellent walks in the forest. Dirt roads and bridle trails probe many parts of it, but the best walks involve bushwhacking. Crissey Mountain commands a surprising western view that reveals hardly a sign of human habitation — only a very few distant buildings. There are several nameless outcrops providing limited views that highlight different segments of the forest, and there is a precipitous bluff rising over a pond that is one of the most inviting places in all New England to while away a warm afternoon, especially in laurel season. Often Jack and I have stayed long enough to see deer browsing on the shore or a file of Canada geese advancing cautiously out onto the pond. There are streams smothered in ferns, and swamps rich in many kinds of birds, and there is a small waterfall where a few rusty remnants of an all but prehistoric sawmill can still be seen and where banks of flowering shadblow make a spring visit imperative. Round trips of 10 or 12 miles can be taken anywhere in the forest, which is relatively open and permits easy bushwhacking.

It is a forest for all seasons. To be sure, nothing can compare with a day in June when the laurel is in flower or an October morning when the hillsides blaze with blood red and yellow, russet and dark crimson. But all seasons are good, and some of our most memorable trips were made on snowshoes in the heart of winter. Long views through the forest are possible then, and snowshoes can be quiet. Consequently winter is the season when we have seen the most deer — family groups of two or three does and their yearlings, or a buck freed of his antlers and wintering alone in a hemlock grove. One cannot claim true familiarity with an area until he knows it at all seasons.

At one time or another Jack and I have seen most of the different forms of wildlife that inhabit the forest. There are a few rattlesnakes — once we saw a four-footer — but most of the snakes are harmless, like the black, the garter, and the red-bellied. Frogs and toads abound in the swamps and woodlands, water snakes and turtles in the ponds. Raccoons, foxes and woodchucks may be seen almost anywhere. Snowshoe hares, common in northern New England, are a surprise here, since only cottontail rabbits inhabit most of Connecticut. Beavers build lodges on some of the ponds, muskrats are found where cattails grow, there are very few otters, and we have spied mink on the streams. Even though the deer are abundant, the forest is not over-browsed. Often we have come upon fawns bedded down in deep fern or standing motionless in clumps of laurel and pink azalea.

At first we went to Canaan Mountain for exercise, for a change of pace and a respite from the daily grind. But soon we found that we were coming because we loved the mountain and its forest, loved them in all seasons, in sunshine and rain, in the heat of summer and the awesome cold of winter. Like many others who frequented the forest on foot or on horseback we loved it for its wildness, for its primeval swamps and waterways, and most of all for the fact that it was unblemished by man.

Finally Jack bought a house on Undermountain Road

where Wangum Lake Brook tumbles down Canaan Mountain. The view from his porch takes in a valley hemmed by hills and sprinkled with trim old farmhouses, suggesting the more picturesque valleys still left in Vermont — or those that once existed in many parts of Connecticut. To gaze down that valley from Jack's porch is to glimpse what Connecticut was like a hundred or even two hundred years ago.

Jack and his family lived there about a year in peace. They believed this would be their home for the rest of their lives and that nothing would change it. The proximity of the forest promised such protection.

It was a fool's paradise. We had forgotten the apprehensions of Aldo Leopold, his haunting fear that no place in America was any longer safe. The blow was struck by an organization known as Northeast Utilities. Their proposal embraced such a grandiose piece of devastation that it taxed credibility. Their target was Canaan Mountain. A reservoir, encompassing 750 acres, would be dyked up not far from the summit. A pipeline would imprison Deming Brook, one of the main tributaries of Wangum Lake Brook. A second reservoir of 750 acres would inundate most of Wangum Lake Brook Valley, and 250 foot swathes would be slashed through the forest to make way for power lines in all directions. The complex would be called a pumped-storage facility. Water would be pumped from the lower reservoir to that on Canaan Mountain whenever extra power was available. From there it would be released to provide hydroelectric power during periods of peak demand.

Canaan Mountain would be disembowelled. Tunnels big enough for trucks would bore into its heart, from which, at a depth of 800 feet below the surface, a vast chamber would be blasted having dimensions 492 feet long, 73 feet wide and 123 feet high. This would house conduits, pump turbines, generators and other accessories.

Of course access roads would have to be built, asphalt-surfaced and wide enough for heavy vehicles. The total effect of the proposal would be a weird mixture of the ingenious and the monstrous — water shooting up and down the mountain through the pipeline replacing Deming Brook, reservoirs cresting and dropping, mud flats emerging and disappearing, cars and trucks speeding through the forest, power lines stretching in all directions, and the heart of the mountain throbbing with six generators and six pump turbines each capable of producing 337,000 kilowatts. In the valley would tower a dam 1,700 feet long and 100 feet high to contain the lower reservoir.

The pumped-storage proposal for Canaan Mountain embodies an issue that is facing all of us today. Either we save the more beautiful parts of our country for recreation in its broadest sense, or we succumb to a total takeover by industry. The issue of Canaan Mountain is no more pointed than that involving every polluted river, every community befouled by poisoned air, every remaining scrap of scenic beauty that is threatened by another multilane superhighway. The issue, in fact, is everywhere.

A host of people are fighting to save the mountain's life. They have pointed out that there exist more desirable and efficient ways of generating power and that there is no actual need to violate the landscape with pumped-storage facilities. Alternatives may cost more; we cannot save our environment without some cost. A salvaged and beautified country which our children can enjoy and love is far more precious than the dollars we might save today.

The struggle to save Canaan Mountain goes on. The outcome is uncertain. But one thing is worth remembering — Canaan Mountain is not an isolated phenomenon. What is happening there can happen anywhere, for the powers of destruction take many forms. The threat in northwestern Connecticut is pumped-storage. The threat in another place may be a superhighway, a poisoned river, a flattened forest. The hour of "no more goose music" is closer than we think.

Hatch and Canaan Mountain prevailed. The mountain remains today much as it is described in the article. The pumped-storage facility was not constructed and the "hour of no more goose music" was pushed back once again.

INTERSTATE ROUTE 93
AND FRANCONIA NOTCH
1958–1980

*ORGANIZATIONS SUCH AS THE AMC support
a number and variety of conservation issues. Small paid staffs and
volunteer members attend to these causes as a part of daily routine, and the
leaders of the Club must work to sustain members' interest and enthusiasm
over the long life of many issues.*

*Occasionally, however, a particular issue triggers an instinctive,
vigorous reaction throughout the organization. With the Sierra Club it
was a dam proposal in the early 1900s in the Hetch Hetchy Valley of
Yosemite National Park. In the 1950s nearly all conservation organizations similarly reacted when it was proposed to impound the Colorado
River as it flows through the Grand Canyon. For the Appalachian
Mountain Club, the galvanizing issue was a proposal for an interstate
highway through Franconia Notch.*

*Franconia Notch has long ranked as one of the most beautiful and
interesting areas in New England. Its striking geologic formations have
attracted countless visitors, and the "Old Man of the Mountains" has
become the scenic symbol of New Hampshire. The AMC was crucial to
preserving the Notch in the 1920s when it was threatened by extensive
logging operations: the Club and its members gave generously, along with
the people of New Hampshire, to purchase the area for an eventual gift to
the state as a park. And so it was especially ironic for the Club to learn
thirty years later that the state planned to expand the two-lane road
through the Notch into a four-or-more-lane interstate highway.*

*An "unofficial" source in October 1957 first informed the Club of
the proposal. It was later learned that a "public" hearing on the subject
had been held several months before. The AMC Council formally
discussed the proposed highway for the first time in January 1958. That
meeting launched more than two decades of Club activity to protect
Franconia Notch. Eventually, the Club negotiated an extraordinary
agreement with the state and federal governments, which permits the*

parkway through the Notch to remain the only stretch of two-lane interstate highway in the nation.

The following excerpts briefly chronicle the struggle over Franconia Notch. Portions of this material were assembled for a 1969 Appalachia *article by C. Francis Belcher; others have appeared since that time.*

✳ 1958

Just thirty years ago the AMC played a prominent role in the drive of "Save Franconia Notch from the Woodman's Axe." The State of New Hampshire appropriated $200,000 toward the purchase of this area which includes the Old Man of the Mountains, The Basin, The Pool, The Flume, and Profile, Echo and Lonesome Lakes. The final amount was raised by contributions in a drive headed by a former AMC president. In addition to contributions by individual AMC members, the Club gave from its own treasury, as did each chapter. But many will recall that the highlight of this campaign came when thousands of school children gave a dollar each to "Buy a Tree."

How ironic that these same children, now thirty years older and thirty years wiser, are among the legislators and highway personnel developing plans for high-speed turnpikes through state parks, and national parks, and forests across the country — including our own Franconia Notch. For example, there is the "Tioga Turnpike" from Yosemite Valley to the Tuolumne Meadows. Closer by is the controversial $275-million-dollar four-lane limited-access Northway, whose proposed route from Albany, New York, to the Canadian border would cut a 25-mile slash through the fine public Forest Preserve lands, unnecessarily splitting the Adirondack Mountains.

Through Franconia Notch one splendid new highway has just been completed at a cost of hundreds of thousands of dollars to New Hampshire taxpayers. It is a broad scenic road providing continuous access to the many attractions of the Notch. Those who fear the proposal to turn the Notch Road into part of the federal interstate defense highway system have been told that federal subsidy (ninety percent) requires a four-lane limited access highway with a center dividing strip, various interchanges and grades and curves permitting 60- and 70-mile-per-hour traffic.

We hope details of the proposed Interstate System in the Franconia Notch will soon be presented completely and candidly to the people of New Hampshire, who once saved this Notch for the State and to whom it properly belongs.

✳ 1966

The State of New Hampshire Department of Public Works and Highways is developing plans for the extension of Interstate Route 93 through Franconia Notch which should alarm all who are interested in preserving the unique scenic beauty of this famous area. In 1959 the Appalachian Mountain Club opposed legislation which was subsequently passed by the New Hampshire legislature authorizing the route through the Notch for this dual-lane highway. The basis for our opposition then was that there had been grossly inadequate studies of alternative routes for this highway around the Notch and of the potentially harmful effects to the topography and appearance of this area. Now the Highway Department is working on the lay-out and design of the route northward from its present end at Plymouth through the Notch, but has done nothing in the intervening seven years to justify any change in our earlier position.

New Hampshire Governor King has recently described this issue as "a clear-cut clash between the economic needs of the area and conservationists." It is most difficult to agree with this statement. The economic needs of the area do not require the desecration of the natural beauty of Franconia Notch. It is commonly agreed that a vastly improved highway to North Woodstock at the south end of the Notch is essential. It is also commonly agreed that Interstate Highway 93 should be extended northward to Littleton and beyond. But agreement on these points does not mean that the Interstate Highway must go through the heart of the Notch.

The position of the Club on conservation matters in the past has represented an effort to be constructive and to accommodate wherever possible the interests of all the public in our natural resources. Our views on this highway represent no departure from this position. There is no need for any conflict in those interests if intelligent, thoughtful planning is carried out. Franconia Notch deserves the best.

✴ 1977

On September 1, 1976, the long-awaited Franconia Notch Draft Environmental Impact Statement (DEIS) was released for public review. The nine-volume, 3500-page document was the product of a two-year, 1.4-million-dollar study. Six alternatives were presented in the DEIS, but no specific recommendation was made. Four were within the Franconia Notch corridor: 1) the no-build, 2) a two-lane parkway, 3) a four-lane parkway, and 4) a four-lane Interstate. The remaining two alternatives were Interstates around the Notch, via Bog Pond and via Kinsman Notch.

The AMC, as a member of the White Mountain Environment Committee (WMEC), a coalition of concerned conservation organizations, was involved in the review of the massive report. It soon became apparent that none of the studied alternatives provided the necessary creative solution. The so-called two-lane parkway was largely three, four, or five lanes and involved three substantial realignments within Franconia Notch State Park.

The WMEC and the AMC structured their own alternative, based on the mandate of the Department of Transportation Act of 1966 that any project involving park land must include "all possible planning" to minimize harm to the park. Working with consultants, the WMEC and the AMC developed an innovative solution that was feasible, responsible, and consistent. The proposal calls for a two-lane roadway through the Park, with improved Park facility access, visitor centers at each end of the Park, and the option to institute a shuttle bus system for sightseers if Park use intensifies. The concepts recommended by the WMEC and AMC have been endorsed by State and federal agencies including the New Hampshire Division of Parks, the Environmental Protection Agency, and the Department of the Interior. A final recommendation from highway officials is expected in mid-1977. The selection of the WMEC-AMC stance could signal a new beginning for Franconia Notch State Park and an end to the decades of conflict.

❊ 1980

In 1977 the AMC reached a negotiated agreement with the New Hampshire Division of Public Works and Highways and the Department of Transportation whereby Franconia Notch Park will be carefully protected and a two-lane parkway will be constructed through the critical areas of the Notch. This will be the only piece of two-lane interstate highway in the country. AMC representatives will continue to work with the White Mountain Environment Committee and the New Hampshire Divisions of Public Works and Highways and the New Hampshire Division of Parks during the design phase of the project.

Wilderness: Paradox of Preservation

EARLY REPORTS of the Club's Councillor of Improvements repeatedly expressed the fear that not enough people would be drawn to the White Mountains for recreation. Without enough people attracted to mountain tramping, forest growth would close in quickly and obliterate the newly created trails. That concern was, of course, short-lived. Today, the problem is just the opposite — what to do with so many people in the mountains.

Wilderness preservation seems to be characterized by paradox. The struggle to establish a national policy of wilderness preservation culminated in passage of the Wilderness Act in 1964. The act permanently protects our few remaining wild lands from development. We have since learned, however, that the ultimate threat to wilderness may come from within: those who love the wilderness may eventually love it to death. Fragile vegetation is trampled and destroyed, soils are compacted and eroded, and water quality is threatened by sedimentation and pollution. The solitude so closely associated with a wilderness experience in many cases has given way to crowding and conflicts among wilderness visitors.

In response to these "population" problems, the AMC and other groups have become interested in wilderness management. But wilderness management is in itself paradoxical. Wilderness connotes a land free from human control; management suggests just the opposite. To what extent can wilderness be managed before it loses its very meaning?

In 1970 Philip Levin, a former editor of *Appalachia*, published in the journal a tongue-in-cheek look at the extremes that wilderness management might eventually reach. Management of wilderness, he suggested, would be guided by the Use Saturation Theory (dependent on participant/unit-area ratios and participant-efficiency-coefficients), a computer reservation system, and the Pinkham Notch Trail Control Data Processing Center. Levin followed this article with another in 1973 recommending abolishment of the Four-Thousand-Footer Club and its kindred organizations. These programs, he· suggested, and AMC educational efforts in general, encourage additional use of wilderness that in many places is already overused.

Levin's articles began a debate on the pages of *Appalachia* over the role of wilderness management. John Nutter, then the Club's director of education, responded quickly, and he was followed by William Burch, professor of forestry and environmental studies at Yale University. Levin, in turn, prepared a response to each, and the debate continues. The three selections in this section show each point of view.

TOWARDS A FUTURE WILDERNESS: NOTES ON EDUCATION IN THE MOUNTAINS
JOHN B. NUTTER
1973

THE WILDERNESS ACT OF 1964 for the first time permanently protected certain lands remaining free of human development. The act defined wilderness as "an area where the earth and its community of life are untrammeled by man." Further on, the act states that wilderness should present "outstanding opportunities for solitude." Congress initially designated about nine million acres as the National Wilderness Preservation System (NWPS). With the recent addition of vast Alaskan lands, the NWPS has grown to eighty million acres. The Great Gulf, about 5,500 acres in the White Mountains of New Hampshire, was one of the few areas in the eastern United States included in the initial NWPS.

In 1975, the Eastern Wilderness Act extended the concept of wilderness protection more fully to include the heavily settled East, and a number of small wilderness areas have been added in the eastern third of the country, including several in the Northeast. The largest and most prominent is the 20,000-acre Presidential Range-Dry River Wilderness surrounding the northern, western, and southern flanks of Mount Washington.

Recreational use of both White Mountain wilderness areas is heavy. Camping in the Great Gulf Wilderness is limited to sixty persons per night, controlled by a permit system.

Restrictions on wilderness use concern John Nutter. As the Club's director of education when he wrote this article, Nutter was keenly aware that wilderness can teach. Firsthand experience with wilderness instills appreciation for the natural world. Appreciation leads to support for wilderness protection as well as for protecting the environment in general. To Nutter, fewer people in the wilderness translates into fewer voices raised for wilderness protection.

RECENTLY, IN AN *APPALACHIA* ARTICLE Phil Levin argued that people be kept out of *his* mountains. "Fewer people (in the wilderness) is precisely what is to be desired." To many, this is an appealing argument, for the wilderness experience is most often described in terms of solitude. Let us now examine that argument in terms of the future of wilderness.

Legislative Wilderness is an attempt by Congress to please as many constitutents as possible. The amount of land in the Wilderness Preservation System is closely, although not directly, related to the number of people advocating that system of land management. The pressure for Eastern Wilderness can certainly be attributed to the recent explosion in backpacking. On the other hand, the intensive opposition to wilderness from off-road vehicle interests can be attributed to their numerical growth. In the resulting legislative battle pedestrians cannot afford to desire fewer people. Furthermore, we cannot exclude from the wilderness those whose support we are seeking.

While Levin deplores thirty campers on a summer weekend at Speck Pond, he does not even mention the threats of timber access roads and downhill ski developments to the wilderness value of the mountains. Since the early days of the AMC, backpackers have joined together to oppose the loss of wilderness. Our successes in preserving wilderness have been out of proportion to our numbers. In the near future, as pressures mount on wilderness from conflicting recreational uses and developments, the forces of our counterpressure must grow.

There are other, more important, reasons for not wanting "fewer" people in the wilderness. Our society needs to nourish the new environmental ethic. To develop that ethic we must develop a positive attitude toward the natural world. We must be aware of more than the fact that pollution is bad and ugly. Ask a high school student today what ecology means and he or she will often answer "pollution."

Wilderness has the capacity to raise the consciousness of those who experience it. It awakens our senses to the continuity and change of natural forces, to the harmony of an order where man does not dominate. Wilderness can transform attitudes, and arouse us to base our daily environmental decisions on new values. As Aldo Leopold said, "Perhaps the most serious obstacle impeding the evolution of a land ethic is the fact that our educational and economic system is headed away from, rather than toward, an intense consciousness of land." Wilderness has much to teach and we have much to learn.

IN DEMOCRACY IS THE PRESERVATION OF WILDERNESS
WILLIAM R. BURCH, JR.
1974

IN 1970 GEORGE STANKEY, a U.S. Forest Service researcher, published a paper entitled "A Strategy for the Definition and Management of Wilderness Quality." The paper was based on a study conducted in response to dramatically expanding use of wilderness areas. Stankey found in his study that perceptions of wilderness vary widely among the population. To some, wilderness may be a relatively isolated corner of Central Park, while others may settle for nothing less than a remote mountain range in Alaska. How then should wilderness be defined and managed?

Stankey suggested that wilderness be managed in accordance with those whose views of wilderness are most strictly or "purely" defined. He noted that this purist definition of wilderness is most consistent with the notions of primeval land and solitude given statutory recognition in the Wilderness Act. On this assumption, wilderness must be managed closely, and use must be restricted when it begins to threaten resources or restrict opportunities for solitude.

Like John Nutter in the previous article, Bill Burch rebels at such purist views of wilderness and their implications for wilderness management. "Purism" to Burch is elitism, a charge often hurled at preservationists. Playing on the words of Thoreau, Burch suggests that wildernesss must serve broad values to ensure political survival in a democracy.

    Burch pleads for a more fluid concept of wilderness, a definition that evolves with society. Just as we interpret the Constitution more broadly than when it was written, so should we view the Wilderness Act. "Solitude" today has a vastly different meaning than it did when the nation was being settled, and it will almost certainly mean something else still in the year 2000 and beyond. Public-land managers must not be oblivious to the nature of the society for which wilderness lands have been preserved. Wilderness must not go the way of the dinosaur.

WILDERNESS IS A MYTHICAL construction. It exists only at the sufferance of human society. Our air pollutants drift into it; we control its insect infestations and wildfires. We build trails and fireplaces and heliports. We survey and map and construct signs. We manage it and its temporary human inhabitants. We regulate its hunting and fishing. We leave it to winter storms, and like us, it reflects the press of time. Wilderness is our Japanese garden, our artificial imitation of nature, where the hand of man controls the vagaries of natural processes to achieve a human conception of timeless pristine nature.

    As George Stankey has stated, "...wilderness remains largely a function of human perception." Unfortunately, he does not make a logical connection between such a fact and problems of management and allocation. Human perception has certain invariant physiological properties, but more importantly, it is highly variable, being dependent upon variations in the culture and group structure surrounding the perceiver. And try as we might to impose fixed meanings upon the objects being perceived, it is a solution bound to defeat. There are no management tricks for holding back the future or for keeping the confrontations of the larger society out of the wilderness.

    Hippies in Yosemite, bikers in Bryce Canyon, pot-smokers and nudists in the North Cascades are but harbingers that another cycle of changing wildland clientele is occurring. And managerial groups seem eternally out-of-phase with such changes in taste. At the turn of the century elaborate lodges were constructed for the fashionable folk who arrived at the wilderness in their private Pullmans; then in the 1920s they were displaced by less fashionable folk in Fords and tents who needed primitive sanitary facilities and fireplaces; then came the Airstream–mobile home folk of the 1950s with their demands for mock suburbia in the wilderness. In the 70s we have the counterculture people. We should look to the 80s and 90s as bearing the fruits of the many programs to make the wilderness relevant to the inner-city minority children, for if these programs are successful, then when these children become adults, they will be bringing their own special perceptions to the wilderness. The question is not one of seeking some low common denominator of taste; rather it is one of constantly expanding the opportunity for diverse tastes.

All matters of human judgment have their purists and critics of taste who attempt to objectify that which is purely intuitive and emotional. Wilderness taste is merely a special case of this general form. Yet there seems little value in creating a Byzantine holy hierarchy of nature lovers with a small priesthood of super-purists at the apex, then trailing away through the moderate purists on down to the indifferent, vulgar masses with their Jones Beaches and Coney Islands. Indeed, reading through such categories one believes it is the sensitive mass confronting a vulgar minority, rather than the reverse. At least the mass in the White Mountains and the Adirondacks realize it is quite one thing to hold out roads and urban developments, but quite another thing to deny wilderness access to those whose attitudes are not quite up to standard. Indeed, we of the wilderness mass think that the capacity of wilderness to transform attitudes is such that, given enough time, even the most vulgar will be converted; that even the most privatized of purists may eventually discover their membership in the human community.

A wilderness experience is paying unusual costs to obtain one's goal. As a displaced Westerner I have evolved my own strategies for minimizing the densities of Eastern "wilderness." Early spring is a period of great solitude because there are no children's camps swooping into the Adirondacks, while a massive hatch of black flies and mosquitoes thin out all but the most determined. You also learn that nature is seldom benign. Another good time is late fall, around Columbus Day, which often brings snow and ice to the high-peak region and brings out only the more serious campers. Winter camping and climbing in the Adirondacks and White Mountains have their own special dangers and foolishness which make you very happy to encounter another party. In the midsummer the best strategy is to figure out where the people are going, and go the opposite...this means avoiding trails and bushwhacking cross-country. In the heavily vegetated Northeast I find that with a few minutes' travel up a stream or river I have great acres of solitude. The secret to solitude in somewhat crowded wilderness is to know that the function of pathways is to concentrate traffic which leaves the great bulk of wilderness rarely used. I would hope that the purists in the large Western wilderness areas could find their way equally well off a trail.

I am prepared to admit that such strategems may debase my wilderness experience. Still I collect my specimens of plants and twigs and stones: I find solitude; I am surrounded by an infinitude of nature. The stars are my roof — I am suitably exercised in mind and body. I learn to make do.

Much as I might wish to have the wilderness to myself and my group, I wish even more to share its joys and beauties with my fellow citizens. Further, I want to go when I want to without some bureaucrat assigning me a time schedule. Part of my wilderness freedom is the ability to go whenever I wish. And for this I am willing to pay costs of possible density. Though there may be some merit in zoning, I suspect that by drawing a line on the map and labeling it the "real" wilderness we will only encourage greater crowding rather than less. A better solution seems the collection and publication of studies which tell those who desire solitude where most of the folk are going or not going and permit them to plan accordingly.

Finally, it seems a rather unrealistic notion to take the language of the Wilderness Act as defining anything other than the intentions of congressmen to please as many constituents as possible while offending as few as possible. The language of our laws is not intended to provide precision, but to provide a suitable mixture of idealistic rhetoric and vague enough prescriptions to provide some application to reality. And woe to the agency which deviates too far from these prescriptions or hangs too close to them. I feel confident that managing wilderness for purists alone was not part of congressional reality, nor had it better be for the managing agencies. Indeed the assurance of sufficient numbers of visitors is going to be an important part of the survival of the system and of the agencies which manage them.

There are, of course, certain absolute moral principles which can withstand no political trading, no democratic compromise — the dignity of human life, the basic realities of ecosystem constraint, and so forth. But there are many other ideologies presented as moral absolutes which are only culturally relative. Cotton Mather would not like the modern era's violation of his moral absolutes. And one suspects that the modern advocates of total personal freedom combined with demands for absolute moral integrity in social institutions, political leaders, church leaders, moms and dads, are advocating moral standards possible only in a theocracy. And that, of course, takes care of personal freedom.

The moral principles of wilderness purists are matters of political debate rather than revealed truth. And in matters of political debate they have done rather well considering their numbers.

My point is simple — faced with the realities of increasing populations who have ever-diversifying tastes, with increasing material, political, and spiritual expectations, we should ask about the ways in which wilderness functions to preserve and expand the life of democracy. We know intuitively, and on many dimensions empirically, that in preserving wilderness we are preserving our own humanity. For we join an expanded community of life.

Yet wilderness cannot be separated from other issues of humans and natural exploitation. The destruction of wild places, animals, and plants is not dissimilar from exploiting our fellow man, whether in West Virginia stripmining, Vietnam pacification, Indian reservations, urban ghettos, or Spanish-American highlands. If we insist that wilderness is an island entire of itself, a sacred thing set above and beyond the political life of man, then, like all false idols, it will deserve its fate. And we shall all be equally diminished.

INWARD TO WILDERNESS

PHILIP D. LEVIN

1975

IN 1974 PHIL LEVIN *began to prepare a response to the previous articles on wilderness management by John Nutter and Bill Burch. What was conceived as a two-part paper to be published in 1975 expanded to a four-part series appearing in* Appalachia *from 1975 through 1978, a reflection of the thoughtfulness and personal concern with which he approached the issues involved. The excerpt appearing here is from the first installment, where Levin lays the foundation of his wilderness philosophy.*

To Levin, wilderness is a constant — a moral absolute — unlike the "relativistic" notions of Nutter and Burch. Wilderness is human heritage, the wellspring from which we all developed and where we are all subconsciously rooted. Wilderness retains its full meaning only in a primeval, unspoiled state. To allow, indeed to encourage, the perception of wilderness to change with the times is to abandon a "nexus with our origins" and to lose the essential idea that underlies the battle for the Wilderness Act.

As in many debates of this kind, disagreements may be more apparent than real. Each side states its case in the extreme so that differences are obvious and points are clear. When the debaters move beyond theory to apply their principles of wilderness management, areas of common ground emerge.

In his series of articles, Levin develops specifics for wilderness management. Like Burch and Nutter, he believes the public should not be denied access to wilderness. Artificial restrictions on use, such as permits, are a desperate last resort. Neither, though, should access to wilderness be made artificially easy through highly engineered trails, elaborate sign systems, and designated camping areas. Wilderness should be met on its own terms. Levin proposes a "concentric" wilderness, defined much as the contour lines on a topographic map define the mountains themselves. The outer circles, by their very nature, are relatively accessible to all. Here, high-standard trails and huts are appropriate to accommodate the large numbers who come for an introduction to wilderness. Inner circles have fewer facilities, are more remote and natural, and are, therefore, more difficult to reach and to traverse. Finally, there is the core — wilderness with no trails or other facilities, areas that only the most skilled and fervent enthusiasts will attain.

The concentric wilderness proposed by Levin denies minimum access to no one. Further access depends only on interest and the effort the user is willing to invest. In Levin's system, wilderness use is rationed as it always has been, through natural "frictions" that each individual must overcome. In this way, we must each "earn again what we have inherited," and the ultimate purpose of wilderness preservation will have been fulfilled.

FOR EVERY APHORISM that the ingenuity of mankind has invented, someone with a different slant of vision has proposed its opposite. To Heraclitus' axiom that nothing is constant except change itself, a Gallic aphorism declares, "Plus ca change, plus c'est la meme chose" — which pretty well sums up where we find ourselves in the unending debate over how to "use" our White Mountains and our entire northeastern "wilderness." For all the attention it has received, the issue is still largely virgin. At stake are the use patterns in our northeastern wild areas during the rest of our lifetimes, the lifetimes of our children and grandchildren, and conceivably long thereafter. What we do in New England, where population pressure on our wild areas may be unprecedented, could very well influence what is done in the rest of this country and in other areas of the world. Thus we are all participants in a great venture into unknown terrain. Every piece of knowledgeable input, no matter how idiosyncratic, contributes to the ultimate resolution.

It was Darwin who first injected into our awareness the notion of relativism on a planetary scale. With the turn of the century Einstein brought the entire perceived and unperceived universe within his theory of relativity. Then somewhere on the battlefields of two cataclysmic wars we were stunned to learn that God Himself was missing in action, bringing into doubt the hierarchical ethical systems which culminate in belief of His existence. What is left? I see the current wilderness debate as being between those, including myself, who, for whatever reason, still cling to the concept that there are islands of immutability in human affairs, and those who downplay the notion of permanence in a universe which is otherwise wholly relativistic. On one side are those who seek, in wilderness, an escape from the city and its petty, pragmatic, and relativistic value system. Aligned against us are those who do not particularly fear the transplantation into a wilderness environment of existing societal patterns and scenarios. These ideas and theories on wilderness are more subconsciously than consciously formulated and adhered to. But whatever may be the respective inner motivations of the adherents to our opposed philosophies on wilderness management, the debate must turn on the objective merits of the ideas presented.

In our society the presumption is for novelty. It is the stuff that dreams and great adventures of the intellect — in fact, whole careers and great fortunes — are made of. It is at once the glory and the misery of the Western World. It is interesting to contemplate how the last twenty-five centuries of Western history are truly a turbulent succession of violent mood swings, projected onto a national and supra-national scale, each mood inconsistent with its predecessor, and the whole cultural and historical development as random and unpredictable as the very course of evolution itself. It is fully conceivable that, but for the West, the world would have changed little in that time — latter-day "pre-Columbian" civilizations might still inhabit The New World, inner Africa would still lie undiscovered and China itself would sit timeless, without Mao and the Revolution. All this in lieu of the cataclysms which threaten us daily. I do not intend to place a value judgment on this fact, except to illustrate that restlessness and its offspring, novelty, are our very cultural wellspring, our social heritage. As has so often happened in the past (and as is happening now to our wilderness) we are capable of destroying all that is meaningful and valid for no other reason than that it smacks of permanence. Over the better part of the past millennium, we have not truly grasped the idea of immutability. No matter how adaptable to future shock we think we are, if we do not understand the value of permanence, then we do not really understand change. This is particularly frightening today when we possess the power to bring about total and irrevocable change. Wilderness managers, intoxicated by the headiness of novel ideas and relationships, are perfectly capable, in all innocence, of forcibly subjecting wilderness to a drawingboard idea of wilderness. That, I suggest, is what will happen if we follow the theories of Burch and Nutter.

Wilderness, within fairly restricted parameters, is a constant — not a variable (a fact which does not negate the existence of different types of wilderness: tropical, desert, maritime or alpine, for example). Human perception being the varied phenomenon it is, people will perceive wilderness in many different ways. But that does not mean that we should impose those perceptions on wilderness. This is the point which Eisley, Brower, and Matthiessen have made so brilliantly. It is also the point on which Burch and Nutter have gone utterly astray. There is a recurrent theme in existential literature describing how man, having imposed his will upon the world around him, finds himself confronted by a wilderness of mirrors, reflecting, of course, only his own image. I assume that most of us would find this thought anathema, particularly in the context of a wilderness which reflected only the handiwork and untutored appetites of man. But this is actually what Burch and Nutter are arguing for. Wilderness — or unspoiled nature — is at the heart of all man's heritage, regardless of his epoch or his culture. Not all of us will wish to see it this way, but unless those of us who want to can find some affinity between our wilderness experience and a DaVinci background, a Sung mountainscape, a Thoreauvian insight, an Ansel Adams photograph, or a folksong from the Auvergne, we will have lost our wilderness.

It is possible that my ideas represent a minority view. We do not know. But even if this should be so, what I am arguing for — a nexus with our origins through the constancy of unspoiled nature — this should not be abandoned. There are limits to majority rule, limits beyond which there are ideas and potentialities which can destroy not only the social compact by which the majority rules, but also the majority itself. It would be ironic if we saved wilderness from the exploiters only to lose it to the managers and the masses. It could happen. If in fact a majority wants traditional concepts of wilderness discarded, then I would propose to educate the majority. Teachers have always been a minority.

The error committed by my two opponents in this debate is the passion for a relativistic approach to wilderness administration. From the proposition that we *can* do what we like with and to our wilderness, Burch and Nutter argue that we *may* and (following the opinion polls) *should* do what we like with it. I have tried to show some of the consequences which flow from this devastating fallacy. But perhaps the most eloquent hymn ever raised to the godhead and omnipotence of relativistic man was created by Dostoyevski in his novel *The Possessed*. His character Kirillov, realizing that all things were possible to him in the absence of a moralistic universe, felt that he had thereby become a god, and to establish once and for all his life-and-death power over his own destiny, committed suicide. Dostoyevski was expressing a profound truth: the lifelessness of a moral system which eschews fixed values and the limits which such values would impose. I believe it is not overly dramatic to suggest that a similar fate awaits our relationship with wilderness under a literal application of the theories of Burch and Nutter.